Cover to Cover

Through the Bible in 365 Days

John A. Carroll

Cover to Cover

Through the Bible in 365 Days

by John A. Carroll

Paperback Version: ISBN-13: 978-1519759085 (First Edition - December 2015)
Paperback Version: ISBN-13: 978-1-7321724-0-1 (Second Edition - July 2018)

4 Seasons image – licensed from Shutterstock.com
Original Cover Design – Susannah Clements

Published by John A. Carroll
jacarroll71@gmail.com

For Mary, world's greatest wife

Table of Contents

Foreword

Food for the soul, one right-sized plate full at a time! John Carroll has seen into our souls & felt our deepest need. How can we get more of Jesus in heart & life? The incarnate Word has given us His written Word to draw us ever closer. With lives so busy that we cannot breathe much less think, John has measured just enough & prepared it for tasty eating. Never too little or too much, the meals here prepared are just what we need. Holding us by the hand & taking us on a tour of the selected portion, John does not leave us with just an emotion, but he challenges our minds & lives. Are you lazy-minded, lacking serious reflection? John does not abandon you, but leads you to the mind of God. Is your heart cold even when facing living truth? John calls you out, insisting that you wake up & see the Lord. I hope you will find this helpful aid to the habit of regular Bible reading a real encouragement. John Carroll has touched many lives with the penetrating eyes of a pastor and missionary. Here, he reaches out through the page for our good and God's glory!

Dr. W. Duncan Rankin

Adjunct Professor of Systematic Theology, Erskine Theological Seminary
Adjunct Professor of Systematic Theology, Reformed Theological Seminary
Professor of Systematic Theology, BRITE—Blue Ridge Institute for Theological Education

Preface

Is this you? You wanted to grow spiritually so you set a goal to read through the Bible. You decided to finish it in a year. You determined not to fail. You were excited and eager as you started out.

But one month later, you were behind schedule. You determined to double your speed and catch up.

During the next thirty days the wheels came off your life and crowded out your reading plan. It was slow going in the second half of Exodus. Oh, and Leviticus? That was a hard read. Some days you read just to get it done without much joy or understanding.

Four weeks later a pattern of not reading had emerged. You were discouraged. You said, "I'll try again someday."

You truly wonder if you will ever succeed in reading the Bible "cover to cover" in one year and actually benefitting from reading it every day.

If the above description sounds familiar, this book is for you. You are not alone. You are not the only one who has struggled to maintain a regular time of Bible reading. You are not the only one who has bogged down in some of the tedious sections of the Old Testament, desperately wondering if those passages are really "profitable for teaching, for reproof, for correction, and for training in righteousness" (2 Timothy 3:16).

I can assure you that it is do-able to read the Bible through in one year and to gain great benefit each day from your reading. Please read the introduction to learn how this will work.

Introduction

As a missionary and pastor, I have long sought to encourage all who desire to know God in truth to commit to regular personal Bible reading. *Cover to Cover: Through the Bible in 365 days* offers a plan for reading through the Scriptures and models a practical four-step method for gleaning truth from each reading. Here's how this book does that:

- Simplicity. Our reading schedule starts in Genesis and goes through the sixty-six books of the Bible in order to Revelation. We will not be reading from different parts of the Bible simultaneously (although that is a popular way to read). This plan is simple. It is easy to keep your place.
- Uniformity of daily assignments. The readings are each about eighty-five verses long so you can expect a similar time commitment each day.
- Fellowship. Within the limitations of the printed page and the author-reader relationship, I share my own daily reflections and challenges with you from the passage we are reading. I hope you will read the daily assignment in your Bible, then, time permitting, use the four-step method below. Finally, turn back to this book and take a look at what I got from my reading.

I suggest using this four-step method as you read. You will need to have your Bible, a pen or pencil, and a notebook.

Step 1. As you prayerfully read the assignment, mark verses that you wish to reflect on more deeply.

Step 2. Selection. When you have completed the reading, choose one of your marked verses for further thought. I usually focus on a selection of one to three verses maximum each day.

Step 3. Reflections. Write out your thoughts and questions about the selected passage. What does this passage teach about God, mankind, sin, faith, salvation, eternal life, etc.

Step 4. Challenge. Note how this passage applies to your life. What truths do you need to remember and believe? What commands do you need to obey? What sins should you confess and forsake? How can you be a doer and not just a hearer of God's Word (James 1:22)?

Optional Step 5 is to read what I selected, reflected on and was challenged by. It is not necessary that you read my thoughts and comments, but I hope you will read God's Word and seek to apply it to your life and circumstances.

Don't expect to find here a commentary on every chapter of the Bible. I have merely included some brief thoughts from one passage that stood out to me in my reading each day for a year. I humbly offer it to you as an example of the gems I discovered in going through the Bible in 365 days. [1]

May God bless your reading and study.

---

[1] This material was originally posted in 2013 on my blog at http://ThistleDewFarm.us. Some editing has been done since the original posting.

January 1/Day 1

God Created Man

Today's reading: Genesis 1:1-3:24

My selection: Genesis 1:27

God created man in his own image, in the image of God he created him; male and female he created them. And God blessed them.

My reflections: These three chapters set the context not only for the rest of the Bible but for all of human history. Volumes have been written about these brief passages, but I must pause at verses 27-28 of chapter one to reflect on who man is, what he is, and why he exists.

1. Man was created (therefore, not self-existent, not self-sufficient, not a random result of time and chance).

2. Man was created in God's image (therefore not a mere animal, not worthless).

3. Man was created male and female (therefore not asexual, homosexual, nor bisexual).

4. Man was blessed and commissioned by God to multiply and to have dominion over the earth (therefore, not purposeless, not useless, not solitary).

How many of the current problems facing our society stem from our losing sight of one or more of these foundational claims of the Bible?

My challenge: We cannot instantly solve all of these ills, but I challenge you to start this year of Bible reading with thanks and praise to God for His good and hospitable creation, corrupted though it became and continues to be by man's sin. Praise Him for His coming kingdom in which all the good of original creation and more will be established forever.

January 2/Day 2

Worship that Pleases God

Today's reading: Genesis 4:1-5:32

My selection: Genesis 4:4-5

4 And the Lord had regard for Abel and his offering, 5 but for Cain and his offering he had no regard. So Cain was very angry, and his face fell.

My reflections: There is much I would like to know about this incident that God has not told us. What prompted the brothers to worship in this way? Why did they each choose different kinds of offerings? Why did God not accept Cain's offering?

None of this is clear.

However, what is clear is, first, that an offering is needed for the one who seeks to worship God. Second, not every offering is acceptable. Third, God indicated here whether the offering was acceptable or not and, in the case of Cain, showed him grace and mercy, giving him the opportunity to repent. From the rest of the Bible we see that, though for a time God prescribed animal sacrifices as offerings before Him, these merely pointed to the ultimate and only truly, acceptable sacrifice, the Lamb of God, Jesus Christ.

Jesus Christ is the perfect offering for sin. We come before God on the basis of His offering Himself for us on the cross. Our own offerings are not just inadequate, they are offensive to a God who is pleased with nothing less than the offering of His Son for sin. [See John 1:29-34; Ephesians 2:8-9; Hebrews 10]

My challenge: Thank Him for the perfect offering for sin. Believe in the Lamb of God who takes away the sin of the world. Come to God by Him alone. This is worship that pleases God.

January 3/Day 3

Salvation: Enduring and Undeserved

Today's reading: Genesis 6:1-9:17

My selection: Genesis 8:21

The Lord said in his heart, "I will never again curse the ground because of man, for the intention of man's heart is evil from his youth. Neither will I ever again strike down every living creature as I have done.

My reflections: Noah apparently could not wait to show his gratitude to God for preserving him, his family, and the animals through the flood. His first recorded act is to build an altar and make offerings that were pleasing to the Lord.

God graciously made a covenant with Noah following this act of worship. But God's graciousness was not and never is based on any worthiness in man or any illusion that man is upright in himself. God was pleased with the sacrifice of Noah but was not deceived that man would or could be perfectly holy. In fact, part of this covenant included a provision that has been seen as the basis for human government and capital punishment in the case of murder (9:5-6). God anticipated continuing murder after the flood.

My challenge: God knew Noah's heart, and He knows your heart and mine. Have you seen how the Lord shows you grace and mercy despite your persistent sin? If you are trusting in Jesus Christ, give thanks for God's undeserved salvation through His Son, a salvation even more precious and enduring than the temporary preservation of life from drowning in a flood, a salvation of complete forgiveness and deliverance from eternal destruction.

January 4/Day 4

Covering for Sin

Today's reading: Genesis 9:18-12:9

My selection: Genesis 9:23

Then Shem and Japheth took a garment, laid it on both their shoulders, and walked backward and covered the nakedness of their father. Their faces were turned backward, and they did not see their father's nakedness.

My reflections: Here is an illustration of what we saw yesterday, that "the intention of man's heart is evil from his youth" (8:21). Noah showed no self-control in foolishly becoming drunk and disrobing where he could be seen. Canaan made a bad thing worse.

Canaan may have seen his father inadvertently (it is not said), but it seems his sin was to report the incident to his brothers and to make his father look shameful before them as well. Shem and Japheth showed respect and creativity in solving the problem rather than exploiting an opportunity for evil. The result was blessing for Shem and Japheth and a curse upon Canaan.

My challenge: Shem and Japheth loved their father and, literally, covered him and his many sins. They portrayed what Jesus Christ would do for all His people: show mercy and cover sin.

We, who trust Christ for the covering of our sin, are called to be like Him in our relationships with others. [See 1 Peter 4:8]. Remember it was because of God's love for us that, in Christ, He has covered our sins. Do the same for others.

January 5/Day 5

God's Mercy through Suffering

Today's reading: Genesis 12:10-16:16

My selection: Genesis 12:17

But the Lord afflicted Pharaoh and his house with great plagues because of Sarai, Abram's wife.

My reflections: Abram foolishly leaned "unto [his] own understanding" as he tried to protect himself by lying to Pharaoh (Proverbs 3:5-6 KJV). God intervened to protect Pharaoh from the consequences of Abram's folly. So even Pharaoh and his house were blessed by plagues which they correctly interpreted to be a warning that they were in danger of committing an illegal or immoral action. Abram's plan to protect himself backfired and he, Sarai, and their entourage were sent out of Egypt in humiliation.

God is merciful and gracious to His sin-prone children. God showed Abram that He does not need His people to deceive, lie, and manipulate in order to protect themselves.

My challenge: Think about how you have seen God's goodness in sending trials, obstacles, and setbacks in your life. Thank God that He is able to stop us in our foolishness and that the trials He sends are for our good, but do not presume that He will always rescue us from the immediate consequences of leaning to our own understanding.

January 6/Day 6

God's Covenant People: Who Are They and What Do They Have?

Today's reading: Genesis 17:1-19:29

My selection: Genesis 17:7

And I will establish my covenant between me and you and your offspring after you throughout their generations for an everlasting covenant, to be God to you and to your offspring after you.

My reflections: God graciously chose Abraham and made with him a covenant which extends to his offspring.

But who are his offspring? Can I be included?

The Apostle Paul in Romans 2 and Galatians 3 shows that these offspring are not the biological descendants of Abraham, but rather his spiritual children by faith. Some, of course, may be both biological and spiritual children of Abraham, but the decisive element for inclusion in the covenant people is faith not genetics. Yes, I can, by faith, be included.

What does it mean to be included in the covenant? What do covenant people have?

It means to have God as our God, to belong to Him, to be His children. Born in sin and, to put it bluntly, by nature children of the devil (John 8:44), we need deliverance from the power that the serpent gained over mankind at the fall (Genesis 3). In Genesis 3:15, God promised that the seed of the woman would crush the serpent's head. That seed was Jesus Christ who definitively defeated Satan by dying on the cross. He rose again leading His people to eternal life. Now all who by faith are in Jesus Christ are included in the covenant with Abraham.

My challenge: God's covenant with Abraham had in view blessing for all the families of the earth (Genesis 12:3). This is the good news of the gospel, that God has made a covenant to save all who believe in the One who crushed the serpent's head. These are His covenant people. Are you among them? If not, believe in Him. If so, rejoice in His salvation and proclaim the good news of the gospel.

January 7/Day 7

Selfish or Selfless?

Today's reading: Genesis 19:30-22:24

My selection: Genesis 19:30

Now Lot went up out of Zoar and lived in the hills with his two daughters, for he was afraid to live in Zoar. So he lived in a cave with his two daughters.

My reflections: While his uncle Abraham was surveying the remains of Sodom and Gomorrah (vs. 27), Lot was settling in a cave in the hills. Although the angels had reluctantly given him permission to live in Zoar, Lot, seeing the destruction of his former city and the judgment on his wife, in fear decided to head for the hills. He set up housekeeping in a cave with his two daughters.

These are the same daughters that, in their last night in Sodom, had been offered for gang rape by their father to a mob of perverse men (19:8). Lot saw his daughters as expendable resources available to solve his problem with the locals in town. Fortunately, the offer was rejected and the daughters escaped with their lives and their father. But they had grown up in Sodom and the values and attitudes grew in them. Taking them out of Sodom did not take Sodom out of them. They plotted to get pregnant by their father. The children they bore would father the tribes of the Moabites and the Ammonites, tribes that would be mortal enemies of Israel.

Lot and his daughters all demonstrated an appalling disrespect for each other and a willingness to sacrifice others in their selfish pursuit of their personal goals.

My challenge: Let it not be said of you, "he took care of Number One at all costs." Jesus Christ "made himself of no reputation" to serve those He came to save. Make His mindset your own. (Philippians 2:5-8KJV).

January 8/Day 8

Guidance through Signs

Today's reading: Genesis 23:1-24:67

My selection: Genesis 24:14

Let the young woman to whom I shall say, "Please let down your jar that I may drink," and who shall say, "Drink, and I will water your camels"—let her be the one whom you have appointed for your servant Isaac. By this I shall know that you have shown steadfast love to my master.

My reflections: Abraham's servant was commissioned to choose a wife for Isaac and bring her back to him. Am I glad this system was not in place when I was single! Nevertheless, the servant, who showed real trust in God and sought His direction in prayer, asked for a confirming sign from the Lord. This can be a dangerous practice if the sign has nothing to do with the matter being decided. For example, if a young man driving down a road prays that if he should marry a certain person the *next* traffic light would be green, that sign would have nothing to do with the matter being decided.

In the case of the servant, the sign he requested did relate to the character of the woman for whom he was looking. The sign, if fulfilled, would be a good indicator of the diligence and kindness of the woman. It was fulfilled to the letter and everything else fell into place as well. So, Isaac got a wife, Rebekah, and she proved to be faithful.

Looking for guidance through signs is dangerous but, as a final confirmation of a decision on which Scripture is silent, it may be used. If it is used it should always have some bearing on the matter in question.

My challenge: Seek to know and do God's will as revealed in the Bible and confirmed by godly counsel and circumstances. Rarely, if ever, rely on signs.

January 9/Day 9

Foolish Decisions: Consequences and Forgiveness

Today's reading: Genesis 25:1-26:35

My selection: Genesis 26:34,35

34 When Esau was forty years old, he took Judith the daughter of Beeri the Hittite to be his wife, and Basemath the daughter of Elon the Hittite, 35 and they made life bitter for Isaac and Rebekah.

My reflections: Esau made bad choices and he made them consistently. He let his hunger cloud his wisdom and sold his birthright. Unlike his father, Isaac, he did not allow his father to play any role in his choice of a wife. He married two Hittite women possibly defying his parents' advice and certainly ignoring family tradition. Esau and his wives, Judith and Basemath, made life bitter for Esau's parents. He was off to a bad start in life.

Perhaps you live today with the consequences of regrettable decisions. The truth is, in small and large ways, we, as sinners, all live with such consequences. Some of these consequences cannot be alleviated at all. We bear them like indelible scars. But, whether or not the consequences can be alleviated, the sinful decisions that caused them can be forgiven. Christ died to save His people from their sins (Matthew 1:21). Believers, those who recognize their sin, repent, and trust in Jesus Christ's death for forgiveness, are delivered from the guilt and debt of offenses of every kind.

My challenge: Bear the inevitable ongoing consequences of your sin, but do so with the confidence that by believing in the One who saves His people from their sin you do not bear the guilt of that sin. As you face important decisions, do not be an Esau, who did it his own way, but seek to act wisely by studying the Bible, making use of the means of grace, and by listening to godly counsel.

The Worldwide Scope of the Covenant

Today's reading: Genesis 27:1-29:14

My selection: Genesis 28:14

In you and your offspring shall all the families of the earth be blessed.

My reflections: The Lord God had previously given His covenant to Abraham and reiterated it to Isaac and, now, to Jacob. It is significant that each time the covenant is explained, the Lord promises that blessing will extend, through it, to all the families of the earth. It is striking that this obvious feature of the covenant was almost completely lost by the Jews in later centuries. Paul described the relationship between Jews and Gentiles as one of having a "dividing wall of hostility" (Ephesians 2:14). Christ fulfills this vision of a ladder connecting heaven to earth (John 1:51) and in Him that wall was broken down.

My challenge: Have we, evangelicals, reconstructed a wall of hostility with those who do not yet believe? Have we erred as did the Old Testament Jews in being too inward focused? Or have we also watered down the gospel so that some are teaching that people of other non-Christian religious traditions may be saved despite having no identification with Christ or His Church? We are prone to go to extremes.

Seek to make disciples of all nations, but be faithful to the Scripture. Only through faith in the sacrifice of Jesus Christ, the Son of God, may sinners be saved. Through the gospel of Jesus Christ blessing is coming to all the families of the earth.

The Incredible Power of Love

Today's reading: Genesis 29:15-31:21

My selection: Genesis 29:20

Jacob served seven years for Rachel, and they seemed to him but a few days because of the love he had for her.

My reflections: When love exists, no sacrifice is too great. When love exists, time and hard labor are not obstacles. Love overcomes anything.

Paul gave his famous biblical description of love in 1 Corinthians 13:4-8. But what is called love in our western society is quite contrary to the qualities he listed. It is focused on self-fulfillment, instant gratification, and pleasure. It is conditional, suspicious, jealous, controlling, and possessive. This is not what Jacob felt for Rachel. It is not what Paul described.

My challenge: Are you in love? If so, does your love look like Jacob's? Does your love look like that described by Paul? Biblical love (the love of God) is not a mere feeling. It is active. If you love, show it by serving patiently. No one loves perfectly, but seek to grow in godly love. True, biblical love has power to overcome daunting obstacles.

January 12/Day 12

Change of Heart

Today's reading: Genesis 31:22-33:20

My selection: Genesis 32:10

I am not worthy of the least of all the deeds of steadfast love and all the faithfulness that you have shown to your servant, for with only my staff I crossed this Jordan, and now I have become two camps.

My reflections: Most of the tenor of Jacob's life has been one of a conniver who thinks he has been cheated by others or only has taken what was his due. Here we see a change of heart as reflected in his prayer to the Lord for deliverance from the threat of his estranged twin brother, Esau. For, perhaps the first time, he acknowledges that God has done great deeds of steadfast love and faithfulness to him. Jacob seems to recognize that all has been by grace and mercy not because he earned it or deserved it.

The fear of Esau was the greatest test he had ever faced, and this test brought with it a change of heart. Jacob shows that he really does recognize his sin and need for God's protection.

My challenge: As you look at your life to this point, do you think you have been blessed or cheated? Do you see God's grace, or have you merely gotten what is "fair"? Do you feel humbly grateful for God's blessings on you or do you feel you have gotten less than you earned and deserved? Jacob, at this point, sets a good example to us in gratefulness to God. Praise Him for His love and faithfulness which is truly more than we deserve.

January 13/Day 13

War: Just or Unjust?

Today's reading: Genesis 34:1-36:30

My selection: Genesis 34:31

But [Simeon and Levi] said, "Should he treat our sister like a prostitute?"

My reflections: This is a sad story of human depravity. The incident brought great loss to everyone involved. Dinah foolishly (in retrospect) takes a tour of the land, apparently, unchaperoned and unprotected. Shechem, the spoiled, self-indulgent, and perverse prince of the land, captures and rapes her. He then appeals to his father, Hamor, to get her for his wife at any cost.

Jacob acts in cowardice to make a deal with Hamor while apparently ignoring the great sin that was committed against Dinah. The brothers make a deceptive deal that appealed to the whole kingdom of Hamor because it seemed to promise easy wealth. Next, Simeon and Levi kill the men who had been circumcised and take all the spoils including the women and children. Jacob finally shows a little backbone in objecting to what they had done, but his complaint is too late and makes no difference. It's hard to see any good in this entire story. It is hard to find a wise person or a godly action anywhere here.

There is a political view that says all war is evil or that all who die in war should be honored equally. Certainly, this is based on a relativistic view of morality. If there are no absolutes, then who is to say that anything is wrong? Was Dinah wrong? Was Shechem wrong? Were Simeon and Levi wrong? Were all of them partly wrong? Were all of them partly right? This doesn't work. We know that no matter how you judge Dinah for her naiveté or her father for failing to protect her, Shechem was scum. Perhaps the right thing would have been to declare war against Hamor and attack for the action of their prince, with his execution being the objective.

We need to beware of unjust wars while recognizing that there are some just wars. But neither side in a war is perfectly just. One side may be more just (or less unjust) than the other, but there are no perfect holy nations or armies. It seems that there is a difference between a Hitler and an Eisenhower. World War II was more clearly a war of an evil tyrant who was taking people and nations captive and executing a whole race of people without cause. The USA acted quite altruistically since the war in Europe never spread to our land. We ought not to take it lightly when we send troops to Afghanistan or Iraq. Was Vietnam justified? Was the Korean War justified? Was the Gulf War justified? Are we becoming a nation which more easily sends troops into battle, not to defend freedom, but to protect our economic interests? Or are our motives mixed and, while not perfectly altruistic, not completely unjustified?

My challenge: Pray for our president and political leaders who must make decisions about sending our troops into war. May they fight whenever necessary and only when necessary.

January 14 /Day 14

Judgment, Mercy, and Repentance

Today's reading: Genesis 36:31-38:30

My selection: Genesis 38:26

Judah identified them and said, "She is more righteous than I, since I did not give her to my son Shelah." And he did not know her again.

My reflections: Judah was quick to pass judgment on his daughter-in-law, although he had been equally guilty of sin. His judgment would have killed her and his child that she was expecting. Certainly, the hypocrisy of Judah was great and disgusting, and he was quickly shown up before all of his family and all who would read this passage for years to come.

Judah did show promptness in acknowledging his sin and in reversing his judgment. In spite of all this sordid mess, he would be established as head of the royal family of Israel from which comes the Lord Jesus Christ. Great sin and great mercy are shown here. See Matthew 1:3for the genealogy of Jesus Christ including Judah and Tamar.

My challenge: Are you quicker to judgment than to repentance? Do you show more mercy on yourself than on others? It behooves us, who profess faith in Christ, to show humility and promptness in recognizing our faults. Show mercy. Repent promptly.

As James wrote: "For he shall have judgment without mercy, that hath shewed no mercy" (James 2:13 KJV).

January 15/Day 15

God's Presence, Consistent Character, and Success

Today's reading: Genesis 39:1-41:36

My selection: Genesis 39:23

The keeper of the prison paid no attention to anything that was in Joseph's charge, because the Lord was with him. And whatever he did, the Lord made it succeed.

My reflections: Joseph went from a comfortable life with his family, to a pit, to the slave traders, to Potiphar's right-hand man, and, now, to prison in a foreign land. Talk about ups and downs! But all these vastly changing circumstances did not change Joseph's character or God's blessing upon him. Neither comfort nor prison could affect the one upon whom the Lord showered His favor. God was always with Joseph and Joseph was always faithful and successful.

My challenge: Do you change with your circumstances or does your character remain the same in plenty or little, in trial or in blessing? Paul could say "I have learned, in whatsoever state I am, therewith to be content" (Philippians 4:11 KJV).

The late R. Dwight Hill, who discipled me in college, often said, "Circumstances do not make or break a man, they merely reveal him for what he is." Focus on the Lord, not on your circumstances. Be steadfast despite the ups and downs of your life. Apparent defeat today may lead to unparalleled promotion tomorrow. It did for Joseph, as we shall see in our next reading.

January 16 /Day 16

Nagging Guilt

Today's reading: Genesis 41:37-43:34

My selection: Genesis 42:21

Then they said to one another, "In truth we are guilty concerning our brother, in that we saw the distress of his soul, when he begged us and we did not listen. That is why this distress has come upon us."

My reflections: Joseph's brothers had carried the secret and guilt of their sin toward him for many years. Time did not make the guilt go away. One wonders how many times over the years they had relived and regretted their action toward Joseph, as they watched their father living in a permanent state of mourning. Now, when adversity came their way the thought of what they did so many years earlier immediately came back to them to haunt and torment them.

Scripture warns of the danger of hiding sin and not confessing (Psalm 32) but also promises that, when confession is made, God forgives and cleanses us from all unrighteousness. There is a remedy for guilt and it is repentance, confession, and faith in the atoning work of Christ, the perfect sacrifice for the sin of all who believe in Him.

My challenge: Be quick to repent and thoroughly confess sin to God and to all who have been affected by it. Psalm 32:5 (KJV) tells us: "I acknowledge my sin unto thee, and mine iniquity have I not hid. I said, 'I will confess my transgressions unto the Lord; and thou forgavest the iniquity of my sin.'"

January 17/Day 17

Our Suffering; God's Viewpoint

Today's reading: Genesis 44:1-45:28

My selection: Genesis 45:5

Do not be distressed or angry with yourselves because you sold me here, for God sent me before you to preserve life.

My reflections: Joseph messed with his brothers' minds throughout his interactions with them. But his purpose seems to have been to test their repentance for what they had done to him. Certainly, the agony they were experiencing, as they considered how the loss of Benjamin would impact their father, helped Joseph make these statements here. Joseph, after revealing his identity to them, comforted his brothers in their torment and showed the grace of forgiveness to them.

Although Joseph's comment in Genesis 50:20, which occurs years later, is more frequently quoted in regard to God's sovereignty in using evil for good purposes, the thought is well-developed here by Joseph.

My challenge: Have you processed the suffering you have received unjustly? Joseph worked through what had been done to him. Pray for wisdom to see the good in the bad you have experienced. You will know you have done that when you can thank God wholeheartedly for what you have suffered.

January 18/Day 18

Reassurance in the Midst of Change

Today's reading: Genesis 46:1-48:22

My selection: Genesis 46:3

I am God, the God of your father. Do not be afraid to go down to Egypt, for there I will make you into a great nation.

My reflections: See the graciousness of God to an old man! The Lord spoke to Jacob in visions in the night. Jacob was not unresponsive. He said, "Here am I." God identified Himself again as the God of his father. He gave direction to Jacob to go down to Egypt without fear. The Lord told Jacob what He would do with his family in Egypt: "make [them] a great nation." God promised His presence with Jacob in Egypt and that He would bring him back to the land of Canaan after dying in Joseph's care.

God graciously gave this old man reassurance and direction at a time when He was sending him on a journey to a foreign land. The elderly are reticent to leave familiar surroundings, but Jacob had known the Lord for many years and trusted Him to complete His promises to him.

My challenge: You may be called to unforeseen and uncomfortable circumstances, but God works out His unchanging and sovereign purposes. Walk today in the knowledge that He has a purpose in what He calls you to do. If you are His child, He will not ever leave you or forsake you (Hebrews 13:5).

January 19/Day 19

God's Hand in Human History

Today's reading: Genesis 49:1-Exodus 1:22

My selection: Exodus 1:8

There arose a new king over Egypt, who did not know Joseph.

My reflections: Once again, God works through trials and adversity for His good purposes for His people. We saw it with Joseph being sold into slavery in Egypt but eventually rising to assist Pharaoh and to use his position for the good of his family. Now, through the paranoia of the new Pharaoh, the people of Israel are subjected to brutal slavery that will increase their willingness to leave Egypt and forge their bond with one another as a nation in formation.

My challenge: The hand of God in history may not be obvious in the short term. Thus, we walk by faith in Him who promises to be with us to the end of the age. Must you always see in order to trust? You may not demand that God always allow you to see what He is about. We walk--not by sight--but by faith (2 Corinthians 5:7). So, walk.

January 20/Day 20

Self-confidence vs. God-confidence

Today's reading: Exodus 2:1-4:31

My selection: Exodus 2:12

[Moses] looked this way and that, and seeing no one, he struck down the Egyptian and hid him in the sand.

My reflections: Moses' early life was marked by God's providence and Moses' depravity. God providentially protected him from death at birth and from the death penalty after murdering an Egyptian. Moses' depravity is evident in that his first recorded act was murder. It was not a promising start. He certainly had the makings of a leader, but he lacked wisdom and self-control. After fleeing from Pharaoh, he lived in relative obscurity. By the time God called him, Moses had lost all that fire and over-confidence of his youth. He needed much prodding from God to begin the task for which he was called and gifted. In all of this, God was gracious and patient with him.

My challenge: What is God calling you to do? Is your trust in Him or do you hesitate because of your lack of self-confidence? Self-confidence, whether in scarcity or abundance, needs to be replaced with confidence in the Lord who will bring about His purposes in and through your life for His own glory. It's not about you. It's about Him.

Keep Proverbs 3:5-6 (KJV) in mind: "Trust in the Lord with all thine heart; and lean not unto thine own understanding. In all thy ways acknowledge him, and he shall direct thy paths."

January 21/Day 21

Handling a Leadership Crisis

Today's reading: Exodus 5:1-7:25

My selection: Exodus 6:12

Moses said to the Lord, "Behold, the people of Israel have not listened to me. How then shall Pharaoh listen to me, for I am of uncircumcised lips?"

My reflections: Moses' leadership crisis is complicated and difficult, but not unusual. He is commissioned by God and given clear directions and resources. This is on the positive side of the ledger. On the negative side, he cannot get the cooperation of Pharaoh, and he is fast losing the support of the people of Israel. Furthermore, Moses sees himself as an inadequate speaker.

What does he do? He must turn to the Lord for strength and reassurance.

We know from the rest of the story that the people will always be fickle and hard to lead. Pharaoh will not let them go, really. But the trials they are currently facing will forge the Israelites into a nation who will be willing to go. The plagues God will send to Egypt will cause Pharaoh to blink long enough for the people to get out of the land and get some distance.

My challenge: The Christian leader must not focus on his own inadequacy but on God's purposes and power. His wisdom means He chooses the highest ends and the surest means for obtaining them. He changes people but, at least in this case, He did so through an unreasonable, paranoid king and the toughening impact of his severe policies on an enslaved people. There would be supernatural intervention, too, through the timing of the plagues. Meanwhile, the best thing Moses can do is keep his focus on the LORD. The same goes for you.

January 22/ Day 22

Seeing the Same Things; Drawing Different Conclusions

Today's reading: Exodus 8:1-10:20

My selection: Exodus 10:1-2

[1] Then the Lord said to Moses, "Go in to Pharaoh, for I have hardened his heart and the heart of his servants, that I may show these signs of mine among them, [2] and that you may tell in the hearing of your son and of your grandson how I have dealt harshly with the Egyptians and what signs I have done among them, that you may know that I am the Lord."

My reflections: On several occasions the Scripture says that Pharaoh hardened his heart in response to the plagues. Here God says He hardened Pharaoh's heart. Pharaoh was not a robot. He did what he wanted to do according to his own natural inclinations. He may have deluded himself with the thought of being a courageous leader of the nation, resisting the pressure of the enslaved Israelites to be released to worship the Lord. Whatever his thought processes, Pharaoh hardened his heart.

But it is also true that God hardened Pharaoh's heart, in that God left Pharaoh in his natural state so that his heart was hard and foolish. The result would be that the Israelites would someday tell the stories of the plagues to their grandchildren. They would all know who the Lord is through these events.

God rules over the hearts of all. Unless He chooses to change a heart, it will remain unresponsive, defensive, unrepentant, and unbelieving just as Pharaoh's was. Pharaoh saw God's power but did not believe. The Israelites saw and believed. As an agnostic friend once told me, "we see the same things, but draw different conclusions."

My challenge: If God has given you faith in Him and a hatred for sin, give thanks to Him. He has not left you in your natural state. This is also called regeneration or the new birth (John 3:3; 1 Peter 1:23). Be sure and relate to your family and friends your testimony of God's work in you which resulted in a soft heart that believes and not a hard one that rebels.

If you do not believe, ask God to give you the grace to believe and repent of your sin. Keep reading the Bible and attending a church where you hear the gospel. Concern about your spiritual life is evidence of God's work in you.

January 23/Day 23

Salvation Depicted

Today's reading: Exodus Exodus 10:21-13:16

My selection: Exodus 12:23

For the Lord will pass through to strike the Egyptians, and when he sees the blood on the lintel and on the two doorposts, the Lord will pass over the door and will not allow the destroyer to enter your houses to strike you.

My reflections: All the firstborn sons in the land of Egypt were marked for death. Nothing was required in order for their executions to occur on the designated night. But those who heard and believed the message, the faithful Israelites, would be spared by taking action, offering Passover lambs and putting the blood on the lintel and two doorposts of their homes. There was sure death outside the blood-marked doors but sure salvation within.

Observations:

1. All mankind is under the condemnation of death due to sin.

2. Nothing needs to be done for the sentence to be executed. Our sins of omission (what we fail to do that we should) and commission (what we do that we should not) add to our guilt but the reduction or avoidance of sin cannot remove the sentence.

3. There is sure salvation in the blood of the Lamb, Jesus Christ. There is certain destruction outside of Him. [See John 1:29; 1 Corinthians 5:7].

4. The blood must be applied by grace through faith for salvation to be received.

My challenge: Give thanks to God for His giving us a picture of salvation in the historical Passover of the Lord in Egypt. Praise God for His great salvation in His Son, the Lamb of God, Jesus Christ, the King of kings and Lord of lords. Take refuge in Him.

January 24/Day 24

Clear Leading; Hidden Reasons

Today's reading: Exodus 13:17-16:36

My selection: Exodus 13:17

When Pharaoh let the people go, God did not lead them by way of the land of the Philistines, although that was near. For God said, "Lest the people change their minds when they see war and return to Egypt."

My reflections: God's apparent zigzag direction had a purpose. The Lord led them but not by the most direct route geographically. He knew their hearts and minds. He knew they needed to make a clean break with the past and with Egypt. He reinforced that they could never go back by leading them through the Red Sea. The sea opened, they crossed, and the sea closed behind them. "No turning back, no turning back."

This closure was reinforced as the waters of the Red Sea swirled over and drowned the army of Pharaoh. God had left a marker of death in Egypt behind the Israelites with the slaying of the firstborn males and, now, the destruction of the army.

My challenge: God does not always reveal the reasons for His guidance but that does not mean He has no reasons. Believing disciples follow and trust His guiding hand even when it does not appear to be the most efficient or logical way.

Has God's path for you seemed inefficient and inexplicable? Trust Him that He has a purpose in all things even the zigzag pathways of your life. It is enough that we know what He wants us to do, even when we do not know why.

January 25/Day 25

One People of God

Today's reading: Exodus 17:1-20:21

My selection: Exodus 19:5

Now therefore, if you will indeed obey my voice and keep my covenant, you shall be my treasured possession among all peoples, for all the earth is mine.

My reflections: God's purpose in bringing Israel out of Egypt and slavery was to bring them to Himself so that they might obey His voice, keep His covenant, and be His treasured possession among all peoples. Through this relationship and their response to Him they would be a kingdom of priests and a holy nation. Peter uses this same language in referring to the Church (1 Peter 2:9). It was always God's purpose in choosing Abraham to transform Israel, the Old Testament church which is continued in the redemption of people from every tribe and tongue, into the Church of Jesus Christ. There is one Church, one purpose. Here we see the unfolding of God's purpose and the unity of Scripture that is emphasized in covenant theology, but, I believe, is missed by those who erroneously maintain a separate purpose and plan for ethnic Israel and the true spiritual Israel.

My challenge: What God did for the Israelites in forming them into a nation was part of the plan which resulted in the coming of the Messiah, Jesus Christ, in His life, in His atoning death, in His resurrection and in His ascension to the right hand of God the Father. Our hope is in Him who will come again to judge the living and the dead and to gather His one people to Himself for eternity. If this is your hope, give Him thanks today. Pray that His Kingdom will come fully and soon.

January 26/Day 26

Words from Heaven

Today's reading: Exodus 20:22-23:13

My selection: Exodus 20:22

The Lord said to Moses, "Thus you shall say to the people of Israel: 'You have seen for yourselves that I have talked with you from heaven.'"

My reflections: God talked with them from heaven. What an amazing thing for the Israelites to experience!

Yet we are not left out of this blessing.

The premise of Scripture is that God exists and communicates verbally with His people through His Word. His Word may not be ignored. His Word may not be twisted. It is good news that there is a God and that He is not silent. It is bad news for all who do not believe and obey the message. He is holy. He is worthy of worship. Israel and all who hear their testimony recognize there is no alternative to obedience. Yet for the believer there is great joy and peace in believing.

My challenge: Give thanks to God for His Word. Treasure it. Study it. Obey it carefully today.

January 27/Day 27

Acceptable Offerings

Today's reading: Exodus 23:14-25:40

My selection: Exodus 25:1-2

Speak to the people of Israel, that they take for me a contribution. From every man whose heart moves him you shall receive the contribution for me.

My reflections: The Lord ordered Moses to instruct the people to make contributions as their hearts moved them, but these contributions had to be of certain specified commodities, for example: gold, silver, bronze, certain skins, yarns, and woods (Exodus 25: 3-7).

There was freedom to contribute for those whose hearts were moved to do so but only according to the list of items needed. Moses in vs. 9 was ordered to follow the pattern for the tabernacle and its furniture exactly as he had been shown.

God will not accept offerings on our terms.

1. Offerings must be from the heart (2 Corinthians 9:7).

2. Offerings must be of the kind He specifies to build the tabernacle.

My challenge: We are foolish if we attempt to make offerings to God without regard for His Word and will. Do you give to the Lord from a sincere, cheerful heart? Do you give in order to build up His Church, which is the New Testament equivalent of the Old Testament tabernacle? Check your offering practices and attitudes. Be sure they actually comply with God's Word.

January 28/Day 28

The High Priest

Today's reading: Exodus 26:1-28:30

My selection: Exodus 28:29

So Aaron shall bear the names of the sons of Israel in the breastpiece of judgment on his heart, when he goes into the Holy Place, to bring them to regular remembrance before the Lord.

My reflections: Aaron was the designated high priest who would go into the Holy Place to bring to the Lord the names of the sons of Israel, all the tribes of God's chosen people. He also bore the judgment of the people before God as symbolized by a breastplate containing the mysterious Urim and Thummim through which the priest received oracles from God.

All this was a mere shadow of what would one day come when the true and perfect High Priest of a higher order than Aaron, the Lord Jesus Christ, would enter, not an earthly tabernacle but, the heavenly one bearing on His heart the judgment of His people, the true spiritual Israel. There will be much more about this in the New Testament (Hebrews 4:14 ff).

My challenge: God had an amazing and wise purpose for laying out the details of the Old Testament priesthood. He was putting in place a graphic depiction of the ministry of His Son, Jesus. As Paul cried out in Romans 11:33 (KJV): "O the depth of the riches both of the wisdom and knowledge of God! how unsearchable are his judgments, and his ways past finding out!"

If you know Christ as your High Priest who bears your name and your judgment before God, give Him praise for the great salvation that is yours in Him.

January 29/Day 29

Glory and Beauty

Today's reading: Exodus 28:31-30:21

My selection: Exodus 28:40

For Aaron's sons you shall make coats and sashes and caps. You shall make them for glory and beauty.

My reflections: All of the instructions for the tabernacle and furnishings were extremely detailed and orderly. The vestments of the priests were no less so. Aaron and his sons were to reflect glory and beauty in their dress, showing the solemnity of their office and work. They were to be ordained (or set apart) for their service of mediating between God and His people. They were marked as being the designated men to offer the sacrifices before God.

My challenge: Although the Old Testament priesthood was only a shadow of the priesthood of the Incarnate Son of God, it was to be carried out with the highest dignity. In the New Testament, the believers are called a holy priesthood (1 Peter 2:5). Since the Reformation, evangelicals have held to the doctrine of "the priesthood of the believer." All believers are members of the body of Christ with immediate access to God through Christ who alone is our mediator. As members of a holy priesthood called to make disciples of all nations, we believers have a grave responsibility to reflect the glory and beauty of the Lord in all our actions and speech.

Let us seek to fulfill this high calling today.

January 30/Day 30

Keeping the Sabbath

Today's reading: Exodus 30:22-33:11

My selection: Exodus 31:13

You are to speak to the people of Israel and say, "Above all you shall keep my Sabbaths, for this is a sign between me and you throughout your generations, that you may know that I, the Lord, sanctify you."

My reflections: Under the old covenant, God told His people to keep His Sabbaths on pain of death. While we could debate whether we should keep Saturday or Sunday as a holy day of worship, rest, and acts of necessity, it troubles me that modern evangelicals disregard any kind of Sabbath or Lord's Day. It is common for church goers to bolt out of worship and head for the restaurants. I hear of professing believers hitting the supermarkets or stadiums on Sunday afternoons or evenings without a second thought. Any suggestion that there may be something amiss with this will bring protests of Pharisaism and legalism.

Sadly, they are not only offending God's law, but also missing the blessing intended by keeping the Sabbath holy.

My challenge: What is your practice in keeping the Sabbath or the Lord's Day? Are you overlooking one of His commandments? Is this why your life is frantic, and you lack time for prayer, Bible study, and worship? Let us pray: "Lord, awaken your people--beginning with me--to the priority of keeping your Sabbaths for worship, corporate and private, for rest and for service for your glory."

January 31/Day 31

Seeing God's Glory

Today's reading: Exodus 33:12-35:35

My selection: Exodus 34:29-30

29 When Moses came down from Mount Sinai, with the two tablets of the testimony in his hand as he came down from the mountain, Moses did not know that the skin of his face shone because he had been talking with God.30 Aaron and all the people of Israel saw Moses, and behold, the skin of his face shone, and they were afraid to come near him.

My reflections: Moses' face shone after being in the Lord's presence. Others could see it and were afraid to come near him, but Moses himself did not realize how they saw him after he talked to God. Paul referred to this, in 2 Corinthians 3:7-18, contrasting the glory of the ministry of death and the ministry of the Spirit. Even that Old Testament ministry of condemnation, with law carved in letters of stone, held a frightening glory. The New Testament ministry of righteousness has a surpassing glory.

My challenge: What do we know of this glory? Far too little, I am afraid.

In the gospel, all who believe are assured of acceptance before God and access to His throne. Should that not drive us to prayer and result in radiant faces?

In Christ, we are brought near to God, the veil is removed, and we see the glory of the Lord. And this glory surpasses that which could be seen through Moses. This glory does not fade out but is permanent. It produces in us boldness and freedom and a progressive transformation into His image. Pray with me, "Lord, grow us in the knowledge and experience of your glory."

February 1/Day 32

God's Gifts and His Glory

Today's reading: Exodus 36:1-38:20

My selection: Exodus 36:2

And Moses called Bezalel and Oholiab and every craftsman in whose mind the LORD had put skill, everyone whose heart stirred him up to come to do the work.

My reflections: Respect is shown here for the abilities of workmen and craftsmen but, above all, the Lord is credited for having put into them the skill and intelligence to know how to do the work. This includes designing, engraving, constructing, weaving, etc.

As one who does not have many manual skills, I can appreciate these abilities. On our home remodel project, we had a trim carpenter who has a deformed right hand. Two of his fingers are extremely large stubs. Nevertheless, his work is impeccable. The skill is in his mind, not his hands, as we learned from Joni Eareckson Tada who, though a quadriplegic, does wonderful paintings holding a brush in her mouth.

My challenge: God gives gifts to His people for His glory. He stirs up their hearts to do the work. The gifts vary greatly but they all work together for Him, to bring Him praise and glory. Have you identified your God-given gifts? Is your heart stirred to use them fully for His glory?

Seek to discover and use your gifts faithfully.

February 2/Day 33

Listening and Finishing

Today's reading: Exodus 38:21-40:38

My selection: Exodus 40:33

He erected the court around the tabernacle and the altar, and set up the screen of the gate of the court. So Moses finished the work.

My reflections: Two things strike me here.

1. Moses paid attention to God's instructions. God gave great detail to Moses in the specifications of the tabernacle, the furnishings, and the priestly garments. How do we know? Moses wrote down those details. This shows that he was paying attention to what God was commanding him.

2. Moses completed the task. Moses was not a mere starter who left a trail of unfinished projects behind him. He saw it through to the end. He made sure all the workers did their work according to the plan.

My challenge: Since God has gone to great lengths to redeem a people for Himself, praise Him for His mercy and grace to us. Since God calls us to do His will with care and thoroughness, do today what He has commanded in His strength for His glory sparing no effort. If you know God wants you to do it, do it and finish it.

February 3/Day 34

The Offering that Pleases God

Today's reading: Leviticus 1:1-5:13

My selection: Leviticus 1:13

The entrails and the legs he shall wash with water. And the priest shall offer all of it and burn it on the altar; it is a burnt offering, a food offering with a pleasing aroma to the Lord.

My reflections: Here in Leviticus, the Old Testament church was given clear laws for how offerings were to be made. The goal of an offering was to please God. Offerings made according to law were pleasing to the Lord. Unlawful offerings do not please God no matter how sincere the worshiper. In Genesis 4, we saw that God accepted Abel's offering but not Cain's.

My challenge: We, as New Testament Christians, still need an offering in order to come to God, but that offering was made once for all by Jesus Christ. God was pleased with that offering. It was, of all offerings, the one sufficient offering for sin. Thus, God is not only *not* angry with His redeemed people, He is pleased with the offering which His Son made on our behalf and He is pleased with us who trust in that offering. Rejoice in His mercy and grace. Christian, your offering pleases God.

February 4/Day 35

Keeping a Clear Conscience

Today's reading: Leviticus 5:14-7:38

My selection: Leviticus 5:17

If anyone sins, doing any of the things that by the Lord's commandments ought not to be done, though he did not know it, then realizes his guilt, he shall bear his iniquity.

My reflections: Ignorance of the law is no excuse. This principle is still held to in the legal system in the United States. Citizens are responsible to know the law. Immunity is not granted on the basis of ignorance, otherwise, there would be an incentive to be (or claim to be) ignorant.

Forgiveness is possible through offerings and restitution.* Offerings were made to the Lord and restitution was made to those who had been harmed by the sin. Sin committed always is an offense to God and often is toward others as well. Although it is costly and painful to confess sin and make offerings and restitution, what joy to be forgiven! Before God our sin is atoned for in Christ. Let us not take lightly our responsibility to confess our sin. Before man we need to make restitution appropriately.

My challenge: Can you say with Paul, "I always take pains to have a clear conscience toward both God and man" (Acts 24:16)? Confess sin promptly. Make restitution fully. Keep your conscience clear.

* Restitution is reparation made by giving an equivalent or compensation for loss, damage, or injury caused; indemnification.

February 5/Day 36

How Not to Approach God

Today's reading: Leviticus 8:1-10:20

My selection: Leviticus 10:2

Fire came out from before the Lord and consumed them, and they died before the Lord.

My reflections: The same fire that came out from before the Lord and consumed the burnt offering showing acceptance of the offering, here came out from before the Lord and consumed the disobedient and presumptuous sons of Aaron.

Who says we do not need to fear the Lord? Who says the fear of the Lord is mere reverence and respect? Ask Aaron about that. Our God is a consuming fire. He will not give His glory to another. Those who are called to minister before Him must do so with great care and caution lest they be consumed for their sinful actions which they call ministry.

We read in Hebrews 12: 28-29: "Let us be grateful for receiving a kingdom that cannot be shaken, and thus let us offer to God acceptable worship, with reverence and awe, for our God is a consuming fire."

My challenge: Never lose the fear of the Lord, but, if you are trusting in Jesus Christ for forgiveness of sin and eternal life, balance fear with confidence that God has also accepted you in Christ and made you His child. Come into His presence with boldness but never casually and not without fear and awe. [See also Hebrews 10:19-22.]

February 6/Day 37

Responsible Care for Your Health

Today's reading: Leviticus 11:1-13:46

My selection: Leviticus 11:2

Speak to the people of Israel, saying, "These are the living things that you may eat among all the animals that are on the earth."

My reflections: Here God through Moses gives His people laws concerning diet and health. Although it is a fallen world, there are better and worse ways to live and flourish. Certainly, it is not wrong to be concerned about our health and well-being in this world. This does not indicate love for this world but recognition that God has put us here for a time and that (to quote the late R.C. Sproul) "right now counts forever." Even the mundane matters such as nutrition, rest, exercise, and preventive health care are important in our service to God and to one another.

I hear people say, "There's no need to take care of your health because God is going to take you when your time is up." The second part of the statement is true, but not the first. You will die at God's appointed time, true. But you will almost certainly feel better and be more productive if you care for your body properly.

My challenge: Let us glorify God in how we care for our health and the health of our families. Let us show appreciation for those who prepare and serve healthful meals to us and to those who help us take care of our health. If you have a spouse who encourages you to stay in good health by nutrition and exercise (as I do), then be appreciative. Do not resist that encouragement.

February 7/Day 38

The Practical Nature of God's Love

Today's reading: Leviticus 13:47-14:57

My selection: Leviticus 13:50

The priest shall examine the disease and shut up that which has the disease for seven days.

My reflections: The laws about leprosy extended to inanimate objects as well as people. Clothing and houses were to be examined for disease. Two observations:

1. God's love extends to concern for the health and well-being of His people. The creation itself is fallen, and material things are affected by contamination and disease. This law, as all biblical commands, should be understood as another evidence of God's love.

2. God's love includes designating responsible authorities to lead and care for His people. God assigned the task of diagnosis of leprosy to the priests. There needed to be a recognized, qualified official to rule on matters of disease. This was not a job for the lazy or the fearful.

My challenge: Thank God for His loving care of His people. God's people need spiritual leaders who care for the people and are not afraid to work or to risk involvement. If you have a pastor who serves with diligence and courage, thank God for him.

February 8/Day 39

The Day of Atonement

Today's reading: Leviticus 15:1-17:16

My selection: Leviticus 16:34

And this shall be a statute forever for you, that atonement may be made for the people of Israel once in the year because of all their sins. And Moses did as the Lord commanded him.

My reflections: This is the apex of the Aaronic priesthood, the annual Day of Atonement. Here two truths are pictured more vividly and concretely than anywhere else in the Bible:

1. Sin requires a perfect blood sacrifice. Blood had to be shed. That sacrifice had to be unblemished.

2. Sinners need to have their sin removed far away forever. The scapegoat symbolically and dramatically showed the sins of the people being taken away from them, never to be seen again.

In the gospel we learn that Jesus Christ is the Lamb of God who shed His blood to atone for sin and who takes away the sin of the world through His death and His high priestly function of offering the perfect once-for-all sacrifice for sin.

My challenge: Never think of the Old Testament sacrificial system as a mere relic of a by-gone era. It points wonderfully to a greater and fuller truth fulfilled perfectly and eternally in Jesus Christ. Praise God for His unspeakable gift!

February 9/Day 40

The Judgment and Mercy of God

Today's reading: Leviticus 18:1-20:27

My selection: Leviticus 18:3

You shall not do as they do in the land of Egypt, where you lived, and you shall not do as they do in the land of Canaan, to which I am bringing you. You shall not walk in their statutes.

My reflections: Why was God's judgment so severe on Canaan and the surrounding people? The behaviors that are condemned in the law here were those practiced by the peoples of Egypt and Canaan including: incest, homosexuality, bestiality, prostitution, child sacrifices, and necromancy (conjuration of the spirits of the dead for purposes of magically revealing the future or influencing the course of events*). God's patience with all this had come to an end and judgment on them was imminent. The wicked cultures would be obliterated, and their land given to the Israelites who had been carefully instructed in the law of God.

God does not allow us to define sin by a poll of the majority. He alone may say with authority what is and is not good and ethical. In a modern democracy, like the USA where the shifting sands of public opinion define good and evil, our moral survival depends on the influence of God-fearing people who take the law of God as revealed in the Bible as good policy for our society.

From God's viewpoint, mercy is being extended right now as wickedness, as He defines it, goes from being seen as merely acceptable to being noble. The solution to the problem of evil in the world is not to redefine evil as good but to call all people everywhere to repentance and faith in Jesus Christ, whose death on the cross bought forgiveness for all kinds of sin committed by all who would believe in Him.

My challenge: If you are reading this and are caught in any or all of the practices which are condemned in these chapters, do you not fear the judgment of God to come? If you do, it is evidence that God is giving you the grace to repent and believe in the gospel of Jesus Christ who assured an adulteress of forgiveness and charged her to renounce her sin (John 8:11). Heaven will be filled with sinners who have committed all the wickedness condemned in the law, but who also hate their sin and who through faith have found forgiveness in the One who took upon Himself the sin of His people. Our sin is great, but His love and atonement are even greater. Repent and believe today!

If you are a Christian, do not fear to call sin "sin" (including and especially your own), but also remember to proclaim hope for sinners through Jesus Christ for "if anyone is in Christ, he is a new creation. The old has passed away; behold, the new has come" (2 Corinthians 5:17). No doubt you (like me) are still struggling with your sinful flesh, but do not despair; He is at work in you, forgives you, and will receive you into His presence where the new creation that has come is completed (1 John 3:1-3).

*Merriam-Webster, I. (2003). *Merriam-Webster's collegiate dictionary.* Includes index. (Eleventh ed.). Springfield, Mass.: Merriam-Webster, Inc.)

Resting, Worshipping, and Feasting

Today's reading: Leviticus 21:1-23:25

My selection: Leviticus 23:2

Speak to the people of Israel and say to them, "These are the appointed feasts of the Lord that you shall proclaim as holy convocations; they are my appointed feasts."

My reflections: Here is a summary of the feasts that God prescribed to Israel. How interesting that these were commanded--not optional! We know that Israel neglected them to their own detriment and would bring judgment on their nation for that neglect. In other words, although you would think feasts and days of rest would be anticipated, they were not, at least not consistently. It seems that they learned quickly that by neglecting their Sabbaths and Passovers they could squeeze out more time to make money.

God knew that they would not worship, rest, and celebrate without making it a matter of law.

My challenge: This chapter also reminds us that there is to be a weekly and annual flow to life with feasts to commemorate historic events, including God's interventions in history and His creation. We do well to keep the Sabbath and to allow time for the Lord weekly and on special annual occasions. Rest, worship, and celebrate. Do not feel guilty about resting. Feel guilty for not resting.

February 11/Day 42

God's Ownership of His People

Today's reading: Leviticus 23:26-25:55

My selection: Leviticus 25:55

For it is to me that the people of Israel are servants. They are my servants whom I brought out of the land of Egypt: I am the Lord your God.

My reflections: God set a limit on the length of time an Israelite could be held as a servant by a stranger or foreigner, although it was voluntary slavery. If redemption (the purchase of freedom) did not occur first, then the servant was set free at the year of jubilee, which occurred every fifty years. The reason given was that the people of Israel were to be the servants of the Lord their God who brought them out of the land of Egypt. He bought them, and they belonged first of all to Him. Through economic hardships, they might (for a time) sell themselves as servants, but they could not belong permanently to a stranger.

My challenge:

1. Know your true identity. We, as God's people, need to see ourselves as His servants. Though we have jobs in the marketplace, we belong to Him, and we work for Him.

2. Maximize availability. Because we are His people, we should seek to be as available as possible to Him for His purposes in our lives. If I have enough to leave the marketplace, I free myself to pray and to serve God and others in new ways using my gifts.

3. Develop generosity. Because we are His people, we should assist our brothers and sisters who seek to serve Him. This may be by giving strategically to genuine cases of need or by teaching others to apply sound financial principles to their personal lives.

February 12/Day 43

The Pride of Power

Today's reading: Leviticus 26:1-27:34

My selection: Leviticus 26:19

I will break the pride of your power, and I will make your heavens like iron and your earth like bronze.

My reflections: Here, in Leviticus 26, is a detailed list of the promised blessings for obedience to God's law focused particularly on worship and commandments 2, 3, and 4. This is followed by an even longer list of punishments for disobedience. Both lists are comprehensive and cover physical and mental health and economic well-being.

As the selected verse above indicates, there is pride in power which is why those who are powerful in this world must be careful to fear God and worship Him. God's people are held to a standard of holiness and reverence that they must not allow to be obscured by the power they acquire in this world through His blessing. There would be warnings to the people (e.g. Deuteronomy 8) not to allow the blessings of God to turn into sources of pride and thus bring down the curses of God.

My challenge: Join me in this prayer. "Lord, everything I have is yours beginning with my very breath. Let me not grow proud in what I am, what I have done, or what I have obtained. All is yours. May I use it for your service today, maintaining the humility of a steward."

Contentment and Productivity

Today's reading: Numbers 1:1-2:34

My selection: Numbers 2:34

Thus did the people of Israel. According to all that the Lord commanded Moses, so they camped by their standards, and so they set out, each one in his clan, according to his fathers' house.

My reflections: In a perfect society, everyone would be productive and content. In our imperfect world, discontentment about one's status and standing contributes to the lack of willingness to bloom where you are planted. We struggle with who we are, but we will never resolve the struggle until we know and accept who we are in relationship to others, including God, our Creator.

The Lord spoke to Moses giving him a plan. Moses instructed the people, and the people did what was ordered. At least for a moment in time, the people seemed to have been both productive and content. God was at the center and they were willing to take their assigned places in camping and marching even though there was obvious ranking.

The plan called for four tribes to take leadership: Judah (on the east), Reuben (on the south), Ephraim (on the west), and Dan (on the north). The Levites camped in the center and marched in the middle after Judah and Reuben and before Ephraim and Dan.

The Lord's commands to Moses made worship a priority. Both literally and symbolically, God and worship were at the center of their life. Order was also important. Everyone could not be first. Each one had a place, but they were not all equal. Here are two key elements if the people of God were to be productive and content:

the centrality of worship and the acceptance of a division of labor and rank.

My challenge: I cannot make my society follow these principles of worship and acceptance of roles, but I can begin with myself and, to the degree I am able, with my friends and family. A failure to keep God at the center of life goes hand-in-hand with discontentment about my role and rank in life. The fear of God makes one more willing to accept His assigned role and rank in His kingdom and to be productive and content. Are you content? Are you productive? Are you blooming where you are planted? Think about that.

February 14/Day 45

Almost Forgotten

Today's reading: Numbers 3:1-4:33

My selection: Numbers 3:4

Nadab and Abihu died before the Lord when they offered unauthorized fire before the Lord in the wilderness of Sinai, and they had no children. So Eleazar and Ithamar served as priests in the lifetime of Aaron their father.

My reflections: I heard this quote many years ago when I was a student: "They died and when they were gone it was as if they had never lived." I don't know the name of the author, but it is almost true for Nadab and Abihu. Almost--because, although they left no offspring, they did leave a terrible example written down, here a second time so far in the Scriptures, to be read and pondered for the rest of human history and beyond. [See February 5 reading.] They presumptuously and arrogantly misused their office as priests.

My challenge: God's servants, whether ordained ministers or lay people, have an obligation to do what they are called to do, to do it well, and not to seek to turn it into some kind of mechanism for self-glorification or advancement. Beware of seeking great things for yourself.

February 15/Day 46

The Blessing of God's People

Today's reading: Numbers 4:34-6:27

My selection: Numbers 6:24-26

[24] The Lord bless you and keep you; [25] the Lord make his face to shine upon you and be gracious to you;[26] the Lord lift up his countenance upon you and give you peace.

My reflections: This traditional blessing was given by the Lord to Moses for Aaron and his sons to pronounce upon the people of Israel. It is wonderful as it recognizes that true blessing comes from God and from being in His favor.

1. Presence. Blessing from God includes His face to shine upon them and His grace to be shown to them. It involves His countenance to be lifted up towards them. They are not alone. God sees them, and He sees them with love and favor.

2. Protection. Being kept by God implies safety and security for His people.

3. Peace. The Hebrew word here is "barak", the peace which is the result of this blessing. Peace is given by God. It is the true peace which is internal not merely outward, depending on the up-and-down circumstances of life. Jesus repeated this theme with His disciples. "Peace I leave with you; my peace I give to you. Not as the world gives do I give to you. Let not your hearts be troubled, neither let them be afraid" (John 14:27).

My challenge: This blessing is not unconditional. In pronouncing it, the priests were putting God's name on the people. Blessing came to them because they were included in the people who had received His name. In the gospel of Jesus Christ, we learn that to have God's name is not a matter of being born into the line of Israel. It depends upon believing faith through the grace of God by which Jews and Gentiles are made God's people. The Church of Jesus Christ, the Israel of God, is blessed with God's presence, protection, and peace. Is this blessing yours? Believe in the promised Messiah, the Lord Jesus Christ, through whom come all the blessings of God.

February 16/Day 47

Communication with God

Today's reading: Numbers 7:1-89

My selection: Numbers 7:89

And when Moses went into the tent of meeting to speak with the Lord, he heard the voice speaking to him from above the mercy seat that was on the ark of the testimony, from between the two cherubim; and it spoke to him.

My reflections: The completion of the tabernacle, the furnishings and the vestments of the priests was celebrated over a twelve-day period with each of the twelve tribes providing sacrifices for one of the days. All this culminated with Moses entering the tent of meeting to speak with the Lord. He heard the voice speaking to him from above the mercy seat between the two cherubim.

God's communication is not given in the same manner all through history, but it is always clear and unmistakable to the believer. He spoke audibly to some, like Moses and the prophets. He spoke both audibly and tangibly in His Son, the Lord Jesus Christ. He spoke through the Apostles as they were inspired by the Holy Spirit to write the New Testament.

My challenge: We err if we seek some other kind of personal communication with God, ignoring the means of communication He has already given: His Word and prayer. I have felt God's presence at times in my life more vividly than usual. I have been impressed at times with God's direction for me through His Holy Spirit in accordance with His Word. But I do not seek or expect some kind of personal audible "word" from Him as He gave to Moses. He has spoken through His Son. The Bible is His Word to me and to all whether we believe it or not. Hear His Word. Pray to Him. He has spoken finally and definitively through His Son and His Word. He welcomes us to come before His throne in prayer. [See Hebrews 1:1-2; 4:14-16].

Traveling Prayers

Today's reading: Numbers 8:1-10:36

My selection: Numbers 10:35

Whenever the ark set out, Moses said, "Arise, O Lord, and let your enemies be scattered, and let those who hate you flee before you."

My reflections: Moses made it a custom to pray as they broke camp and when they rested from the march. One of their great dangers was enemies who might attack them on the way. He prayed for the Lord's enemies to flee before Him. The words used here are interesting. He did not refer to them as Israel's enemies, but the Lord's enemies. He did not pray for victory in war over them, but that they would not even oppose them. He prayed for them to be scattered. They are identified as those who hate the Lord.

Upon resting, Moses did not assume God's continued presence with them, but prayed that He might "return" to them.

My challenge: How presumptuous we can be in our going and coming when we do not pray for the Lord's protection! When we rest we may falsely feel safe, but we should always be aware of our need for His presence. Do not be presumptuous of God's protection and presence but pray for both.

February 18/Day 49

Leadership: Success vs. Obedience

Today's reading: Numbers 11:1-13:33

My selection: Numbers 13:30

Caleb quieted the people before Moses and said, "Let us go up at once and occupy it, for we are well able to overcome it."

My reflections: Caleb showed leadership characterized by faith, wisdom, and courage in opposing his fellow spies. The Lord had told Moses to send the spies into the land of Canaan which He promised them as His gift (Numbers 13:2). Caleb believed that God was giving them the land. The mandate for the spies was not to determine the viability of the invasion but the nature of it. The ten spies saw giants and danger, not God and His promises. Their report was, of course, self-contradictory. They said that the land devours its inhabitants. If the latter were literally true no one would be living in it, and the spies themselves would not have returned safely.

Alas, wise and believing leaders are not always able to turn the tide of human events. The people would listen to the voice of the doubters and refuse to enter the land. Nevertheless, God would make Caleb a shining example by preserving him strong and healthy through the forty years of wilderness wanderings. He and Joshua alone would see the Promised Land as a reward for their faith. Caleb did not "succeed" but he did obey and for that he was rewarded.

My challenge: Do not think your leadership has failed, if you have been obedient. Success is in God's hands. Obedience is in ours. As a leader, do what is right, whether or not it is successful.

February 19/Day 50

The Place of the Law

Today's reading: Numbers 14:1-15:41

My selection: Numbers 15:32

While the people of Israel were in the wilderness, they found a man gathering sticks on the Sabbath day.

My reflections: The law could not save, but it could, and did, condemn. Furthermore, the commandments were not prioritized as if some were more important than others. Breaking the Sabbath, knowingly and openly, was an act of direct rebellion against God. It was no less of a sin before God than making a graven image, blaspheming His name, or adultery.

We err when we think the law can save (Romans 3:19-20). We err when we think the law is irrelevant (Matthew 5:17-20). We, as Christians, trust in Christ for forgiveness, but we seek to obey the law for His glory and our own good. We fail to keep it perfectly, but we must not take lightly what He has commanded. Curiously, I recently had a conversation with a businessman who says he seeks to keep the Ten Commandments but, apparently, he sees no problem opening his business and working every Sunday.

Certainly, Jesus shed light on the fourth commandment in His teaching, which we will see when we get to the gospels. He declared Himself "Lord of the Sabbath" and said that the Sabbath was made for man and not man for the Sabbath. He confirmed exceptions for emergencies (like an ox in a ditch), for works of service {like healing), and works of necessity (like picking grain for immediate consumption).

My challenge: Take seriously God's law, not as a basis for salvation and acceptance before God, but as an essential source of guidance for doing His will. Be thankful that Jesus Christ fulfilled the law perfectly and has taken upon Himself the punishment for our failures to keep it. Let your law keeping efforts be done as an act of gratitude to God.

February 20/ Day 51

The Dangers of Role Discontentment

Today's reading: Numbers 16:1-18:32

My selection: Numbers 16:9

Is it too small a thing for you that the God of Israel has separated you from the congregation of Israel, to bring you near to himself, to do service in the tabernacle of the Lord and to stand before the congregation to minister to them?

My reflections: Here rebellion broke out again, this time led by a Levite who, though a worker in the tabernacle, was not a priest, and two members of the tribe of Ephraim. The former wanted promotion to the priesthood and the latter wanted political power. They joined together in a common cause to bring down Moses.

Once again, the theme of contentment (or the lack thereof) arose. Moses specifically confronted the Levite, Korah, on the issue. Lack of contentment includes the unwillingness to accept the role God gave him to play while focusing on, what he considers, a greater role in the life of Israel.

As a consequence of this evil craving, Korah, Dathan, and Abiram did not gain more power and prestige. Moreover, they lost all that they had including their lives.

My challenge: What are your God-given roles? Are you fulfilling them to the best of your ability? Are you distracted with an unholy desire for some other role? How can re-focusing on your place in God's kingdom help to reduce the coveting of some other place? How can coveting a role not given to you endanger your place in your family, the church, your job, and your community?

Beware of coveting good things not meant for you. Be content. Be faithful to the roles and tasks to which God has called you.

February 21/Day 52

Contaminating Purification: A Contradiction?

Today's reading: Numbers 19:1-21:35

My selection: Numbers 19:7

Then the priest shall wash his clothes and bathe his body in water, and afterward he may come into the camp. But the priest shall be unclean until evening.

My reflections: The priest became "unclean" as he offered a sacrifice for purification. How can that be? Is this some kind of contradiction? No! This is one more indication that mankind needed a better sacrifice than what the old covenant and the law of Moses provided. The Old Testament sacrifices were not adequate to remove sin. God was establishing the fact that all are sinful, and no one is able to make an offering which is sufficient to remove sins, perform spiritual cleansing and achieve acceptance before a Holy God.

My challenge: Jesus Himself was made sin for us that in Him we might become the righteousness of God (2 Corinthians 5:21). His was the only sacrifice that did not contaminate the Priest. Praise God today for His great salvation through the sacrifice that cleanses us of our sin.

Note: For further reading on this see Hebrews 4:14-10:18 which discusses in detail the superiority of Christ to Aaron (4:14-7:28) and the superior priesthood of Christ (8:1-10:18).

God Unchanging/Unchangeable

Today's reading: Numbers 22:1-24:14

My selection: Numbers 23:19

God is not man, that he should lie, or a son of man, that he should change his mind. Has he said, and will he not do it? Or has he spoken, and will he not fulfill it?

My reflections: Balaam was an enigmatic character. He had some knowledge of the God of Israel, and he could sometimes make accurate statements about Him, such as the verse above. He may be the perfect example of the person who believes truth intellectually while being spiritually lost. In James 2:19 we learn that even the demons believe (in an intellectual sense, not savingly). They even show fear before God as they tremble.

As Balaam's words indicate, it is foolish to think of God as one who can be pressured or manipulated into changing what He has said. His Word is established. He is the only unchanging one. It is a good thing, too, because if He were not unchanging and unchangeable, we would live in total uncertainty. He is neither arbitrary nor fickle. As the 19th Century Scottish poet, Walter C. Smith, wrote in the third stanza of "Immortal, Invisible":

To all, life Thou givest, to both great and small;
In all life Thou livest, the true life of all;
We blossom and flourish as leaves on the tree,
And wither and perish—but naught changeth Thee.

My challenge: Worship Him. Obey Him. Glorify Him. Trust Him. He is worthy of worship, obedience, glorification, and trust. Always has been. Always will be.

February 23/Day 54

Temptation, Sin, and Judgment

Today's reading: Numbers 24:15-26:65

My selection: Numbers 25:18

[The Midianites and the Moabites] have harassed you with their wiles, with which they beguiled you in the matter of Peor, and in the matter of Cozbi, the daughter of the chief of Midian, their sister, who was killed on the day of the plague on account of Peor."

My reflections: The Midianites and Moabites had invited the Israelites to the sacrifices to their gods. Soon there was sexual involvement as well as false worship. The Midianites could not persuade Balaam to call down the curses of God on Israel, but they could defeat them by attracting them through prostitution and pagan feasts. The Midian nation knew exactly what they were doing. They had harassed Israel "with their wiles." God judged Israel but ultimately spared them and commissioned them to bring judgment on Midian. Later Balaam would die in battle at the hands of the people he had been hired to curse. [See Numbers 31:8, 15-16].

My challenge: How are you being tempted by evil forces through the appetites of the flesh? Are you aware of the "schemes" of our enemy, Satan (Ephesians 6:10-11)? Do not be duped. There are godly and ungodly ways to satisfy our physical and social needs. Seek godly and God-glorifying ways to be satisfied.

February 24/Day 55

Daily Offerings: Then and Now

Today's reading: Numbers 27:1-29:40

My selection: Numbers 28:2

Command the people of Israel and say to them, "My offering, my food for my food offerings, my pleasing aroma, you shall be careful to offer to me at its appointed time."

My reflections: The Lord gave Moses very specific instructions for daily, weekly, monthly, and annual sacrifices, all of which are a foreshadowing of the ultimate, once-for-all offering of our great High Priest, the Lord Jesus Christ.

Christians are called to be no less devoted to daily worship than our Old Testament brothers and sisters. In his Epistle to the Romans, Paul, after carefully laying out the gospel and the basis for our standing with God by grace through faith, gives this call to the New Testament version of sacrifice: "I appeal to you therefore, brothers, by the mercies of God, to present your bodies as a living sacrifice, holy and acceptable to God, which is your spiritual worship. Do not be conformed to this world, but be transformed by the renewal of your mind, that by testing you may discern what is the will of God, what is good and acceptable and perfect" (Romans 12:1-2).

By the mercies of God, we are justified before Him. We are able to present ourselves as a holy and acceptable offering to God because, by grace through faith, Christ has purified us. It is a privilege and a responsibility to offer ourselves daily to Him as a living sacrifice.

My challenge: Does your daily devotional time include a presentation of yourself to God as a living sacrifice? Keep in mind that your sacrifice of yourself is holy and acceptable through Christ. Rejoice, your offering pleases God.

February 25/Day 56

Special Protection for Women

Today's reading: Numbers 30:1-31:54

My selection: Numbers 30:15

If he makes them null and void after he has heard of them, then he shall bear her iniquity.

My reflections: I am sure some of my feminist friends will bristle at this passage; but wait. The law actually protected women both married and single from shady deals, as well as rash commitments. They had a safety net in case they made a vow or contract that was unwise or ungodly. There has been much made in our times of the inequality of pay scales for women in comparison to men, but here the women had protection even when they freely made a bad deal. Men had no such advantage but were required to keep their word without an escape hatch (Numbers 30: 1-2).

Furthermore, when a woman made a vow and her husband disavowed it, he would take responsibility for the consequences. She would be free from the vow, but any repercussions for the disavowing would fall to the husband.

Finally, while some will see this law as holding women in disdain, as if they were more prone to make rash vows than men, there is also a built in (and valid) assumption that men tend to procrastinate in decision making. Men whose wives or unmarried daughters make vows had until sundown to make a decision about sustaining or voiding the vow. If nothing was said by the end of the day, the vow would stand.

My challenge: God wisely gave this law not as an insult to women or to unfairly empower men, but in recognition of the human tendencies and weaknesses of both. I, for one, long for a society in which men love and protect their wives, sisters, and daughters instead of abusing and competing with them. When will we see a time in which women cannot be tricked and cheated in business dealings and contracts? If the law of Numbers 30 held true, anyone dealing with a woman would have to beware lest the deal be voided and exposed for what it is.

Pray as Jesus taught us, "Thy kingdom come."

February 26/Day 57

Seize the Day

Today's reading: Numbers 32:1-33:56

My selection: Numbers 33:1

These are the stages of the people of Israel, when they went out of the land of Egypt by their companies under the leadership of Moses and Aaron.

My reflections: If this list of stages in Israel's journey seems long and tedious, imagine how it would have been to camp and move and camp and move and camp and move for forty interminable years! The nation paid a severe price for their disbelief. But the journey was ending. A new generation was on the brink of entering the land.

My father, on his death bed, said he was stunned by the brevity of life, although he had lived nearly 81 years. Life can seem long in youth and middle age, but in the end, it is a mere vapor. As Israel stood on the border of Canaan, there were only two adults, Joshua and Caleb, who were alive at the time of the spy mission at Kadesh Barnea. It was a young nation whose elders had all died in the wilderness.

My challenge: Life is brief but not insignificant. We are here for a time and called to believe God, obey God, trust God, glorify God, and love God. Now is the time. Use it well. Seize the day!

February 27/Day 58

Why Reputation Matters

Today's reading: Numbers 34:1-36:13

My selection: Numbers 35:23

He was not [the deceased's] enemy and did not seek his harm.

My reflections: A key factor in determining the guilt of an accused manslayer was the history of his relationship with the victim. If they were not enemies in the past, this would weigh in favor of the manslayer. If there had been a history of enmity between them, this would indicate possible guilt in the case.

Two observations here:

1. It pays to do everything possible to maintain peace with others. [See Romans 12:16, 18].

2. It is important to exercise extreme care when involved with others in any kind of dangerous activity. We are called to preserve life and that includes keeping the rule "safety first." This should include driving within the speed limit as well as sports and work situations where others can be harmed.

My challenge: To cause the death of another is a horrible thing. Beware of setting up any situation that would bring a lifetime of regret. Try to resolve conflicts promptly. Be known for peacefulness.

February 28/Day 59

Getting in Sync with God

Today's reading: Deuteronomy 1:1-3:11

My selection: Deuteronomy 1:43

I spoke to you, and you would not listen; but you rebelled against the command of the Lord and presumptuously went up into the hill country.

My reflections: There were two ways that Israel got out of sync with God. First, they caved in to fear and refused to go into the land. Second, they refused to accept the consequent punishment and defiantly attempted to go into the land in their own strength and without God's blessing.

Christians need to understand that disobedience has consequences. God's will includes not only a *what* but also a *when.* His people need to obey not only what He tells them to do but also when. To fail to do this may mean a door closes and does not reopen even though they come later to their senses and repent.

My challenge: What is God leading you to do? When does He want you to do it? Are you seeking to be in sync with Him? Sometimes we need patience to wait for His go ahead. Other times, we need faith and bold courage to go ahead in spite of our sense of weakness. Get in sync with God.

March 1/Day 60

The Fear of God in Prayer

Today's reading: Deuteronomy 3:12-5:33

My selection: Deuteronomy 5:24

Behold, the Lord our God has shown us his glory and greatness, and we have heard his voice out of the midst of the fire. This day we have seen God speak with man and man still live.

My reflections: The heads of the tribes of Israel expressed a true view of God. They recognized that what had occurred at Mt. Sinai was a unique event: they had seen the glory and greatness of God. God had spoken to them, yet they had lived. They did not miss the significance nor the fact that to survive an encounter with God was not an everyday thing. They lived to tell about it.

God is a God to be feared. People today have largely lost this view. What seems to be the common view now is: either God does not exist or, if He does, He exists to make us happy. The heads of the tribes got this right as God confirmed (Deuteronomy 5:28.)

My challenge: Do you fear God? If He is not a God to be feared, He is not a God of power. If He is not a God of power, your prayers are futile. There is little difference, practically speaking, between a weak god and no god. We pray to Him because He is powerful but also because through Christ we are welcome to bring our petitions to Him.

Pray to God, but fear Him, too.

March 2/Day 61

More Dangerous than Adversity

Today's reading: Deuteronomy 6:1-9:6

My selection: Deuteronomy 6:10,12

[10] And when the Lord your God brings you into the land that he swore to your fathers, to Abraham, to Isaac, and to Jacob, to give you—with great and good cities that you did not build... [12] then take care lest you forget the Lord, who brought you out of the land of Egypt, out of the house of slavery.

My reflections: God warned the Israelites to beware of forgetting Him, the source of their wealth and blessing, once they had settled into the land. They would go into a place with cities, houses, furnishings, wells of water, vineyards, and orchards. None of this did they work for.

It is very difficult for people to appreciate what is given to them. There is danger in being given things, in that it can result in ungratefulness and presumption. In the case of Israel, they would eventually forsake God and replace Him with idols--the very idols that the defeated nations had trusted in. Go figure.

My challenge: Sin is not logical. As my friend, Pastor Fred Greco says, "Sin makes you stupid." It starts in the heart with ungratefulness and spreads to false worship. If we are blessed with abundance, may God help us to never forget Him. Don't be stupid. Be alert to the fact that there is more spiritual danger in times of prosperity than in times of adversity. Whatever your circumstances, worship and praise God for all that you are and have.

Response of the Broken-hearted Pastor

Today's reading: Deuteronomy 9:7-11:32

My selection: Deuteronomy 9:18

Then I lay prostrate before the Lord as before, forty days and forty nights. I neither ate bread nor drank water, because of all the sin that you had committed, in doing what was evil in the sight of the Lord to provoke him to anger.

My reflections: Moses, who functioned as a pastor and preacher to Israel as well as their national leader, had every cause to be devastated by their idolatry. Aaron and the people had witnessed the great working of God in their exodus from Egypt. But while Moses was on Mt. Sinai, they grew impatient and defaulted to a version of idolatry they had, no doubt, seen in Egypt.

How did Moses respond? Anger and fear were his emotions: anger toward Aaron and the people and fear toward God. But he did not become paralyzed or passive. He broke the stone tablets upon which the law was written, out of anger. Then He lay before the Lord, seeking mercy for the people.

My challenge: What pastor of unbelieving church members or what parent of unbelieving children cannot identify with Moses? If that is you, how are you responding? Do you seek the Lord in serious prayer? It is fruitless and futile to berate ourselves for the faithlessness of those in our care. We can teach and model the gospel (and we should!) but we cannot make those in our care believe, repent, and obey. Faithful spiritual leaders will turn to God in prayer. Moses did. Israel eventually made it to the Promised Land. Do not let your anger become sinful (Ephesians 4:26). Instead--like Moses--pray.

March 4/Day 63

Biblical Worship

Today's reading: Deuteronomy 12:1-14:29

My selection: Deuteronomy 12:1

These are the statutes and rules that you shall be careful to do in the land that the Lord, the God of your fathers, has given you to possess, all the days that you live on the earth.

My reflections: What follows here are regulations for the proper worship of God in Ancient Israel. Scripture regulates worship. Here in the law, God told His people where, when, and how they were to worship. Although the Old Testament priesthood and worship were mere shadows of what would be fulfilled in Christ, the principle of regulating worship by Scripture is still in effect.

I once visited a church that was in the middle of constructing their worship center. The pastor proudly showed me around. He had a confessional booth reminiscent of a Roman Catholic Church. There was an "altar" where people could come and kneel to receive communion. There was a baptistery behind the pulpit which would facilitate baptism by immersion. His hodge-podge sanctuary revealed the confusion of theology in his mind rather than a concern to regulate worship according to Scripture. He may have thought he would be more successful since the church would draw people of various religious traditions.

My challenge: Does your church seek to heed Scripture in ordering worship or does it merely follow the latest fad for packing the pews? If a church will ignore the Bible on the matter of worship, how can you trust it on the matter of salvation or other theology? Find out what your church believes about the regulative principle of worship.

Poverty and Generosity

Today's reading: Deuteronomy 15:1-18:22

My selection: Deuteronomy 15:11

For there will never cease to be poor in the land. Therefore I command you, "You shall open wide your hand to your brother, to the needy and to the poor, in your land."

My reflections: At first glance it seems like the law contradicts itself here in saying that, if they obey, there will be no poor in the land (vs. 4) and then saying there would always be poor in the land. There would always be poor, but there was always to be generosity toward the needy (vs. 11). The generosity would insure that, although there would always be poverty, there would always be immediate relief and care for those who were suffering because of it.

This system called for local, tribal, or family attention to the needy. The people of Israel were never to ignore a needy brother. Local and family involvement in welfare would help insure that the system was not abused and that those who were assisted were not also enabled to slide into chronic dependency.

Two things would always be true: the existence of poverty and the command to generosity. The law did not anticipate an earthly kingdom in which either poverty or generosity would cease to exist.

In modern western society, our impersonal welfare system allows the wealthy to dispatch their obligations to the poor without personal involvement. It allows the poor to work a faceless system and feel that they have a right to permanent assistance--a handout rather than a hand up. Poverty is not diminished, and generosity is not encouraged.

My challenge: Shall we pray? Lord, help us, who have more than enough, to be generous and involved as we have opportunity. If we are in need, let us seek to be conscientious in using the assistance we get to improve our financial footing so that we can be among those who assist rather than those who need assistance. Help us all to be content with what we have and to beware of the love of money.

March 6/Day 65

Capital Punishment for Rebellion

Today's reading: Deuteronomy 19:1-22:12

My selection: Deuteronomy 21:21

All the men of the city shall stone [the rebellious son] to death with stones. So you shall purge the evil from your midst, and all Israel shall hear, and fear."

My reflections: This section of the law lists a number of crimes which our legal system does not recognize or punish severely (e.g. cross-dressing 22:5). Here we have the law concerning a rebellious son. In this case the offenses include disobedience to parents, lack of response to parental discipline, gluttony, and drunkenness. It is not surprising that these behaviors should be found punishable. It is surprising that they should be ultimately punishable by death by public stoning.

I, for one, am glad that we apply the moral law (Ten Commandments) to our Christian behavior and, to some degree, it influences our legal system. I am glad we have a system which is more patient with rebellious children. However, we see that the law of Israel in the Old Testament theocracy did not tolerate chronic rebellion, idleness and substance abuse by youth. This law seems to say that once these behaviors have settled in they are impossible to root out. Make this offender a horrible example for the rest of the nation.

Today we spend huge amounts of money and effort to try to rehabilitate the chronically rebellious, lazy drug addict. There seem to be more cases of failure than of success. The generally recognized approach to psychotherapy assists clients to shift blame to others for their problems and thus reduce guilt while decreasing motivation or hope to change. Our law releases youth at age 18 from any obligation to their parents.

My challenge:

1. Youth, be warned. Rebellious children need to know that their behavior is serious and, once deeply rooted in one's character, is hard to eliminate. This is why in Ancient Israel it would result in public stoning to death. Maybe some of our youth will be motivated by this warning to stop blame shifting and start working to change.

2. Parents must discipline their children because of the seriousness of rebellion in their children. It must not be encouraged or tolerated in the toddler, much less the teenager.

I know of no record in the Bible that this law was ever applied. There are a number of cases where it was ignored to the detriment of the nation (the sons of Eli, David's sons Ammon and Absalom). Parents, beware. Children, beware. The gospel gives hope to the worst sinner. Forgiveness comes through Christ, and He is able to save those who come to God through Him. Nevertheless, there will be great suffering and temporal loss to parents of rebellious children and to children who rebel against their parents.

March 7/Day 66

Marriage Laws: Ancient Israel vs. Modern America

Today's reading: Deuteronomy 22:13-25:19

My selection: Deuteronomy 22:22

You shall purge the evil from Israel.

My reflections: While there are many apparent inequities in Deuteronomy 22:13-30, the laws here highlight the importance of sexual purity before marriage, the legal status of a betrothal or engagement, and the permanency of marriage. What a stark contrast to the practices of western culture in the 21st Century! The media and pop culture depict casual sex with no consequences. The dating scene has created categories of commitment like: being "in a relationship," living together unmarried, engaged but living together, etc. There is no bright line between single, engaged, and married. All of this is blurred to our confusion. People hurt and are hurt.

My challenge:

1. Value and protect your virginity and that of those you love. Being able to give yourself to one person for a life time is a wonderful, God-honoring thing. Sexual experience before marriage, not only is not helpful, it is sinful.

2. Have clear lines between friendship, engagement, and marriage. Do not allow a blurring of the lines so that one or both of the people involved are not sure where they stand. Parental involvement is essential. An engagement is not marriage, but it should be entered into with the same seriousness as marriage.

3. Never get married if you consider a divorce a likely, attractive, or, even, possible option. Marriage is for adults but in the best of cases both are sinners who will need to work at growing in love, patience, and commitment. A good marriage is not achieved in days, weeks, months or years but in decades of struggle, forgiveness, and unshakeable commitment.

4. When you have failed in one or many ways to be perfect, remember the gospel: good news of forgiveness, cleansing, and renewal in Jesus Christ. Apply it to yourself and to your spouse. A spiritual life, centered around the true and living God of the Bible, is crucial for lifelong endurance of the joys and trials in a marriage relationship.

March 8/Day 67

The Path to Blessing

Today's reading: Deuteronomy 26:1-28:14

My selection: Deuteronomy 28:1

If you faithfully obey the voice of the Lord your God, being careful to do all his commandments that I command you today, the Lord your God will set you high above all the nations of the earth.

My reflections: This verse opens a list of blessings promised to Israel contingent upon their faithful obedience to the law and to the worship of the Lord alone. The blessings extend from their individual lives to their national success, from their personal work to their international relations. A very optimistic picture is painted here as the Israelites stand on the border of the Promised Land. These blessings were never fully achieved for any significant length of time, although there seem to have been brief periods in which they experienced enough of them to taste what could be if they were completely and consistently faithful.

Sadly, even a taste of the good life is not enough to overcome the depravity of human nature. It takes a fundamental change to make a fallen sinner even desire to be consistently obedient. That change can only come when the Holy Spirit regenerates the spiritually dead giving a new heart and mind that repents of sin and believes the gospel. The Spirit has come upon the Church and regenerates people wherever the gospel is preached. But there is more to come. Jesus told us to pray that God's kingdom would come and that His will would be done on earth as it is in heaven.

I long for the kingdom to come fully, a kingdom that will never end in which righteousness dwells. Meanwhile, obedience and faithfulness to the Lord does bring blessing. God is calling out a people for Himself who will live in a new heavens and earth where the knowledge of the Lord will cover the earth as the waters cover the sea.

My challenge: Today, seek to repent and to believe the gospel. There will be a taste of heaven and a promise of more blessing to come.

March 9/Day 68

A Heart to Understand

Today's reading: Deuteronomy 28:15-29:29

My selection: Deuteronomy 29:4

To this day the Lord has not given you a heart to understand or eyes to see or ears to hear.

My reflections: God gave His people a long list of curses that they would experience should they break His covenant with them (Deut. 28). But without a heart to understand, eyes to see, and ears to hear they would not make the connection between their suffering and their sin. It is the grace and mercy of God that grants wisdom to see one's true spiritual condition and need. It is the grace and mercy of God that enables a spiritually dead sinner to repent and believe the gospel. God must give it.

My challenge: Has God given you a heart to understand? Do you think your sufferings are a result merely of the fallenness of this world rather than the means by which you are called to seek God more fully? Is your response to trials "I must plan better, prevent more, or prepare more wisely"? The one who has a heart to understand will respond, "Lord, show me my sin, forgive me, and grow me in grace to know You better."

All sin results in some kind of suffering, but not all suffering is a judgment of sin. Remember Job? Yet all suffering is sent to drive us to the Lord, not merely harden us with better planning and prevention. When we have a heart to understand we will react to trials with faith and a deepened desire to know and serve God better. We will call upon Him to grow our heart to understand.

March 10/Day 69

Bringing Delight to God

Today's reading: Deuteronomy 30:1-32:47

My selection: Deuteronomy 30:9

The Lord will again take delight in prospering you, as he took delight in your fathers.

My reflections: It's easy to forget that the Lord takes delight in His people when they walk in His ways. He has warned them about the dangers of complacency and compromise that allow the culture of pagan nations to seep in and seduce them to idolatry and unfaithfulness. He has promised that He will restore them when they repent and turn back to Him. But He also tells them, through Moses, that He will delight in prospering them no less than He delighted in Abraham, Isaac, and Jacob.

The thought of God delighting in prospering me is almost beyond comprehension. I take it on faith. It should spur obedience that has double motivation: to avoid the wrath of God and to bring joy to Him.

My challenge: Is your obedience motivated only by fear or is it also motivated by love? Fear of God is essential but so is love for God. Let your obedience today be prompted by love for God that longs to bring delight to Him.

March 11/Day 70

Characteristics of Godly Leadership

Today's reading: Deuteronomy 32:48-Joshua 2:24

My selection: Deuteronomy 34:9

Joshua the son of Nun was full of the spirit of wisdom, for Moses had laid his hands on him. So the people of Israel obeyed him and did as the Lord had commanded Moses.

My reflections: At Moses' death, leadership of Israel was transferred to Joshua. Here we have a commentary on both Moses and Joshua that gives us several characteristics of godly leadership:

1. Wise. Joshua was full of the spirit of wisdom. The task before Joshua would require great wisdom as the people were about to enter the Promised Land and face hostile nations. James 3:13-17 speaks of the qualities of the wisdom from above.

2. Duly installed. Moses officially ordained Joshua to take his place by the laying on of his hands. This action made the transition to Joshua seamless. From what we read in the Book of Joshua, he seems to have had no serious resistance to his leadership. Leaders who do plan for their replacement are wise. That planning should include clear communication both to the new leader and to the people who will follow him.

3. Authoritative. Joshua was effective because his leadership was in accordance with what the Lord had told Moses to do. His authority came from God through Moses. Moses' epitaph exceeded that of any other prophet of Israel and Joshua respected that. Joshua did not seek to outdo his mentor but merely carry on the Lord's assigned task into the new land.

Leadership is exercised at all levels. Your calling is not that of Moses or Joshua, but, at some level, you are given the authority and responsibility to manage yourself, your time, and your money. You may be a leader in your home and family, in the marketplace, or in a profession. You may have employees, or you may not. But you do have a sphere of leadership to exercise.

My challenge: What is your God-given task? Are you full of the spirit of wisdom? Are you functioning with a clear mandate to act (i.e. are you duly installed)? Is your leadership authoritative but not self-seeking (derived from the Lord's commands)? Are you content to do it without seeking to outshine others? Is God's glory what you long for in your situation? How does seeking God's glory today affect your attitudes and actions in your job or role? Pursue the characteristics of godly leadership in your sphere of responsibility.

March 12/Day 71

Godly Leadership: Giving Reassurance of His Presence

Today's reading: Joshua 3:1-6:27

My selection: Joshua 3:10,13

[10] Joshua said, "Here is how you shall know that the living God is among you and that he will without fail drive out from before you the Canaanites, the Hittites, the Hivites, the Perizzites, the Girgashites, the Amorites, and the Jebusites. [13] When the soles of the feet of the priests bearing the ark of the Lord, the Lord of all the earth, shall rest in the waters of the Jordan, the waters of the Jordan shall be cut off from flowing, and the waters coming down from above shall stand in one heap."

My reflections: Joshua wanted to make sure that the people were aware that it was the living God who was among them and that He would drive out the nations who occupied the land. He pointed them to God by reminding them that the ark was going before them. God would stop the waters of the Jordan from flowing when the priests stepped into it. Joshua had a monument built to commemorate the miraculous event of this crossing.

Here is wise leadership exemplified. The godly leader points his people to the Lord and keeps His presence, promises, power, and purposes before them. They would see victory in Jericho in a miraculous way.

My challenge: Do you keep the Lord's presence, promises, power, and purposes before others? Start by keeping Him central in your own thoughts today. Those you lead and influence need to see the reality of God in your life.

March 13/Day 72

The Anatomy of Temptation

Today's reading: Joshua 7:1-9:27

My selection: Joshua 7:20-21

20 And Achan answered Joshua, "Truly I have sinned against the Lord God of Israel, and this is what I did: 21 when I saw among the spoil a beautiful cloak from Shinar, and 200 shekels of silver, and a bar of gold weighing 50 shekels, then I coveted them and took them. And see, they are hidden in the earth inside my tent, with the silver underneath."

My reflections: The despicable Achan, to his credit, immediately confessed his sin once it was discovered. He also gave a helpful analysis of the steps to his sin. He said, "I have sinned", and "this is what I did."

1. I saw

2. I coveted

3. I took

4. I hid

It is striking that he could not enjoy the cloak, the silver, and the gold. He had to hide them. As is always true, his sin did not give the enjoyment it promised. In the end it cost lives, including that of Achan and his clan. The best place to stop sin is at the earliest stage - the seeing or the coveting. God promises the crown of life to those who are steadfast in trials. [See James 1:12-15.]

My challenge: How can you cut off potential sin by stopping it at the seeing or coveting stage? How have you experienced the emptiness of indulging in sin? How does this experience of emptiness help you resist temptation? How does the promise of the crown of life help propel you toward steadfastness in temptation?

Today there will be temptation. Be steadfast.

March 14/Day 73

God Uses Sin for Good

Today's reading: Joshua 10:1-12:24

My selection: Joshua 10:6

The men of Gibeon sent to Joshua at the camp in Gilgal, saying, "Do not relax your hand from your servants. Come up to us quickly and save us and help us, for all the kings of the Amorites who dwell in the hill country are gathered against us."

My reflections: Joshua and the people of Israel had acted foolishly and disobediently in making a treaty with their tricky neighbors, the Gibeonites. This resulted in Gibeon being attacked by the alliance of kings under Adoni-zebek. But even this was turned for good in that Joshua had time to prepare his troops and make a surprise attack on the enemy resulting in a great defeat and the conquering of the southern nations. This is not to say a victory (or even greater victory) would not have come without the foolish treaty with Gibeon, only that after the treaty was made God's purposes were not thwarted and His blessing on Israel continued.

My challenge: It is never wise or good to sin, but God is able to forgive and make our dumb or evil choices result in good. Do not waste time playing the "what if" game about your past sin. Confess and move on, knowing God will make all things turn out for good for those who love Him and are called according to His purpose (Romans 8:28).

March 15/Day 74

Equality and Inequality in God's Economy

Today's reading: Joshua 13:1-15:63

My selection: Joshua 14:1

These are the inheritances that the people of Israel received in the land of Canaan, which Eleazar the priest and Joshua the son of Nun and the heads of the fathers' houses of the tribes of the people of Israel gave them to inherit.

My reflections: The system for distributing the land to the tribes was by lot. The areas were not equal in size nor were the tribes equal in population. God controlled the outcome of the drawing but, even so, it would not be even and equal. Resources were distributed by God's providence not on a human fairness scale.

The Lord could have given them a land that was easier to divide, where the acreage per tribe and per family would have been more obviously equal and "fair." God gave differing abilities and resources to individuals as we see throughout Scripture. This is not a mistake. I see no reason to believe that in heaven it will be any different.

Politicians today use envy and fear to stoke support. Liberals promise to make life more fair by laying a heavier burden on the rich and giving entitlements to those who have less. Conservatives promise to make life more fair by insuring equality of process, a level playing field where you get to keep all you supposedly deserve. But in the Bible, we don't see either of these things being promised. There is equality only of purpose for God's people. All are called to glorify God. People are assigned their "talents" and are called to use them to the best advantage for their Master's glory.

My challenge: Are you content with what God has given you? Are you using it to the greatest advantage for His glory? Are you captivated by the purpose of glorifying God so that what others have pales in insignificance?

Resist envy of what others have. Resist pride of thinking you deserve what you have. Instead focus on serving and glorifying Him today with all your resources and abilities.

March 16/Day 75

Godly Leadership: Wise and Fearless

Today's reading: Joshua 16:1-19:31

My selection: Joshua 17:14-15

14 Then the people of Joseph spoke to Joshua, saying, "Why have you given me but one lot and one portion as an inheritance, although I am a numerous people, since all along the Lord has blessed me?" 15 And Joshua said to them, "If you are a numerous people, go up by yourselves to the forest, and there clear ground for yourselves in the land of the Perizzites and the Rephaim, since the hill country of Ephraim is too narrow for you."

My reflections: The tribe of Joseph was actually, legally, two tribes (or half tribes as they are sometimes called) since Jacob (Israel) had adopted his two grandsons by Joseph: Manasseh and Ephraim. They had grown in population and needed more land. The question was, "Whose responsibility is it to see that these two tribes have sufficient land?"

Tribal leaders complained to Joshua that he had short-changed them in the doling out of land. He did not question their need for more land, but he did put the responsibility back on them to clear and conquer territory for themselves.

The leaders of the two tribes argued that they needed more land because they were so many. They implied that Joshua should provide this for them. The additional land he assigned to them was populated by Canaanites with chariots of iron - the ancient equivalent of atomic bombs. They argued that they could not conquer such well-equipped people. Joshua wisely turned their earlier argument back on them. In essence he said, "If you have so many people you need more land, then you have enough people to conquer the land you need."

Joshua was wise and fearless in answering the people of Joseph. A wise leader will not do for people what they should do for themselves. He will see through their flimsy arguments and stand firm. He will also encourage them that victory and success are possible.

My challenge: Are you wise and fearless in your leadership? Do you challenge those you lead to grow in faith and maturity? Do not enable immaturity, dependency, and laziness, but hold those you lead to reasonable standards that they can achieve by faith, diligence, and self-control.

March 17/Day 76

God's Faithfulness to His Covenant and People

Today's reading: Joshua 19:32-21:45

My selection: Joshua 21:45

Not one word of all the good promises that the Lord had made to the house of Israel had failed; all came to pass.

My reflections: God kept all His promises to Israel. They entered the land, overcame the inhabitants, and established themselves, all by His power and providence. There were still some enemies in the land who had been dominated but not destroyed. They were made to do menial labor. There would be problems with creeping idolatry, but, for a small window of time, there was rest and peace in the land.

My challenge: For the Christian, the final victory has been secured by the Lord Jesus Christ. He has triumphed over the enemy and has purchased redemption by His blood. He has gone to prepare a place for us in His Father's house. Are you resting in His victory today even as you wait for the complete fulfillment of the covenant promises?

Rejoice today, if you know your name is written in heaven. God is faithful. He cannot fail. There is a rest for the people of God. Some have already gone into that rest. We will soon be there, too.

March 18/Day 77

Good Intentions Gone Bad

Today's reading: Joshua 22:1-24:33

My selection: Joshua 24:27

Joshua said to all the people, "Behold, this stone shall be a witness against us, for it has heard all the words of the Lord that he spoke to us. Therefore it shall be a witness against you, lest you deal falsely with your God."

My reflections: As death approached him, Joshua wisely reminded the people of their obligation to keep the Lord's covenant or suffer the dire consequences. God had given them the land, but He would expel them from it if they committed idolatry. The people enthusiastically affirmed their commitment in spite of Joshua's warnings that this would not be easy, and any violation would not be tolerated by God.

The people intended to keep the covenant. They intended to be faithful. But, alas, as we will find in the Book of Judges, their intentions faded out, and they soon slid into idolatry. As predicted, all the warnings came true as they zigzagged through the centuries until they were taken captive and removed from the land.

My challenge: Why were their good intentions insufficient? Why are ours also insufficient? They and we are sinful people. Good intentions are the work of our fallen flesh which apart from God's Spirit and power cannot accomplish anything. Jesus said, "Abide in me, and I in you...for without me ye can do nothing" (John 15:4-5 KJV).

Have you failed at your good intentions? Abide in Christ. He is the One who died for the failed good intentions of His people. Abide in Him. He is the One who will bear fruit in you today.

March 19/Day 78

Limits to Legacy

Today's reading: Judges 1:1-3:30

My selection: Joshua 2:10

All that generation also were gathered to their fathers. And there arose another generation after them who did not know the Lord or the work that he had done for Israel.

My reflections: The generation that followed Joshua lacked personal knowledge of the Lord and His mighty acts at the Red Sea and Mt. Sinai. This did not mean they had no knowledge of their history. Perhaps they could recite it verbatim, but their knowledge was impersonal at best. So, they did evil in the Lord's sight serving the Baals. They did not fear God, love God, nor believe God.

Had the older generation failed to pass on the knowledge of God? Was the fault with the new generation who did not believe? Without a personal relationship with God by grace through faith, the family legacy was mere head knowledge.

My challenge: Are you striving to pass on the truth of the gospel to the next generation? Do you pray for them knowing that, apart from the grace of God, they will not believe? Do you trust God to work in those who come behind you?

Use every means to leave a gospel legacy to your children and grandchildren but recognize that it is God who must call them to Himself. We are not able or responsible to make them believe. Jesus tells us: "No man can come to me, except the Father which hath sent me draw him" (John 6:44 KJV). Pray that He may draw them.

March 20/Day 79

Whose Glory? The Story of Deborah and Barak

Today's reading: Judges 3:31-6:40

My selection: Judges 4:9

[Deborah] said, "I will surely go with you. Nevertheless, the road on which you are going will not lead to your glory, for the Lord will sell Sisera into the hand of a woman."

My reflections: This is a fascinating and humorous interchange between the prophetess and judge, Deborah, and her chosen military commander, Barak. There is also a surprise ending to the story.

Deborah asked Barak to lead the army of Israel against the latest oppressors, the Canaanites. He agreed to go on the condition that she would accompany him. Deborah agreed but she warned him that--in spite of certain victory--he would not get any glory. She went on to prophesy that the enemy would be captured by a woman. Her words come true in the gruesome account.

My challenge: Would you take a great risk knowing there was nothing in it for you? Do you serve God with no thought for your own glory? Do not ask "What's in it for me?" Serve God today seeking His glory alone.

PS. Here is the surprise ending. Centuries later, Barak was remembered for his faith in Hebrews 11:32. God listed him among the faithful saints of old, despite Deborah's prophecy that he would not be recognized. Faith pleases God who has the last word on who gets glory.

March 21/Day 80

A Soft (and Wise) Answer

Today's reading: Judges 7:1-8:35

My selection: Judges 8:3

God has given into your hands the princes of Midian, Oreb and Zeeb. What have I been able to do in comparison with you?" Then their anger against him subsided when he said this.

My reflections: Gideon had won a great victory. The men of Ephraim were probably jealous. Gideon did not react to them but wisely remained patient and even complimented them.

What a great example of Proverbs 15:1, "A soft answer turns away wrath."

A similar incident occurs in Judges 12:1 with a totally different outcome: war and death. What a great example of the second part of Proverbs 15:1, "A harsh word stirs up anger."

My challenge: Who needs a soft answer from you today? Watch for ways to turn away wrath.

Beware the Seduction of Power

Today's reading: Judges 9:1-10:5

My selection: Judges 9:2

Which is better for you, that all seventy of the sons of Jerubbaal rule over you, or that one rule over you? Remember also that I am your bone and your flesh."

My reflections: Gideon had to be coaxed by God to take a leadership role in Israel. This was not true of his sons. There arose a controversy between the illegitimate son of Gideon, Abimelech, and his seventy other sons. Abimelech won over his mother's relatives in Shechem to make him their ruler. Once established he killed the seventy sons of Gideon (his half-brothers). Eventually, however, even the people of Shechem would grow dissatisfied with Abimelech and he would be overthrown.

An aspiring leader must seek the Lord's direction and timing to move into a position of authority. Gideon, timid and hesitant as he was, could not avoid the role that God had designated for him. Abimelech, aggressive, violent, and conniving as he was, could not hold on to the role not designated for him.

Jesus' disciples fought among themselves for first place, but Jesus told them loving service not hostile infighting was the path to greatness (Mark 10:42-45).

My challenge: Do you aspire to a powerful position? Are you willing to be a servant and wait for God to give you the position He has for you? Are you resisting God's calling to you for a position of influence? Will you trust Him to sustain you in that role?

Seek to serve Christ faithfully whether in a very visible position or in obscurity.

Jephthah's Foolish Vow

Today's reading: Judges 10:6-13:25

My selection: Judges 11:40

The daughters of Israel went year by year to lament the daughter of Jephthah the Gileadite four days in the year.

My reflections: Jephthah shows an appalling lack of understanding of God and His ways. He made a rash vow, apparently, to gain God's favor in the battle. To do this implies the one making the vow believes that God can be pressured or needs to be pressured to act in some way. God is free from any constraint. He does not need a man to make a vow in order to carry out His will.

What exactly did Jephthah vow to do? Did he vow to offer his daughter as a sacrifice to God, or did he merely vow not to give his daughter in marriage so that she remained a virgin all her life? I believe it was the former, but there may be some dispute about this.

Either way, Jephthah should not have made this vow and, having made it, he should not have carried it out. The victory in the battle proved to be the Lord's will, and it would have happened despite the vow.

My challenge: Do not make vows in order to attempt to coerce God. Trust God that His plans and purposes will be carried out. He has given us ample promises to answer our prayers in Jesus' name according to His wise will. Trust Him always to do what is best for His children.

March 24/Day 83

Everyone Is Doing It!

Today's reading: Judges 14:1-17:13

My selection: Judges 17:6

In those days there was no king in Israel. Everyone did what was right in his own eyes.

My reflections: The theme of the day in the period of the Judges was "everyone did what was right in his own eyes." Samson, though called to be a judge, was a prime example of political leadership corrupted by evil. The Ephraim family in chapter 17 was another example of religious corruption as they set up their own personal temple and priest in their own home rather than obey the law of God.

Enlightenment thinking laid the foundation for people doing what seems to be self-evidently right and true. There may have been a time when there was some consensus based on a Christian legacy in western civilization that vaguely reflected the Bible. That is certainly not the case now and has not been for many years. Who is to say what is self-evidently right and true?

Ancient Israel had the law of God, but they did not know it or heed it. The problems they encountered were many. The modern church has the law of God. Do we know it? Do we heed it?

My challenge: Pray today that God would revive His Church and turn His people to a fervent passion for obedience. It would change our world.

The Ambitious Minister

Today's reading: Judges 18:1-19:30

My selection: Judges 18:19-20

[19] And they said to him, "Keep quiet; put your hand on your mouth and come with us and be to us a father and a priest. Is it better for you to be priest to the house of one man, or to be priest to a tribe and clan in Israel?" [20] And the priest's heart was glad. He took the ephod and the household gods and the carved image and went along with the people.

My reflections: The Levite who had illegally been installed as priest to the household of Micah in Ephraim received an offer he couldn't refuse, to be the priest for a whole tribe rather than merely for one family. This promotion delighted him. Besides, there were 600 armed men ready to pounce on him and his master should they cause any trouble.

Having already wandered from obedience to the law of God, the unnamed priest had neither the character nor the commitment to resist this new opportunity.

My challenge: If you are a minister of the gospel, do you serve the Lord and obey Him whether or not it advances your status, financial prosperity, or security? Are you eager to promote yourself? Do you consider whether the offer for a more prestigious position is in accord with the ways of God as revealed in His word? Are you caving in to pressure from powerful forces to act in ways that are not true to God's word?

Minister, be faithful. Make obedience to God your sole aim, not personal advancement or the appeasing of powerful people.

Christian, pray for your pastor and all those who serve the Lord that they may be faithful and content to serve in the place and way they have been called.

March 26/Day 85

Can Failure Be God's Will?

Today's reading: Judges 20:1-Ruth 1:22

My selection: Judges 20:18

The people of Israel arose and went up to Bethel and inquired of God, "Who shall go up first for us to fight against the people of Benjamin?" And the Lord said, "Judah shall go up first."

My reflections: The people of Israel were properly outraged by the evil that had occurred in Gibeah. They sought to punish those responsible, but the tribal leaders of Benjamin defended the guilty and blocked any execution of justice. Israel prepared to fight them. Again, Israel properly sought God's direction for how to begin the battle. Twice the Lord told them to go into battle and twice they were brutally defeated. Finally, in the third battle, Israel was victorious.

Does God ever decree failure for His people who do His will? This incident would indicate that God may, at times, decree apparent failure for His people, even in a good and noble endeavor. We may not assume that it is never God's will for us to "fail" at something He has told us to do. Success, as we understand it, may not be His will. Failure may be. Israel did eventually succeed, but it would have been wrong to conclude after one or two failures that they were on the wrong track, that they had misunderstood His directions.

I believe that the Lord was using the two early defeats in battle for another secret purpose. What secret purpose? We are not told. However, there is another notable incident in biblical history where we are told how apparent defeat really led to victory. Jesus' death on the cross seemed like complete defeat at the time. Now we can see that it led to the ultimate defeat of Satan, the crushing of the serpent's head after the bruising of Jesus' heel. [Acts 2:22-24; Genesis 3:15.]

My challenge: Has God called you to serve Him in some way that does not seem to be successful? If it is His call, remain steadfast in spite of apparent failure. Our calling is to be faithful. Success is not always what it seems. Success is to obey and keep on obeying.

March 27/Day 86

Respect for Women

Today's reading: Ruth 2:1-1 Samuel 1:20

My selection: Ruth 2:22

Naomi said to Ruth, her daughter-in-law, "It is good, my daughter, that you go out with his young women, lest in another field you be assaulted."

My reflections: Reading between the lines, one can easily see that, in Israel during this period of the Judges, a poor woman gleaning in the harvest alongside of the men would be in danger of being assaulted if she did not have the protection of the landowner. The poor had the right to gather behind the reapers (Leviticus 19:9-10; 23:22; Deuteronomy 24:19), but in actuality, they were not safe from being accosted. God protected Ruth, but we are reminded of what little fear of God existed in those days in Israel. Legal rights and status do not change the hearts of men who can treat women as if they were products to be consumed or exploited.

Christian men should be different if they understand that women in general, and their mothers, wives, sisters, daughters, and female friends in particular, were created in God's image and are due equal respect not merely legally but socially and personally. Boaz modeled this beautifully in protecting Ruth from his workers. He did not allow her to be abused or exploited.

My challenge: Men, are you treating the women in your life with respect? Are you protecting them from exploitation as much as depends on you?

Women, do you know that you are worthy of respect as a woman? Are you alert and resistant to those men who are selfish and abusive? Is there a Boaz in your life who looks out for your best?

Jesus Christ, our ultimate Redeemer, is the One who truly frees us from the bondage of our sin as Boaz freed Ruth from the bondage of her poverty and childlessness. He is the model for all Christian husbands.

Ephesians 5:25,33 (KJV): "Husbands, love your wives, even as Christ also loved the church, and gave himself for it; Nevertheless, let every one of you in particular so love his wife even as himself; and the wife see that she reverences her husband."

A husband that loves like Christ will be easy to "reverence" or respect. A woman who holds out for a husband like that will find it easy to respect him.

March 28/Day 87

The Sovereignty of God in Repentance

Today's reading: 1 Samuel 1:21-4:22

My selection: 1 Samuel 2:25

They would not listen to the voice of their father, for it was the will of the Lord to put them to death.

My reflections: People cannot repent without the grace of God in regeneration. Eli could confront his sons. He could plead with his sons. He could reason with them, but he could not cause them to repent and they would not repent because they *could not* repent. Eli was powerless to change them, and they were powerless to avoid the path of destruction they had chosen. Yet God uses means and, in the case of Jonah, He chose to use a resentful prophet to turn the hearts of the pagan people of Nineveh to Himself. Lesson one: proclaim the gospel which includes both law and grace, but know that the results of your proclamation are in God's hands.

The godly understand and accept that God is sovereign in repentance and, thus, in salvation. Eli, for all his failings, was quick to say to Samuel, "It is the Lord: let him do what seemeth him good" (1 Samuel 3:17 KJV). Lesson two: give praise to God that His secret purposes in the life of every person will be completed for His glory.

My challenge: Proclaim the gospel diligently to the lost. Trust God to work in the hearts of those to whom you proclaim it. Accept that God is glorified in both saving sinners and judging sinners.

Will you pray with me? Holy God, may I be consumed with Your glory so that I proclaim the gospel faithfully but trust You completely to do Your will in the hearts of those I love.

March 29/Day 88

God's Glory and Judgment

Today's reading: 1 Samuel 5:1-8:22

My selection: 1 Samuel 5:7

When the men of Ashdod saw how things were, they said, "The ark of the God of Israel must not remain with us, for his hand is hard against us and against Dagon our god."

My reflections: God is committed to His own glory first and foremost. When the Israelites attempted to use the Ark of the Covenant as a good luck charm in battle against the Philistines, the Lord defeated them and let the ark be captured by the Philistines. Once the Philistines had the ark installed in the temple of their god, Dagon, the idol fell before the ark and was broken. The people of Philistia began to suffer from tumors. They began to pass the ark around, and wherever it went, judgment followed.

Although God had made a covenant with Israel, He was first of all committed to His own glory and, when His people failed to obey and honor Him, He brought judgment upon them. God is free, and He will judge whoever dishonors Him.

My challenge: Honor Him today. Take His commands seriously. Do not be presumptuous thinking you could never fall under His heavy hand of judgment.

March 30/Day 89

Godly Leadership: Teaching and Prayer

Today's reading: 1 Samuel 9:1-12:25

My selection: 1 Samuel 12:23-24

23 Moreover, as for me, far be it from me that I should sin against the Lord by ceasing to pray for you, and I will instruct you in the good and the right way. 24 Only fear the Lord and serve him faithfully with all your heart. For consider what great things he has done for you.

My reflections: The people of Israel had demanded a king so that they could be like the other nations. God allowed them a king but, through Samuel, showed His power and displeasure by sending them thunder and rain in the midst of harvest season. Samuel taught the nation with a most memorable object lesson. They did respond well to this message.

1. Full and prompt confession. They confessed that they had sinned in asking for a king and that this was not their only sin.

2. Humble recognition of needed prayer. They asked for prayer from Samuel.

Continuing his teaching, Samuel reminded them of God's faithfulness to keep His covenant with them. He told them that instead of being fearful, they should serve the Lord faithfully with all their hearts. He promised to pray for them and to teach them how they should walk before God.

My challenge: As people redeemed by grace through faith in the Lord Jesus Christ, we must be quick to confess our sins and ask forgiveness. We must not lose heart and become fearful, for God will be faithful to forgive us. We also must not become passive and think that diligent obedience does not matter. We will not obey perfectly, but we must not think obedience is unnecessary. Faith alone saves, but the faith that saves is never alone.

If you are a Christian with leadership responsibilities, your role is to teach and to pray for those you lead. Are you doing that? It is easy to worry and try to pressure others to do what is right rather than teach faithfully and pray fervently. Teach and pray today. Challenge the complacent. Confront the disobedient. Encourage the hopeless. May your ministry be as effective as was that of Samuel.

March 31/Day 90

Saul's Stinking Legacy

Today's reading: 1 Samuel 13:1-14:52

My selection: 1 Samuel 14:47

When Saul had taken the kingship over Israel, he fought against all his enemies on every side, against Moab, against the Ammonites, against Edom, against the kings of Zobah, and against the Philistines. Wherever he turned he routed them.

My reflections: Saul had great military victories as King of Israel. These are often overshadowed by his extremely foolish decisions and evil actions. Both Saul and David were victorious, and both men were sinners whose failures are recorded for all to see. Yet Saul's failures seem to mark his life and legacy while David's do not.

Saul was impatient and failed to trust God when it seemed that Samuel would not arrive in time to make the sacrifice before the battle. Saul impulsively issued a foolish command to the army to fast before and during the battle. Then he rashly committed to execute whoever broke the command. When it turned out to be Jonathan, his son, who had won the day, he didn't consider clemency but moved toward carrying out the sentence. Fortunately, the people themselves rebelled against this decision and forced Saul not to carry out the sentence.

Saul had lost the confidence of the people and even of his own son. From here on he seems to be obsessed with defending his position as king and that obsession clouds his vision and corrupts his thinking. Instead of confessing his sin and repenting, Saul dug in and attempted to hold on to his power, position, and prestige.

As a later king, Solomon, would write, "Dead flies cause the ointment of the apothecary to send forth a stinking savour: so doth a little folly him that is in reputation for wisdom and honour" (Ecclesiastes 10:1 KJV).

My challenge: Although Saul's life brought many victories to Israel, it stunk because of his folly. It doesn't take much. Learn from Saul's example. Trust God. Do His will, His way, if you would be remembered fondly by succeeding generations.

April 1/Day 91

Snared by the Fear of Man

Today's reading: 1 Samuel 15:1-16:23

My selection: 1 Samuel 15:24

Saul said to Samuel, "I have sinned, for I have transgressed the commandment of the Lord and your words, because I feared the people and obeyed their voice."

My reflections: Saul's earlier disobedience to God had resulted in Samuel prophesying that Saul's son would not inherit his father's throne. There would be no dynasty for Saul. But Saul continued as king and had an opportunity at least to redeem himself. Again, he failed to carry out specific instructions. He rationalized and spun the incident to downplay his disobedience but finally made the above statement to Samuel.

Saul's actions here are a perfect example of Proverbs 29:25 (KJV): "The fear of man bringeth a snare: but whoso putteth his trust in the Lord shall be safe." Samuel tells him, that not only his dynasty will end but, that his reign is over.

A leader who fears his people more than he fears God is hamstrung. He will not do the right thing. He will abdicate his responsibility and bring down judgment on himself and others.

My challenge: Do you fear God more than Man? Do you seek God's approval even if the whole world should call you a fool? Are you prepared to suffer the consequences of pleasing Him while displeasing others?

Seek to please God. Fear not Man whose power does not extend past the doors of death but, God. Only His opinion of you matters.

Seeing God's Presence in the Daily Grind

Today's reading: 1 Samuel 17:1-18:30

My selection: 1 Samuel 18:12

Saul was afraid of David because the Lord was with him but had departed from Saul.

My reflections: A theme running through the story of Saul and David is the presence or absence of the Lord with these men. The Lord had departed from Saul and was with David. David, meanwhile, seems to have been led along by God and simply responded in godly ways to the opportunities that presented themselves. As a result, he developed both skill and character that were keys to his later success.

From the psalms of David (e.g. Psalm 19), we can see that he loved the law of God and he stood in awe of the Creator. This began early in his life. His endless hours with the sheep were not frittered away but used for prayer and meditation on God's Word.

David developed skills for battle while he was a shepherd defending his sheep. His ability with the sling prepared him to be victorious against Goliath. He ran to the battle line while, as I envision it, Goliath lumbered up wearing a suit of armor that weighed 125 pounds (5000 shekels). David was both competent and confident because he trusted the Lord and he had experience in killing wild animals.

David developed his musical ability so that he was useful as a musician for Saul. David was a trustworthy son whom his father could send with supplies to his brothers on the battlefront.

None of this was, by itself, very unusual, but all of these qualities and abilities came together in a man who was prepared to lead the kingdom in some of its greatest days. The key element was the presence of the Lord with him. For the most part, he was faithful throughout his life and walked before God.

My challenge: Respond today in godly ways to the opportunities that present themselves. Do not overlook the simple ways that God leads His people through ordinary circumstances. Do not despise the day of small things (keeping sheep, practicing music, learning to use a slingshot) or the mundane or distasteful tasks that seem routine (taking supplies to hostile brothers on the front lines). Use this day to serve the Lord without thought for greatness or glory. Do the things before you for Him and through Him. He may use it for great things but, if not, it is a great enough thing to serve Him in obscurity.

Michal's Character

Today's reading: 1 Samuel 19:1-22:5

My selection: 1 Samuel 19:17

Saul said to Michal, "Why have you deceived me thus and let my enemy go, so that he has escaped?" And Michal answered Saul, "He said to me, 'Let me go. Why should I kill you?'"

My reflections: David's wife, Michal, was Saul's daughter. She protected David's life by revealing a plot to kill him in his bed at sunrise. She assisted David's escape.

Michal understood that if she were caught in all this, she would be in trouble with her father, so she told Saul that David had threatened her life. Saul believed this because it fit into his view of David, that his son-in-law was a bloodthirsty warrior willing to do anything to protect himself, and eventually overthrow Saul, and take the throne.

Michal, unlike Jonathan, did not stand up to Saul and defend David. Her lie only reinforced Saul's determination to kill David. Was he not an abusive husband?

It takes courage to tell the truth. In this case it would also have demanded of Michal confidence in God's power to protect her. She lacked that. She inadvertently increased David's problem with Saul.

My challenge: Tell the truth. Tell it in love, but tell it. God had already planned to give David the throne. His plan would not fail, and Saul could not stop it.

Walking with God in Fear and Faith

Today's reading: 1 Samuel 22:6-24:22

My selection: 1 Samuel 23:12

Then David said, "Will the men of Keilah surrender me and my men into the hand of Saul?" And the Lord said, "They will surrender you."

My reflections: The depth of one's relationship to God is demonstrated in the hard decisions of life. David's fear of and faith in God stands in stark contrast to the people of Keilah, and even his own loyal but misguided followers.

David had, by God's direction and against the advice of his followers, just delivered the people of Keilah from the Philistine invaders. David risked his life and those of his men in fighting the Philistines, but he also risked revealing his location to Saul. Sure enough, Saul heard what happened and prepared to come for David. When David sought asylum in Keilah, a walled city, he learned from God that Keilah would betray him.

Talk about a betrayal! Here he had just freed this city, but they would not be loyal to him. This is just one more example of the evil that is in the hearts of men.

Meanwhile, David continued to show integrity in all his dealings, including sparing Saul's life. In today's reading, it is clear that David was a leader who got his directions from the Lord. He did not resort to doing what was popular among his well-meaning followers. They did not want to pick a fight with the Philistines, and they wanted David to kill Saul in the cave. He did neither. Here is the evidence that he was a man who feared God and loved His law. The people of Keilah were opportunists who could be bought and sold to the highest bidder. David's men were driven by fear and human wisdom. David stood alone before God. No wonder he was called a man after God's heart.

My challenge: What risks do you take to obey God? How do you stand against the tide of popular opinion in your decisions to obey Him?

Christian, take heed to Ephesians 6:10-11: "Finally, be strong in the Lord and in the strength of his might. Put on the whole armor of God, that you may be able to stand against the schemes of the devil."

May God make you victorious in Him today.

Trusting God's Timing

Today's reading: 1 Samuel 25:1-27:12

My selection: 1 Samuel 26:10-11

[10] And David said, "As the Lord lives, the Lord will strike him, or his day will come to die, or he will go down into battle and perish. [11] The Lord forbid that I should put out my hand against the Lord's anointed. But take now the spear that is at his head and the jar of water, and let us go."

My reflections: David's loyalty to his enemy, Saul, was not based on any cowardice on David's part. Rather he spared Saul's life twice because he respected the position the Lord had put him in. David knew that the Lord could bring Saul down in a moment, or Saul might die of natural causes in old age or he could die in battle. There was no shortage of ways the Lord could use to get rid of Saul. David knew he had been anointed to replace Saul as king. He also knew that God's will includes both a *what* and a *when.* Timing is important.

My challenge: In making important decisions do you consider not only what God would have you do but also when?

Wait on the Lord to bring the right time for His purposes for you. Do not rush ahead to try to make the good thing happen ahead of time.

Strengthened in God

Today's reading: 1 Samuel 28:1-31:13

My selection: 1 Samuel 30:6

And David was greatly distressed, for the people spoke of stoning him, because all the people were bitter in soul, each for his sons and daughters. But David strengthened himself in the Lord his God.

My reflections: Think of David's situation at this point. He is a fugitive from Saul. He is living in a foreign country where his protector, Achish, has just been overruled by his fellow Philistine lords who reject David as a reliable ally. His home has been burned and his family kidnapped. His outlaw army has turned against him and they are seriously thinking about stoning him.

There are many ways to die. Some are less horrific than others. Stoning, it seems to me, is a slow painful way to die. It would be accompanied by hateful screams of those who carry out the execution.

But David, completely alone in the world, strengthened himself in the Lord. This is what I admire about him. James 4:8 says, "Draw near to God, and he will draw near to you."

David learned that God was his rock and strength. In the midst of all that grief the Lord gave him strength to seek direction from Him. God gave him that direction and he led his men to victory.

My challenge: Do you find yourself completely alone with no one but God to turn to? He may not instantly resolve all your problems, but He will strengthen you to do His will. Seek Him. Trust Him. Praise Him for His faithfulness.

April 7/Day 97

Seeing Life Differently

Today's reading: 2 Samuel 1:1-3:21

My selection: 2 Samuel 1:16

David said to him, "Your blood be on your head, for your own mouth has testified against you, saying, 'I have killed the Lord's anointed.'"

My reflections: Once again, David shows that he does not look at life through the same lens as the vast majority of people. He took no joy in the death of Saul and Jonathan, even though this brought him closer to the throne which he had been promised.

The Amalekite, on the other hand, probably expected to be rewarded for bringing the news and claiming to be the one who killed Saul. It is not clear whether his version of Saul's death is true or not, but it appears to be false as it seems to contradict 1 Samuel 31:4-5.

My challenge: One who is a man after God's heart, like David, will see things differently than others. God takes no pleasure in the death of the wicked and neither do His people (Ezekiel 33:11).

How is your outlook on life being changed by a godly perspective on this world? Seek to please Him in how you view life. Seek to see life as He sees it.

April 8/Day 98

The Burdens of Leadership

Today's reading: 2 Samuel 3:22-6:23

My selection: 2 Samuel 6:16

As the ark of the Lord came into the city of David, Michal the daughter of Saul looked out of the window and saw King David leaping and dancing before the Lord, and she despised him in her heart.

My reflections: David has finally consolidated his kingdom, and he rules over all Israel. He has victories on the battlefield, but all is not well. Joab completely disregarded David's policy toward Abner and executed him for killing Asahel in battle. Ishbosheth, Saul's son, was assassinated to David's chagrin. His people mishandled the ark and suffered death for that. Now his wife, Michal, has turned against him openly.

One suspects that Michal's loyalty to David was not solid, but now she comes out against him. Did she resent his joy in bringing the ark to Jerusalem or was there some vulgar behavior on David's part which gave her cause to despise him? At any rate, the law had been broken in this marriage. She had been forced to return to David after having another husband. This was an illegal marriage (Deuteronomy 24:1-4). It was also an unhappy marriage.

Being in leadership brings its own set of problems. Those who look on from the outside imagine how wonderful it must be to reign over a kingdom, to lead an army that is consistently victorious, and to have the praise of the people. But it is not quite so smooth. There is a lot of heat on a leader. David did not always make wise decisions.

Those who aspire to major leadership roles must consider what they are seeking. God had chosen David as king, but that did not mean a comfortable life, and it did not reduce the pressure on him to handle complex questions wisely. It did give him some assurance that the Lord had put him in that position and would lead him and sustain him in it.

My challenge: Do you aspire to greater leadership? Is God opening the door for that? What illusions might you have about the personal benefits of advancement?

Follow the Lord. Do not seek position for the sake of power, prestige, or personal advantage but only to serve the Lord and His people. Be willing to be in obscurity with only the recognition of the Lord in the work He has called you to do.

April 9/Day 99

Starting and Finishing

Today's reading: 2 Samuel 7:1-10:19

My selection: 2 Samuel 8:14-15

[David] put garrisons in Edom; throughout all Edom he put garrisons, and all the Edomites became David's servants. And the Lord gave victory to David wherever he went. [15] So David reigned over all Israel. And David administered justice and equity to all his people.

My reflections: David consolidated the kingdom that God had promised to Israel. Here are some important observations:

1. The Lord was credited and praised for these victories. In the midst of all this progress it is said by the writer here, *the Lord gave victory to David wherever he went.*

2. David administered well what he had established. Verse 15 says, *David administered justice and equity to all his people.* This included setting up a well-organized administration with reliable people to take care of the on-going business of the kingdom.

3. David kept his promises. He had pledged to Jonathan to protect his family even though for years Saul had pursued him to kill him. He carried out this promise by giving Mephibosheth a place at his table.

In the wake of great victory, David did not lose sight of the importance of praise to God and faithfulness to his duties.

There is a common paradigm that says some people are good starters and some are good finishers. Perhaps no one is naturally both a great starter and a great finisher. Nevertheless, great, godly leaders make sure that both the starting and the finishing of the work are attended to.

My challenge: Have you completed your commitments? Does God get the praise for the victories He has given you? Do you struggle more with starting or with finishing important projects? Do you find ways to assure that projects get both started and finished? Do you care for the Mephibosheths in your life?

Today, take steps to start an important project that needs doing or to finish one that needs completing. Take care of your Mephibosheth. Be sure to take time to give God praise for His power and guidance in your life.

April 10/Day 100

Sin: Vigilance Against and Forgiveness Of

Today's reading: 2 Samuel 11:1-13:22

My selection: 2 Samuel 12:10

Now therefore the sword shall never depart from your house, because you have despised me and have taken the wife of Uriah the Hittite to be your wife.

My reflections: This sordid chapter in the life of King David demonstrates how quickly temptation and sin can ravage a man's life and the lives of many others. Notice the steps:

1. Lack of discipline and responsibility. David stayed home from the battle. He relaxed in his house and took an afternoon nap.

2. Boredom. I suspect he was bored as he had delegated his responsibilities for military leadership to Joab. This opened the door for what happened next.

3. Gross abuse of power for personal gratification and a deceptive cover-up. David used his rooftop to get a view of a woman bathing. He used his authority as king to learn who she was and to have her brought to him. She came and slept with him. When she became pregnant, he tried to make it look like her husband was responsible. When that plan failed, he again abused his power to attempt to cover-up his sin by having her husband killed.

The prophet Nathan confronted David about his sin. David responded humbly, but the sentence would still have to be served. There would be violence and open sexual sin in his own family. It did not take long before Amnon would rape his half-sister and Absalom would plot his murder. Absalom would go on to mount a coup against David and commit adultery with his father's concubines. Where? On the roof where David had stood spying on Bathsheba.

My challenge: Are you vigilant against sin in your life? Are you delegating what you should be doing yourself? Are you careful not to abuse the authority you have been given? Are you quick to confess your sin?

The gospel of Jesus Christ calls us to repent of our sin and believe the good news that He has taken our despicable sin on Himself. David was restored because of faith in the Messiah who would come, and so will you be. Repent and believe. Your sin may not be like David's or it may be worse, but, in Christ, there is forgiveness and salvation.

David in a Lose-lose Situation?

Today's reading: 2 Samuel 13:23-15:37

My selection: 2 Samuel 15:14

David said to all his servants who were with him at Jerusalem, "Arise, and let us flee, or else there will be no escape for us from Absalom. Go quickly, lest he overtake us quickly and bring down ruin on us and strike the city with the edge of the sword."

My reflections: What a contrast between David's relaxation (2 Samuel 12) and his return to fugitive status in this passage! How his life has been turned upside down as a consequence of his sin! Rather than let Absalom besiege Jerusalem and wage a war of attrition, David flees and returns to a familiar lifestyle which he had known during his youth. He wisely left Hushai as a double agent to confuse Absalom and counteract the advice of the turncoat Ahithophel. He also left the loyal priests as informants.

The chaos that had settled into David's family continued. David would continue to be torn between a blind love for his wicked son, Absalom, and the need to administer justice in the kingdom. There seemed no possible good outcome. He would either lose the kingdom (and possibly his own life) or he would lose his son.

Psalm 94:16-23 may have been David's prayer in that awful time.

My challenge: Take comfort in God's sovereignty in the chaotic situation of your life today. God is never in a lose-lose situation, and ultimately neither are His people. Let His consolations cheer your soul.

April 12/ Day 102

The Teachable Leader

Today's reading: 2 Samuel 16:1-19:8

My selection: 2 Samuel 19:8

Then the king arose and took his seat in the gate.

My reflections: Joab confronts and corrects King David setting him straight for his own good. [See 2 Samuel 12:26-30for an earlier similar instance.] Understandably, David grieves the death of his rebellious son, but he has overlooked his soldiers who risked their lives saving his. They succeeded, but their day of victory has been squashed due to the king's attitude.

David listens and heeds Joab's advice. In another instance, he received the prophet Nathan's rebuke for his sin. [See 2 Samuel 12:13.]

There is certainly a pattern of sin and error on David's part, but more importantly there is a parallel pattern of humility in responding to the faithful counselors who correct him. As Solomon would later write in Ecclesiastes 4:13 (KJV): "Better is a poor and a wise child than an old and foolish king, who will no more be admonished."

It would be easy for a king, like David, to get so intoxicated with his own greatness that he cannot listen to wise and gracious counselors. No one is immune to making sinful or foolish decisions. No one is so wise that he never needs advice.

My challenge: Do you have wise counselors who can help you see when you have veered into foolishness? Do you listen to constructive criticism?

Be approachable. Welcome warnings. Encourage those wise and loving friends who are looking out for your well-being and faithfulness to the Lord. Be teachable.

April 13/Day 103

Small Sin; Big Consequences

Today's reading: 2 Samuel 19:9-21:22

My selection: 2 Samuel 19:43

And the men of Israel answered the men of Judah, "We have ten shares in the king, and in David also we have more than you. Why then did you despise us? Were we not the first to speak of bringing back our king?" But the words of the men of Judah were fiercer than the words of the men of Israel

My reflections: The political atmosphere in Israel was completely unstable. Absalom had won a huge following from all the tribes, but now he was gone. There was a willingness to restore David to the throne among eleven of the tribes, but Judah was reticent to do so. David, seeking to consolidate his support, convinced the leaders of Judah, as his own tribe, to lead the way in restoring his kingdom, but then the other tribes took offense at Judah for leaving them out of the celebration. Sheba from the tribe of Benjamin took advantage of this general feeling of alienation to mount yet another attempt to overthrow David.

The rebellion of Sheba was short-lived, but it shows the political instability that existed in the so-called united kingdom. Indeed, David's grandson, Rehoboam, would see that instability result in a permanent division from which the kingdom would never recover.

Human pride and touchiness can lead to great disaster. Sheba was an astute, but evil, leader who used the jealousy of the 11 tribes to leverage support for his rebellion.

My challenge: Are you aware of how seemingly small, "respectable" sins, like pride, can lead to great consequences? Are you vigilant in not allowing bitterness, resentment, and jealousy to take hold of your heart?

Walk in the light today. Do not allow Satan a foothold in your heart. Be quick to confess and forsake sin as the Holy Spirit shows it to you. Walk in the light (1 John 1:7).

April 14/Day 104

Words from God through David

Today's reading: 2 Samuel 22:1-23:39

My selection: 2 Samuel 23:2

The Spirit of the Lord speaks by me; his word is on my tongue.

My reflections: David knew he spoke words that were inspired by the Spirit of the Lord, reflecting what Peter would later write: "For no prophecy was ever produced by the will of man, but men spoke from God as they were carried along by the Holy Spirit" (2 Peter 1:21).

This doctrine of verbal inspiration of the Scripture is crucial to the faith of reformed and evangelical Christians. It is based in the Bible's own claims about itself. It began with the earliest books of the Bible, the Pentateuch, but continues throughout the Bible. We dare not ignore, neglect, or replace the Scripture. It is God-breathed (2 Timothy 3:16-17). The Church received it and did not create it as the Roman Catholic Church claims. Believers and unbelievers alike stand under its pronouncements and judgments. God's Word brings us comfort and fear.

My challenge: What is your view of the authority of the Bible? Do you take it as given by God and, thus, supreme over every other book? Do you tremble at His Word (Isaiah 66:2)? Do you trust what He has said over human reasoning and wisdom? Do you look to His Word as the basis for your life and faith? Thank God today for revealing Himself to mankind through His Word. Think about how His promises and commands both anchor and charge you in your life.

April 15/Day 105

Growing Old is Not for Wimps

Today's reading: 2 Samuel 24:1-1 Kings 2:12

My selection: 1 Kings 2:10

David slept with his fathers and was buried in the city of David.

My reflections: David's life did not end smoothly.

1. The census. In one of his final acts as king, he brought pestilence on the nation through his ordering a census. In this case he departed from his previous practice of accepting wise counsel. He rejected Joab's objection and forced through the census. He later confessed that this was sinful and took steps to confess and make sacrifices. Nevertheless, it was one of his final acts and it was a foolish one. Being elderly does not automatically make you wise.

2. His health. David suffered from poor circulation and could not maintain his body heat. Many elderly people know what this is like and have to dress with extra layers when younger people are in light clothing.

3. Succession controversy. Adonijah, David's son and Absalom's younger brother, set himself up as king without the support of David. David had chosen Solomon to be king, but he had not taken steps to transfer power to him. Adonijah forced David's hand. Like David, many elderly know the difficulty of relinquishing control in a timely manner.

My challenge: If you are senior citizen, are you taking steps to see that your life ends as wisely as possible? Are you allowing your loved ones to assist you as you go through the transitions of late life?

If you have elderly relatives who depend on you, are you serving them and honoring them to make their life as pleasant as possible?

Do you show understanding of their physical needs without ridiculing them for such things as feeling cold in warm weather or being hopelessly behind the technology curve?

If you are a caregiver for an elderly person, be careful to show love and acceptance to him or her. If you are elderly, accept the assistance of loved ones in transferring power and authority at the end of your life. Do that before a crisis occurs.

April 16/Day 106

Prayer that Pleases God

Today's reading: 1 Kings 2:13-4:19

My selection: 1 Kings 3:9, 10

9 Give your servant therefore an understanding mind to govern your people, that I may discern between good and evil, for who is able to govern this your great people? 10 It pleased the Lord that Solomon had asked this.

My reflections: Solomon's prayer for wisdom to be able to govern justly the kingdom of Israel pleased God. The implications are that not all prayer pleases God and that the elements of this prayer are instructive for us in knowing how we ought to pray.

1. Consciousness of God's promises. The Lord appeared to Solomon and told him to make his request. God has invited His people who have been redeemed by Christ to come before His throne confidently in prayer to receive what they need. Hebrews 4:16 (KJV) "Let us therefore come boldly unto the throne of grace, that we may obtain mercy, and find grace to help in time of need."

2. Gratefulness for God's faithfulness. Solomon begins his prayer by reviewing the ways God has already shown great and steadfast love to David and to him. Prayer that gives glory to God is certainly pleasing to Him. There is no hint of complaining or demanding here on the part of Solomon. It is as if he were saying, "You have already given me far more than I deserve."

3. Humility. Solomon recognized his need for the Lord's wisdom to do his job. Solomon did not ask for gifts that would make him comfortable or a long and easy life but the crucial gift he would need to do what God had given him to do: an understanding mind to discern good and evil so that he could properly govern the people.

The result? God was pleased with this prayer. He granted it, but He also gave Solomon riches and honor so that his reign would be like no other. These were the golden days of the kingdom of Israel, a foreshadowing of the coming of the eternal kingdom in which righteousness dwells.

My challenge: Are your prayers pleasing to God? Are you conscious of His promises, grateful for His faithfulness, and humble in your attitude? Make Solomon's prayer a model for your prayer today.

The Golden Age of the Kingdom

Today's reading: 1 Kings 4:20-7:12

My selection: 1 Kings 4:20-21

[20] Judah and Israel were as many as the sand by the sea. They ate and drank and were happy. [21] Solomon ruled over all the kingdoms from the Euphrates to the land of the Philistines and to the border of Egypt. They brought tribute and served Solomon all the days of his life.

My reflections: Here is a window of peace and prosperity in the kingdom. Solomon ruled without conflict. He ruled with great wisdom. He kept his obligations and promises. He built the temple with great care and beauty. The surrounding kingdoms did not question his dominance. Solomon was just in his business dealings, it seems. He went to Hiram and the Sidonians for timber for the temple, but he paid them for their materials and labor.

In a fallen world, there are few times in human history when we see extended periods of peace and prosperity. Leaders can be relatively wise or foolish, just or evil, but they are all fallen sinners who are only sometimes wise and just, at best.

Jesus came announcing that the Kingdom of God was at hand. We look for a city whose builder and founder is God. We look for a kingdom in which righteousness dwells. It is not hard to imagine a perfect world with a perfect King who would rule redeemed people in righteousness. It is impossible to find one, either currently or anywhere in all of human history.

My challenge: In the USA, our political parties argue back and forth about the merits of one candidate over another and about the merits of greater government control and involvement over greater freedom for individuals. Our country zig-zags back and forth between the values of justice and freedom trying to find the perfect balance.

Meanwhile, we must live for God's glory in this time, fully engaged in this world but with an eye on the next one. Right now matters for eternity. But right now is not eternity.

Trust God. Do His will today. Do not lose heart. We will someday see the true golden age of the Kingdom of God which will never end.

April 18/Day 108

A Prayer for the Gentiles

Today's reading: 1 Kings 7:13-8:61

My selection: 1 Kings 8:41-43

41 Likewise, when a foreigner, who is not of your people Israel, comes from a far country for your name's sake 42 (for they shall hear of your great name and your mighty hand, and of your outstretched arm), when he comes and prays toward this house, 43 hear in heaven your dwelling place and do according to all for which the foreigner calls to you, in order that all the peoples of the earth may know your name and fear you, as do your people Israel, and that they may know that this house that I have built is called by your name.

My reflections: What a kind and loving request Solomon makes for believing foreigners!

Solomon understands that the God of Israel, Jehovah, is the God of all the earth and of all the peoples of the earth. He prays that God will hear the foreigner's prayers when he comes for His name's sake and prays toward the temple. Solomon asks that the praying Gentile find grace, mercy, and provision before God's throne.

This attitude and these words sound especially gracious when we think of the general disdain that the Jews held for the Gentiles in New Testament times. They were dogs. They were unclean. So, Solomon showed love for the Gentiles, but he also shows great love for God and for God's glory. There is nothing better than that a human being should turn to the Lord no matter what his race or ethnicity.

My challenge: Do you pray for the salvation of the lost, especially of the lost who seem very different from you? Do you pray that they will hear of God's great name, His mighty hand and His outstretched arm?

Pray that lost people from every nation may see the greatness of God and turn to Him.

April 19/Day 109

The Sad End of a Great King

Today's reading: 1 Kings 8:62-11:25

My selection: 1 Kings 11:4

When Solomon was old his wives turned away his heart after other gods, and his heart was not wholly true to the Lord his God, as was the heart of David his father.

My reflections: Solomon's reign marked a golden age for Israel, but Solomon's own life ended in failures that set up the division of the kingdom under his son, Rehoboam.

To manage success is hard. David experienced his greatest temptation, sin, and defeat during the best period of his reign (2 Samuel 11). Solomon enjoyed smooth sailing throughout his reign. No wonder he let down his guard and succumbed to the temptations presented him by his many pagan wives and concubines.

My challenge: Years ago, I was told, "Few end well." Experience bears this out. Obedience is a daily matter. One may start well, have many good days, but it is how you end that counts.

Do you count past victories and obedience as permission for present disobedience and impunity? Does your success and status tempt you to cut corners in your spiritual life? "Flee also youthful lusts: but follow righteousness, faith, charity, peace, with them that call on the Lord out of a pure heart," Paul warned Timothy (2 Timothy 2:22 KJV). Solomon failed at this point. By the way, youthful passions are not limited to youth. But you already knew that, didn't you? Jesus was obedient unto death. He said, "If any man will come after me, let him deny himself, and take up his cross daily, and follow me" (Luke 9:23 KJV). Follow Jesus. End well.

April 20/Day 110

What Goes Around...

Today's reading: 1 Kings 11:26-13:34

My selection: 1 Kings 11:40

Solomon sought therefore to kill Jeroboam. But Jeroboam arose and fled into Egypt, to Shishak king of Egypt, and was in Egypt until the death of Solomon.

My reflections: Solomon's father, David, while a king in waiting, had been a fugitive from Saul. Now Solomon assumed the same role as Saul against his anointed replacement, Jeroboam. It only took one generation for the tables to turn and for the same drama to be reenacted only with a different cast of players.

This is another example of how little we learn from history, even recent history. How prone is man to be disobedient to God, which brings judgment, and then to resist repentance and faith to return to the right way! Solomon did not repent. Instead he took steps to assassinate his designated replacement. Did he not know what happened to Saul?

Rehoboam continued the resistance and paid the price by losing ten tribes to his rival. The first good thing he did was to listen to the prophet and to let those kingdoms go.

My challenge: Are you learning to fear God by seeing how He resists the proud and gives grace to the humble?

Trust Him. Obey Him. Be quick to repent and to accept the consequences of your sin.

God's Absolute Justice

Today's reading: 1 Kings 14:1-16:20

My selection: 1 Kings 16:7

Moreover, the word of the Lord came by the prophet Jehu the son of Hanani against Baasha and his house, both because of all the evil that he did in the sight of the Lord, provoking him to anger with the work of his hands, in being like the house of Jeroboam, and also because he destroyed it.

My reflections: Baasha was the means God used to destroy wicked Jeroboam and his family. But Baasha also brought destruction on himself by his evil acts including his assassination of Jeroboam and his family.

God uses evil for good but still punishes the evil doer.

God is completely just but it is not the kind of justice we would do as humans. We weigh evil and opt to let lesser evil go. God punishes all evil even though that evil accomplishes His will.

Humanly, we are tempted to find fault with God for this, but who are we to call Him unjust? We expect Him to be like us, to assign relative values to sin and evil, but He does not.

My challenge: Do you find fault with God? Do you question His wisdom or justice?

Praise Him for His righteous ways. His thoughts are higher than our thoughts and His ways than our ways. [See Isaiah 55:8-10]. Praise God for providing a full sacrifice for sin through Jesus Christ who saves His people from all their sins whether they seem small or large.

April 22/Day 112

Attack the Messenger

Today's reading: 1 Kings 16:21-18:46

My selection: 1 Kings 18:5

As the Lord your God lives, there is no nation or kingdom where my lord has not sent to seek you. And when they would say, "He is not here," he would take an oath of the kingdom or nation, that they had not found you.

My reflections: King Ahab, whose name is synonymous with evil, rejected God's message of judgment upon him through Elijah. God sent a drought, and Elijah went into exile. All through the drought, Ahab searched for Elijah, and, when he found him, he called him the troubler of Israel (1 Kings 18:17). Elijah was steadfast and got his orders from God, but the pressure from Ahab was tremendous. Ahab did not accept correction nor consider that the fault was his own not Elijah's.

Hearing truthful warnings and deserved criticism is not easy. The wise and godly man or woman, unlike Ahab, receives correction. [See Proverbs 2:1-5.]

Doing and saying the right thing is often not easy or popular. The man or woman of God will be like Elijah, unwavering from the truth, "stedfast, unmoveable, always abounding in the work of the Lord" (1 Corinthians 15:58 KJV).

My challenge: Do you receive correction, or do you blame anyone who would dare to point out your sins or weaknesses? Are you vigilant in confessing and forsaking sin? Are you a faithful witness risking rejection to proclaim the gospel to those around you?

Be faithful in hearing God's correction or in giving it. Don't attack the messenger. When you are the messenger, be gracious but also be willing to be attacked. Don't be an Ahab. Be ready to be an Elijah.

April 23/Day 113

The Right and Wrong Use of Power

Today's reading: 1 Kings 19:1-21:29

My selection: 1 Kings 21:20

Ahab said to Elijah, "Have you found me, O my enemy?" He answered, "I have found you, because you have sold yourself to do what is evil in the sight of the Lord.

My reflections: In a flagrant abuse of power, Ahab let his desire for Naboth's land and the evil advice of Queen Jezebel lead to perjury and the murder of an innocent man. But the king and queen would not get away with it. Elijah brought the sentence to Ahab so he could ponder just what the real price of his sin would be. His family would be exterminated. There would be no dynasty of Ahab. Jezebel was singled out for special punishment. She would die. Not only would there be no royal funeral, she would be eaten by dogs in Jezreel, the site of the stolen vineyard.

Governors and rulers have a special responsibility before God. They rule by His consent and must be accountable to Him for their use of authority and power. On a lesser level, all of us (parents, employers, and citizens) hold some level of power and authority for which we are accountable to God.

My challenge: Scripture admonishes Christians as follows,

1. To pray for those who govern. (1 Timothy 2:1-4)
2. To use whatever power we have to do good and be just. (I Timothy 5:17; Ephesians 6:1-9)

Are you using your power wisely or abusing it to satisfy selfish desires and discontentment? Are you praying for those who lead our nation? Be wise in the use of power which is given by God for good. Pray that our leaders may rule in justice.

Bold Obedience

Today's reading: 1 Kings 22:1-2 Kings 2:18

My selection: 1 Kings 22:28

Micaiah said, "If you return in peace, the Lord has not spoken by me." And he said, "Hear, all you peoples!"

My reflections: The prophet Micaiah was called by the kings of Israel and Judah, Ahab and Jehoshaphat, to advise them about the pending battle with Syria. Four hundred prophets had already counseled the kings to go into battle. Under enormous pressure, Micaiah told them that God would not be with them nor bless their efforts in the battle.

The kings ignored Micaiah's prophecy. Ahab had Micaiah put in prison and fed on bread and water. Here are some observations:

1. The man of God tells the truth in spite of opposition from powerful leaders and public opinion.

2. The man of God (unlike King Ahab) listens to the advice of wise counselors. He weighs his counselors rather than count them. One "Micaiah" is better than 400 of the other prophets.

3. The man of God remains committed to God's truth in the face of personal loss and suffering. Ahab's punishment did not sway Micaiah. The prophet risked his life for the truth.

My challenge: Do you seek and follow wise counsel when making important decisions? What is the Lord calling you to do or say for His glory and against the tide of popular opinion? Are you ready to suffer personal loss, if need be, to be obedient and to tell the truth?

Today, be a Micaiah not an Ahab.

Validation of the Prophet's Ministry

Today's reading: 2 Kings 2:19-4:44

My selection: 2 Kings 3:12

Jehoshaphat said, "The word of the Lord is with him." So the king of Israel and Jehoshaphat and the king of Edom went down to him.

My reflections: The spirit of Elijah was on Elisha and the word of the Lord was with him. His ministry was validated by a number of miracles. Notice:

1. Prophecies. He accurately proclaimed what God would do both on a personal level to individuals and a national level to the king.

2. Resurrection. He raised a dead boy.

3. Feeding of multitudes. He multiplied food for the sons of the prophets.

There is a parallel here to Jesus' ministry. Miracles do not occur indiscriminately in the Bible, but at times when God is working through someone whose ministry is validated by signs and wonders. Once that ministry was established it was incumbent upon the people of God to listen and heed the words that were proclaimed.

My challenge: We err if we seek signs merely to satisfy our curiosity or to entertain us. Jesus Christ is God's final word to us (Hebrews 1:1-2). Hear Him. Do not seek another prophet or follow those who claim to have a new word from God.

April 26/Day 116

God's Sovereignty over the Nations

Today's reading: 2 Kings 5:1-8:6

My selection: 2 Kings 6:16

[Elisha] said, "Do not be afraid, for those who are with us are more than those who are with them."

My reflections: During the time of Elisha's ministry, the Lord showed His power over the nations. In this incident, the king of Syria came after Elisha who could report to the king of Israel the words his enemy spoke in his bedroom. The Lord delivered Elisha and taught his servant a lesson as well that the forces of God were superior to those of their enemy.

This victory led to a time of peace with Syria but when it was broken by Syrian aggression, the Lord again showed His power and turned around the desperate situation in Samaria in one day. Famine turned to feasting and the skeptical captain who doubted God's power to fulfill Elisha's prophecy was punished with death.

Throughout these examples, we see that God is sovereign even in seemingly impossible situations. He is not limited or hindered by human power. He is faithful to His Word.

My challenge: Do you trust in His sovereign power in your personal life and in the entire world today? Do you rejoice even when things look bleak knowing that His purposes cannot be thwarted?

As you look at what appears to be the hopeless state of affairs, trust in Him. Rejoice in Him. Be steadfast.

Preaching through Tears

Today's reading: 2 Kings 8:7-10:17

My selection: 2 Kings 8:12

Hazael said, "Why does my lord weep?" He answered, "Because I know the evil that you will do to the people of Israel. You will set on fire their fortresses, and you will kill their young men with the sword and dash in pieces their little ones and rip open their pregnant women."

My reflections: Elisha was faithful to deliver the Lord's message horrifying though it was for him. He wept thinking of Hazael, king of Syria, destroying Israel, killing young men, pregnant women, and children, despite the fact that Israel had incurred the just judgment of God for her wickedness.

The gospel is both good and bad news. The bad news is that all people in their natural state are heading for judgment, condemnation, and eternal destruction. The good news is that Christ Jesus saves all who repent of sin and believe in Him who is the one mediator between God and mankind.

We, who believe, cannot ignore the bad news even as we weep at the thought of judgment falling upon those who reject God's truth. Elisha sets an example of faithfulness in delivering a message which troubled his heart. He did not neglect to tell the whole truth. In the end, it will be seen that sin--falling short of the glory of God--is justly punished. The joy of seeing God's name vindicated will overwhelm the sorrow of judgment upon a vast host who remain as Adam's race.

My challenge: Do you hesitate to give the bad news with the good? Be faithful, even while brokenhearted, in giving the gospel to the world.

The Danger of Settling for First Place

Today's reading: 2 Kings 10:18-13:25

My selection: 2 Kings 10:31

But Jehu was not careful to walk in the law of the Lord, the God of Israel, with all his heart. He did not turn from the sins of Jeroboam, which he made Israel to sin.

My reflections: The final evaluation of Jehu's reign resulted in a mixed grade. He wiped out Baal but kept the golden calves of Jeroboam. He did enough good to warrant the continuation of his dynasty but enough bad to be compared to evil Jeroboam.

Jehu was not focused on pleasing God or being completely obedient. Perhaps he was just good enough to be not as bad as most other kings. He settled for being first place in a field of very flawed rulers. He went part way toward leading the nation to faithfulness but not far enough. As a result, the dismemberment of Israel's territory began (10:32).

My challenge: What is the standard for righteousness in your life? Do you compare your obedience with that of others to get a false sense of spiritual superiority? Or do you make Jesus Christ and God's Word the standard for holiness? To use other people as a measure of perfection will result in either overwhelming discouragement or unwarranted pride. Or some of both. To look to Christ will result in humility, challenge, and encouragement.

God's purpose for you, Christian, is not merely to make you better than others but to transform you into a true reflection of Jesus Christ. As Hebrews 12:1-2 (KJV) says, "Wherefore seeing we also are compassed about with so great a cloud of witnesses, let us lay aside every weight, and the sin which doth so easily beset us, and let us run with patience the race that is set before us, looking unto Jesus the author and finisher of our faith; who for the joy that was set before him endured the cross, despising the shame, and is set down at the right hand of the throne of God."

Don't be a Jehu. Look to Jesus. Seek to please Him. Seek to be like Him. There is joy ahead at the end of the race.

Unbiblical Worship Exemplified

Today's reading: 2 Kings 14:1-16:20

My selection: 2 Kings 16:10

When King Ahaz went to Damascus to meet Tiglath-pileser king of Assyria, he saw the altar that was at Damascus. And King Ahaz sent to Uriah the priest a model of the altar, and its pattern, exact in all its details.

My reflections: Ahaz had such disregard for the law of God that he borrowed the design of the altar used in Damascus, had Uriah build a replica of it and replace the bronze altar that had stood in the Holy Place of the temple.

The regulative principle of worship says that our worship must conform to Scripture. We must do all that God commands in our worship and not do what God prohibits. Some would add that biblical worship may not include what God does not command either implicitly or explicitly. Ahaz certainly violated even the most liberal understanding of the regulative principle. He may have found the Damascus altar more appealing or he may simply have wanted to be trendy in his worship in Jerusalem. Whatever his motive, he erred and so do we if we are not careful to observe the Scriptural norms for worship.

My challenge: To glorify God means not only to worship Him but to worship Him properly. It need not be popular or trendy, but it must be biblical. Be sure you worship where being biblical is an absolute.

God's Mercy to Eclectic Worshippers

Today's reading: 2 Kings 17:1-19:13

My selection: 2 Kings 17:41

So these nations feared the Lord and also served their carved images. Their children did likewise, and their children's children—as their fathers did, so they do to this day.

My reflections: After Israel was defeated and taken captive by Assyria, the land was repopulated with a mixture of peoples from captured nations. They had various gods and forms of worship including the burnt offerings of children. When lions attacked the people, they concluded that they were offending the "god of the land." The Assyrian king sent a prophet of Israel to them to instruct them in the law of God.

The result was not a single-minded embracing of the law of the God of Israel but the addition of Biblical worship to their previous traditions. This is why the Samaritans came to be despised by the Jews, as is easy to see in several incidents during Jesus' ministry. But Jesus presented Himself to them as the Messiah and Savior of the world, and they turned to Him in faith (John 4).

My challenge: Praise God for His mercy and grace to such eclectic and unlikely worshipers that He sent His Son to them and to us.

The Recovery of the Law of God

Today's reading: 2 Kings 19:14-22:20

My selection: 2 Kings 22:10

Then Shaphan the secretary told the king, "Hilkiah the priest has given me a book." And Shaphan read it before the king.

My reflections: During the days of the kings of Judah, the Law of God was not just ignored; it was misplaced and lost somewhere in the temple. Josiah, grandson of the infamous King Manasseh, ordered a cleanup and renovation of the temple. It sounds like he was surprised when he learned about the Book of the Law being found. Had he never heard of this book? He was more than surprised when he learned of the contents. He was shocked and terrified at what he could see was going to come upon the people for their flagrant disobedience.

Josiah's repentance led to a delay of judgment. Indeed, a godly ruler who knows and respects the Bible can make a difference for a time. But this whole incident shows how far a nation can go from God when His Law is ignored, disobeyed, and forgotten.

There was a time in America when the Bible was a mainstay in schools and in many homes. How well-known is the Bible today? It is not read in many homes and not preached in many churches. There is a saying, "He who does not read, is no better off than he who cannot." Insert "the Bible" after the word "read" in that saying.

But there is another danger with regard to the Bible. It is the danger of selective reading, that is, merely cherry-picking certain themes or passages that appeal to us and ignoring the rest. We can effectively distort the Bible's truth by believing in God's love but ignoring His wrath, believing His grace but not His holiness, believing His immanence but ignoring His transcendence.

My challenge: Is the Bible present in your life, your home, and your church? More importantly is it in your mind every day as the absolute authority for truth and guidance? We may not be able to make the Bible a cornerstone of public education again, but do make it the cornerstone of your personal life, your family life, and the constant subject in the church you attend.

May 2/Day 122

Obedience: More than Emotional Fervor

Today's reading: 2 Kings 23:1-25:30

My selection: 2 Kings 23:2-3

[2] And the king went up to the house of the Lord, and with him all the men of Judah and all the inhabitants of Jerusalem and the priests and the prophets, all the people, both small and great. And he read in their hearing all the words of the Book of the Covenant that had been found in the house of the Lord. [3] And the king stood by the pillar and made a covenant before the Lord, to walk after the Lord and to keep his commandments and his testimonies and his statutes with all his heart and all his soul, to perform the words of this covenant that were written in this book. And all the people joined in the covenant.

My reflections: Josiah had been deeply moved by the finding of the Law of God, but he didn't stop with his emotional high. He read all the words of the Book of the Covenant. He made a covenant before the Lord to zealously pursue obedience. He led the people in a similar commitment. He went on to cleanse the temple of all the paraphernalia of Baal and Asherah worship. Then he fired of all the priests who had been involved in such worship. Finally, he destroyed all the idols and Jeroboam's unauthorized altar.

It is possible to be deeply moved by God's truth at various times in our lives. It is also possible for us to content ourselves with occasional mountaintop experiences in which we feel especially close to the Lord. Many of us have seen these kinds of experiences come and go. Emotions may be enjoyable, but they are never a substitute for obedient action, the doing of what God has commanded. Josiah had a unique responsibility and opportunity as king, and he fulfilled it for God's glory. It was one of the bright spots in an otherwise dark history of the divided kingdom which was about to end.

My challenge: Pray for strength to act on God's word. Do not be content merely to feel passionately about walking in His ways. Be a doer of God's word (James 1:22).

Your Place in Human History

Today's reading: 1 Chronicles 1:1-2:2

My selection: 1 Chronicles 1:43

These are the kings who reigned in the land of Edom before any king reigned over the people of Israel: Bela the son of Beor, the name of his city being Dinhabah.

My reflections: In this tedious genealogical list, most people are mentioned only in relationship to who their children were. But there are occasional comments. Here is a comment about the kings who reigned over the land of Edom before any king reigned over the people of Israel.

This is a reminder to the people of Israel or Judah who would read this book that there was life before their time, and there would be life after their time.

What is the significance of a human life? Few make a difference. Few stand out. We are liable in our time to think of ourselves more highly than we ought to think. The people of Israel were not the center of the universe. Neither are we. But this passage is also a reminder that we are not nothing. We do have a part to play in the flow of human history.

Our significance is not likely to be in our great accomplishments but in relation to God and His work in history. We can be faithful. We can make our contribution, small as it may seem to be. It may be merely to walk with God and seek to raise godly children. If we do His will, live for His glory remaining faithful to the end we will have conquered.

My challenge: Pray that you will be faithful today. You are not the center of the universe, but your life does count. Many names are written here. They are not forgotten. The Lord will not forget you either.

Honorable Jabez; Wise God

Today's reading: 1 Chronicles 2:3-4:23

My selection: 1 Chronicles 4:9-10

9 Jabez was more honorable than his brothers; and his mother called his name Jabez, saying, "Because I bore him in pain." 10 Jabez called upon the God of Israel, saying, "Oh that you would bless me and enlarge my border, and that your hand might be with me, and that you would keep me from harm so that it might not bring me pain!" And God granted what he asked.

My reflections: The writer of Chronicles gives priority to David's lineage as the exiles returning from captivity would want to be clear on the royal line. This line ultimately ends in Jesus Christ, the King Eternal. Meanwhile we see that two kinds of people get special attention in the genealogy: the very evil and the very godly. An example of the former is Er, whom the Lord put to death (2:3). An example of the latter was Jabez in the passage cited.

Bruce Wilkinson's bestselling book, *The Prayer of Jabez*, makes it difficult to ignore Jabez as we read through this passage. Jabez' name sounds like the Hebrew word for pain. He was said to be more honorable than his brothers. He certainly is an example for us as one who prayed that God might bless him and keep him from painful harm or evil despite the painful birth he had had.

But the focus of this passage should not be so much on Jabez as on God who granted his prayer. God is able to turn the circumstances of our lives for good. He is gracious to answer the prayers of His people. But He does not always answer prayers in the affirmative. He may answer with "yes", "no" or "not now."

We err if we think that Jabez' prayer was answered because he used the right formula. We err even more if we think that by repeating the prayer of Jabez we will automatically get the same results. The God of Israel and Jabez answers prayers on the basis of His wisdom, grace, and love. He is not a celestial vending machine which will always deliver a cold drink when we deposit four quarters.

My challenge: Praise God that He is wiser than we are and that He will always give His children good things, even if they are not the things we think are good. Make prayer to God your way of life, but do not trust in your prayers. Trust in God.

May 5/Day 125

The Famous, the Infamous, and the Forgotten

Today's reading: 1 Chronicles 4:24-5:26

My selection: 1 Chronicles 5:1-2

[1] The sons of Reuben the firstborn of Israel (for he was the firstborn, but because he defiled his father's couch, his birthright was given to the sons of Joseph the son of Israel, so that he could not be enrolled as the oldest son; [2] though Judah became strong among his brothers and a chief came from him, yet the birthright belonged to Joseph).

My reflections: Reading through the genealogy reminds me of the passing of the generations and, I ask, "What remains?" Some are famous, like Caleb or Jabez. There are the infamous, like Reuben. There are the forgotten, their only claim to fame being that they were in the lineage somewhere.

But the descendants of the famous are not commended for what their ancestors did centuries before. There is a false sense of entitlement to one who says, "Caleb was my great, great, great-grandfather." Neither are the descendants of the infamous more despicable because their ancestor was notorious. Those whose names are merely mentioned, whom we skim over without being sure how to pronounce them, may be forgotten by us but not by God.

Those who are saved are saved by grace through faith, not a result of works so that no one may boast (Ephesians 2:8, 9). History marches on leaving a trail of bones behind, but God is able to save to the uttermost whoever comes to Him through our great High Priest, Jesus Christ (Hebrews 7:25).

My challenge: If you trust in Christ, God knows you. Rejoice in your standing before Him, whatever your human heritage. "The Lord is good, a strong hold in the day of trouble; and he knoweth them that trust in him" (Nahum 1:7 KJV). Be content. It is enough to be known by God.

May 6/Day 126

Music Worthy of God

Today's reading: 1 Chronicles 6:1-7:5

My selection: 1 Chronicles 6:31-32

[31] These are the men whom David put in charge of the service of song in the house of the Lord after the ark rested there. [32] They ministered with song before the tabernacle of the tent of meeting until Solomon built the house of the Lord in Jerusalem, and they performed their service according to their order.

My reflections: Worship in ancient Israel under David was given high priority. This can be seen as there is a long list of men who were appointed for the "service of song" in the house of the Lord. This predated Solomon's building of the temple.

I draw two conclusions from this section:

1. Music and song are an important part of the worship of Jehovah. This does not change with the New Testament. Some cross-cultural missionaries have rejected the importing of foreign music and songs into new cultures, but music and song, of some kind, is an essential part of worship.

2. Time and manpower must be given to the ministry of music for it to be worthy of a great and holy God.

When has there been great music in the Church? Here, I am speculating. There was a song written at the crossing of the Red Sea. There were great Psalms written by David and others who lived during the early days of the united kingdom of Israel. There was great music written during the Reformation. Today we have a large quantity of music being written in the contemporary Christian music industry. One wonders if this music has the quality of durability.

My challenge: God is worthy of our best music. Use music to worship God, privately and publicly. If you are gifted in writing lyrics and music or performing music, use your gifts to the maximum for God's glory. Take time to express appreciation to those who serve the Lord in the area of music.

Death and Comfort

Today's reading: 1 Chronicles 7:6-8:40

My selection: 1 Chronicles 7:21-23

[21] Zabad his son, Shuthelah his son, and Ezer and Elead, whom the men of Gath who were born in the land killed, because they came down to raid their livestock. [22] And Ephraim their father mourned many days, and his brothers came to comfort him. [23] And Ephraim went in to his wife, and she conceived and bore a son. And he called his name Beriah, because disaster had befallen his house.

My reflections: The pain of a parent who buries a child is unspeakable. In the case of Ephraim, his son, Elead, must have been an adult when he was killed by raiding Philistines from Gath. When and where this occurred is not clear to me, but the fact remains that a parent is marked forever by the death of a child, as is recorded here about Ephraim.

Two things helped Ephraim get through this time: the comfort of his brothers and the birth of another son, Beriah, whose name sounds like the Hebrew word for disaster.

There is nothing more comforting to those who grieve than the presence of loving family and friends, nothing, unless it is the birth of another child.

My challenge: If you are grieving the death of a close relative, allow others to comfort you. Is there a grieving person who needs your comfort today? Reach out to the one who is in pain. One need not be eloquent or verbose in speaking with the bereaved. The loving presence of another is better than poetic words.

Ignorant Idols; Blinded Idolaters

Today's reading: 1 Chronicles 9:1-11:9

My selection: 1 Chronicles 10:9

They stripped [Saul] and took his head and his armor, and sent messengers throughout the land of the Philistines to carry the good news to their idols and to the people.

My reflections: When the Philistines found that Saul and his sons were dead, they "sent messengers throughout the land to carry the good news to their idols and to the people." This action strikes me as something between hilarious and ludicrous. The idols don't know what has happened, but the Philistines worship them as if they had affected the victory. Who is more ignorant the idols or the idol worshipers who foolishly attribute to them powers which they do not possess?

Apart from the grace of God, we would not connect the dots either.

My challenge: If you have been enabled by God to see the folly of worshiping another god, give thanks to Him. His mercy is great. Pray for your friends and loved ones who still worship other gods, that the true and living God revealed in the Bible may open their eyes to turn them from darkness to light and from the power of Satan to God (Acts 26:18).

A God of Wrath and A God of Grace

Today's reading: 1 Chronicles 11:10-13:14

My selection: 1 Chronicles 13:14

And the ark of God remained with the household of Obed-edom in his house three months. And the Lord blessed the household of Obed-edom and all that he had.

My reflections: The ark of God represented His presence. He sat invisibly enthroned above the cherubim on the ark's cover (13:6). The Law spelled out warnings to any who would desecrate the ark by looking inside it or touching it.

Uzzah was struck down for his careless, unlawful handling of the ark. His death brought such fear to David that he left the ark with Obed-edom rather than move it to Jerusalem as planned. Remarkably, Obed-edom and his family were blessed by the Lord.

The same ark brought death to one and blessing to another. The difference was obedience to God's law. The same God brings down the disobedient and lifts up the godly. He is not fickle but consistently rewards the righteous while destroying the wicked.

My challenge: The gospel is bad news and good news. First, the bad news: God's wrath will justly be poured upon unbelieving sinners. Next, the good news: whoever believes in His Son will not perish but have everlasting life.

Faith is a gift of God (Ephesians 2:8-9). Have you been given faith to believe in Him? Faith comes by hearing God's word (Romans 10:17). If you have not believed, seek to hear the preaching of the gospel regularly. Pray that God may be merciful to you.

May 10/Day 130

The King at Home

Today's reading: 1 Chronicles 14:1-16:43

My selection: 1 Chronicles 16:43

Then all the people departed each to his house, and David went home to bless his household.

My reflections: David was doing a good job as a military leader, governor, and administrator of a vibrant priesthood in Israel. He utilized his position, not to attempt to usurp the position of the Levites and priests, but to ensure that they were well-organized and were admonished to keep the law of God faithfully in the discharge of their tabernacle duties. After bringing the ark to the City of David, getting it in place, organizing the work of the tabernacle, and giving praise to God, David went to his home to bless his household.

Whether in the church or in the spheres of government and commerce, leaders must not forget their families.

Wives and children are easily neglected by those men who spend most of their time dealing with great, public matters. It is easy for such men to relax at home and forget that their families need a husband and father, just like any other family. It is easy for them to feel that they are spent and have nothing to give at home. It is easy for them to come home wanting to receive more than to give. If this is the case, they will need to reserve some energy for their ministry on the home front lest their wives and children be bitter and resentful.

My challenge: Are you a leader who struggles to have enough energy at the end of the day to come home and bless your family? What changes do you need to make to be able to do that? Are you the wife or child of a man who seems to give his best at work and has little reserve for you? How can you pray for him and encourage him to make his family ministry more of a priority? Husbands and fathers, take care of your wives and children. No one else can be husband and father to them.

May 11/Day 131

The Eternal King

Today's reading: 1 Chronicles 17:1-20:8

My selection: 1 Chronicles 17:14-15

[14] I will confirm him in my house and in my kingdom forever, and his throne shall be established forever. [15] In accordance with all these words, and in accordance with all this vision, Nathan spoke to David.

My reflections: God promised to establish the throne of David's son forever. This was just another in an unfolding list of promises of redemption and grace that began at the fall with Genesis 3:15. A definitive blow would be dealt to the serpent by the seed (or offspring) of the woman. Later, Abraham was called and promised land, descendants, and blessing. Through him all the families of the earth would be blessed. Then through Moses, God established the nation of Israel with the law and the priesthood, all of which was a shadow of what would come through the Messiah. Now David is promised to have the Eternal King come through his lineage.

All of the Bible ties together with the theme of the Redeemer and the redemption of God's elect people. God was revealing His plan gradually. It would be an unchanging plan but not a quick one. We now have the benefit of seeing the fulfillment of much of that plan. And there is more to come.

My challenge: Praise God for His wisdom in bringing to pass His eternal purposes for His glory and our good. See how He is calling out people from every tribe and tongue to know and worship Him. Stay tuned and keep confident.

May 12/Day 132

Properly Placed Hope

Today's reading: 1 Chronicles 21:1-23:32

My selection: 1 Chronicles 22:15-16

[15] You have an abundance of workmen: stonecutters, masons, carpenters, and all kinds of craftsmen without number, skilled in working [16] gold, silver, bronze, and iron. Arise and work! The Lord be with you!"

My reflections: David charged Solomon, his son and successor to the throne of Israel, to build the house of the Lord, the temple. David, although not permitted by the Lord to do the building himself, stockpiled materials, and gold, and silver for the building. He even designated the location of the temple (22:1).

David wisely and diligently worked to insure that Solomon's building project would not fail. He did this "with great pains." This was a great and encouraging example of thoroughness and foresight.

At the same time, knowing the history of what would happen after this makes me sad. Solomon's son, Rehoboam, would lose ten tribes, idolatry would grow, and the long downward spiral would begin culminating in the captivity of Judah and the destruction of that wonderful temple.

Then again, what was the temple for? A place for sinners to be reconciled to God on the basis of a blood sacrifice which would point to the once-for-all sacrifice of the Lamb of God, the Lord Jesus Christ.

Meanwhile, the temple was built, and enjoyed, neglected, and destroyed showing how deeply sinful and needy are God's people. All David's pains could not avoid what would happen.

My challenge: Take pains in your work. It matters because it will not be forgotten by the Lord. Do everything for the glory of God today, but know that, until the King returns and establishes a new heavens and a new earth, all will be transitory and precarious. Be sure your hope is properly placed.

May 13/Day 133

The Blessing of God through Children

Today's reading: 1 Chronicles 24:1-26:19

My selection: 1 Chronicles 26:4-5

4 And Obed-edom had sons: Shemaiah the firstborn, Jehozabad the second, Joah the third, Sachar the fourth, Nethanel the fifth, 5 Ammiel the sixth, Issachar the seventh, Peullethai the eighth, for God blessed him.

My reflections: Obed-edom cared for the ark of the covenant when David's attempt to bring it to the City of David failed. Seeing God blessed Obed-edom, David decided to move the ark to its destination (1 Chronicles 13:14; 2 Samuel 6:11) and make Obed-edom a gatekeeper.

How did David see that God had blessed Obed-edom? God blessed him with eight sons. His grandsons were notable for their leadership and abilities (26:6).

What a contrast to the prevalent attitude toward children in western society today where so many look at them as if they were regrettable interruptions and costly hobbies to be severely limited in number, if not avoided completely! Yet many elderly people who have no children or siblings find it difficult and sad to be at the end of their lives without family or descendants.

My challenge: If you have children or grandchildren, give thanks to God. If you do not, are there children you can serve as an adopted big brother or sister, uncle or aunt or grandparent?

Be sure you invest spiritually in the next generations and pass on your legacy to biological descendants or virtual descendants or both.

May 14/Day 134

Godly Leaders and Biblical Churches

Today's reading: 1 Chronicles 26:20-29:30

My selection: 1 Chronicles 29:14

But who am I, and what is my people, that we should be able thus to offer willingly? For all things come from you, and of your own have we given you.

My reflections: A leader expresses godliness through humility. David, though king, saw God as the true king and rightful owner and source of all things. Furthermore, David, as a godly leader, led his people in worship. This was a golden age in Israel because a godly king led the nation to an orderly and more consistent worship of God according to His law.

Today in the USA, we do not have a theocracy such as existed in Israel. We allow for unbelief and differing theological beliefs. It is not illegal to be an atheist, agnostic, or polytheist. Christianity influenced the founding of our country and has had a big influence down through history. Christians must seek to continue unapologetically to influence for good the public policy of our nation lest we completely lose our moral and ethical compass. The protection of human life and the sanctity of marriage as established by God between one man and one woman are significant. But the encroaching of the culture of death and the normalization of homosexuality could not occur without the acquiescence of a large part of the so-called Christian church.

My challenge: We need godly leaders in politics, but they will be greatly limited if there is not Biblical Christianity in our churches. Pray for revival in our churches. Godly churches will impact our culture and our political leaders.

May 15/Day 135

Starters and Finishers

Today's reading: 2 Chronicles 1:1-5:1

My selection: 2 Chronicles 5:1

Thus all the work that Solomon did for the house of the Lord was finished. And Solomon brought in the things that David his father had dedicated, and stored the silver, the gold, and all the vessels in the treasuries of the house of God.

My reflections: At the time of completing the temple, perhaps Solomon had the words from Proverbs 13:19 (KJV) in mind: "The desire accomplished is sweet to the soul." Finishing a long, difficult project like the building of the temple, must have brought great joy to Solomon. It had begun in his father David's mind. David prepared Solomon for the task, but Solomon had to see it through. Even today, nearly three thousand years later, it is not hard to sense the excitement that this brought.

Solomon was a starter and a finisher. Some of us are better at starting than at finishing. We are the ones who leave a trail of half-completed projects behind as we move on to the next thing. Some of us are better at finishing than starting. We are the ones who weigh the cost of finishing and find it difficult to start since it will have to be carried through to the end.

My challenge: Is there an important task or project that you have left un-started or unfinished? Are you guilty of being overly-cautious and fearful about tackling a challenging objective even though you are convinced God has called you to do it? Learn the sweetness of starting and finishing by faith what God has called you to do - things which bring glory to Him and which will endure beyond your own life.

The Day God Shut Down the Ministry

Today's reading: 2 Chronicles 5:2-7:22

My selection: 2 Chronicles 5:13-14

[13] When the song was raised, with trumpets and cymbals and other musical instruments, in praise to the Lord,

"For he is good, for his steadfast love endures forever,"

the house, the house of the Lord, was filled with a cloud, [14] so that the priests could not stand to minister because of the cloud, for the glory of the Lord filled the house of God.

My reflections: The temple was completed according to plan. The temple personnel were appointed, including priests and musicians. When the priests came out of the Holy Place, the trumpeters and singers lifted up the music of praise and thanksgiving to God in unison. The house of the Lord was filled with a cloud and the priests could not minister because of the cloud which was the glory of the Lord.

As a minister, I know that, all too frequently, the sense of the glory and presence of God is not felt by pastors much less by congregants. Sunday morning worship is business as usual. We rush into His presence as if it were the supermarket where we have come to make a commercial transaction in the shortest amount of time and speed off on our way.

Oh, that God would so visit His people that they could do nothing but fall in worship before Him!

My challenge: Be more diligent in preparing to worship God this coming Lord's Day. Pray that God will give His ministers and His people a great sense of awe in God's presence and an overwhelming awareness of His glory filling the churches where they serve and worship. Maybe God will shut down the ministry-as-usual for a day.

May 17/Day 137

God Uses Foolishness and Evil

Today's reading: 2 Chronicles 8:1-11:17

My selection: 2 Chronicles 10:15

So the king did not listen to the people, for it was a turn of affairs brought about by God that the Lord might fulfill his word, which he spoke by Ahijah the Shilonite to Jeroboam the son of Nebat.

My reflections: Rehoboam's foolish decision to listen to the youthful counselors instead of the older ones illustrates how God works through men to accomplish His purposes and plans. The Lord had already revealed to Jeroboam through the prophet Ahijah that He was going to tear away ten tribes from the kingdom and give them to Jeroboam (1 Kings 11:29-39). Rehoboam acted according to his own inclinations and bears the responsibility for his actions and the consequences. But God's will was done according to the prophecy.

My challenge: We must not become apathetic, foolish, or negligent in our work or decisions with a fatalistic attitude that says, "what we do doesn't matter, because God is sovereign." God is sovereign, but He calls us to faithfulness and wisdom in our work and responsibilities. When we fail we should repent and seek His forgiveness. When we do well we should be confident that our "labour is not in vain in the Lord" (1 Corinthians 15:58 KJV).

We must never claim that since God accomplishes His purposes even by means of the foolishness and evil of men, our foolishness and evil are really good things.

Be faithful today. Be wise today. When you are not, repent, and seek forgiveness knowing that His mercies are new every morning.

May 18/Day 138

Getting Home Safe

Today's reading: 2 Chronicles 11:18-16:14

My selection: 2 Chronicles 16:9-10

9 [Hanani, the seer, said], "For the eyes of the Lord run to and fro throughout the whole earth, to give strong support to those whose heart is blameless toward him. You have done foolishly in this, for from now on you will have wars." 10 Then Asa was angry with the seer and put him in the stocks in prison, for he was in a rage with him because of this. And Asa inflicted cruelties upon some of the people at the same time.

My reflections: Asa in the early years of his reign relied on the Lord for victory. Sadly, later on he foolishly looked to the king of Syria for deliverance. As a result, he was confronted by the prophet Hanani and rebuked for this decision. Asa would have wars for the rest of his reign.

My challenge: Faithfulness is a daily battle that never ends. Neither we nor King Asa may rely on past victories for current challenges. Asa started well but ended badly. In the final two years of his life, he personally was afflicted with a severe disease in his feet. Even that suffering did not turn his heart toward the Lord in faith, but he trusted in physicians alone.

Pray that you may never waver from loving and trusting in the Lord until He takes you safely home. In the words of the great old hymn, "O Sacred Head, Now Wounded" by Bernard of Clairvaux,

What language shall I borrow to thank Thee, dearest friend,
For this Thy dying sorrow, Thy pity without end?
O make me Thine forever, and should I fainting be,
Lord, let me never, never outlive my love to Thee.

May 19/Day 139

The Battle is God's

Today's reading: 2 Chronicles 17:1-20:30

My selection: 2 Chronicles 20:15

He said, "Listen, all Judah and inhabitants of Jerusalem and King Jehoshaphat: Thus says the Lord to you, 'Do not be afraid and do not be dismayed at this great horde, for the battle is not yours but God's.'"

My reflections: King Jehoshaphat was overwhelmed by the opposition forces drawn up against the Kingdom of Judah, but he did the right thing and turned to the Lord in prayer confessing his weakness and lack of wisdom (20:12). Then the Spirit of the Lord came upon Jahaziel who commanded the king and the people not to fear knowing that this was God's battle not theirs. Jahaziel went on to prophesy that the Lord would give the victory. They would go out to battle, but they would not need to fight because the Lord would be with them.

The next day the king preached to the army and called them to believe. The enemy was routed, and the allied armies self-destructed.

God doesn't always give us insurmountable trials and easy victories, but He does call us to trust Him no matter what battle we face. He does promise to be with His people to the end of the age (Matthew 28:20).

My challenge: What army is amassed against you today? Call on the Lord for wisdom and strength (James 1:5; Ephesians 6:10).

Lord, thank you that the battle is not ours but yours. Thank you for your presence. Be glorified today in the battle we fight against the world, the flesh, and the devil.

May 20/Day 140

Two Sides of Unbelief

Today's reading: 2 Chronicles 20:31-24:27

My selection: 2 Chronicles 24:24

Though the army of the Syrians had come with few men, the Lord delivered into their hand a very great army, because Judah had forsaken the Lord, the God of their fathers. Thus they executed judgment on Joash.

My reflections: God is not limited by human resources. This was the case when the Lord sent the Syrians in judgment against Joash. We read:

"Though the army of the Syrians had come with few men, the Lord delivered into their hand a very great army." The reason? "Because Judah had forsaken the Lord, the God of their fathers. Thus, they executed judgment on Joash."

My challenge: Fear and overconfidence are both evidence of failure to trust God. These are the two sides of unbelief.

Do you count on the Lord for deliverance or on human strength? Do not trust in your own power to overcome even apparently weak opposition. Trust in the Lord, His wisdom, and His power today.

May 21/Day 141

Dangerous Presumption

Today's reading: 2 Chronicles 25:1-28:27

My selection: 2 Chronicles 28:11

Now hear me, and send back the captives from your relatives whom you have taken, for the fierce wrath of the Lord is upon you.

My reflections: Favorable circumstances alone, without the light of God's Word, are not a reliable guide when determining how one should act or live.

In a battle between Israel and Judah during the evil reign of King Ahaz, Israel was victorious. But Israel overplayed their hand in victory and drew the wrath of God. The prophet Oded warned them that their killing and spoiling of Judah was uncalled for. Oded told them that their sins were many and their victory did not imply that God was approving of all their evil practices. God merely used Israel as a means to punish Judah and King Ahaz.

There was proper and immediate response to the prophet's message, by some of the chiefs, and the judgment of God was averted.

There is a principle to be observed here as we seek to know God's will in our daily lives. Success in a matter must not, by itself, be interpreted as an indicator of God's favor or a basis for deciding further action. This is why we need to walk in the light of His Word which is the objective measure of truth and righteousness.

My challenge: Just because you can do something does not imply that you should do it. Just because you are successful in something does not mean what you did was a good thing. Beware of drawing a wrong conclusion from apparent success.

Seek to let God's Word light your way today, not an unexamined presumption based on circumstances.

May 22/Day 142

Wholehearted Service

Today's reading: 2 Chronicles 29:1-31:21

My selection: 2 Chronicles 31:20-21

20 Thus Hezekiah did throughout all Judah, and he did what was good and right and faithful before the Lord his God. 21 And every work that he undertook in the service of the house of God and in accordance with the law and the commandments, seeking his God, he did with all his heart, and prospered.

My reflections: Hezekiah systematically led the nation to a revival of the proper worship of God. He began by having the temple cleaned up (I hate to think what is meant by "filth" in the temple), reinstating worship and sacrifices, and holding the Passover feast at the designated time. Furthermore, he invited the people of Israel who had neglected the temple and the Passover for so many generations. While many mocked his invitation, the ones who came and joined in were deeply moved so that they later went about tearing down the idolatrous high places in both Judah and Israel.

All this points to a man who did his work with all his heart. He obeyed the law, he sought his God, he did it with all his heart and he prospered.

My challenge: What does it look like in your life to serve God according to His commandments with all your heart? Is there room for improvement in your attitude? Do you serve joyfully and diligently? Does your service move others to serve or do you just follow along waiting for someone else to take the leadership?

You may not be a king but--as far as you can in your sphere of influence--be like Hezekiah. Set an example of wholeheartedness in serving the Lord.

May 23/Day 143

Starting Well, Ending Badly; Starting Poorly, Ending Well

Today's reading: 2 Chronicles 32:1-34:33

My selection: 2 Chronicles 32:25

But Hezekiah did not make return according to the benefit done to him, for his heart was proud. Therefore wrath came upon him and Judah and Jerusalem.

My reflections: Hezekiah started extremely well but ended poorly. His heart grew proud at the end of his life and the wrath of God was upon him and the kingdom. On the contrary, his son, Manasseh started as one of the most evil kings in the history of Judah, but responded positively to the Lord's discipline (33:1ff).

A good start doesn't guarantee a good finish. A bad start doesn't rule out a good finish.

Paul warned the Corinthians about becoming over-confident in their spiritual achievements and victories. "Wherefore let him that thinketh he standeth take heed lest he fall" (1 Corinthians 10:12 KJV).

My challenge: Life's spiritual battle is severe and long. Be faithful and watchful to the end knowing that our enemy, Satan, will never stop seeking to distract, discourage, and devour us. Start well and end well, but if you already know you have started poorly (and you have because you are a sinner), turn to Christ in faith and repentance. He cleanses repentant sinners and equips them to serve Him for a strong finish in this life (2 Timothy 3:16-17). But beware of pride. You stand accepted before God by Christ's righteousness alone.

Missing the Obvious

Today's reading: 2 Chronicles 35:1-Ezra 1:11

My selection: 2 Chronicles 36:15-16

15 The Lord, the God of their fathers, sent persistently to them by his messengers, because he had compassion on his people and on his dwelling place. 16 But they kept mocking the messengers of God, despising his words and scoffing at his prophets, until the wrath of the Lord rose against his people, until there was no remedy.

My reflections: As Judah went into decline, wickedness was coupled with political instability brought by the powerful forces of Egypt and Babylon. Yet God continued to send prophets to call His people to repentance. The nation, despite its troubles, could not see God's compassion on them. They completely missed the obvious of what was happening to them and why God was continuing to give them His message. Instead they mocked His messengers, despised His words, and scoffed at His prophets.

Then came the wrath of God against His people in greater fury than ever, and they were destroyed. Many lives were lost. Survivors were taken captive. Jerusalem was in ruins, and the temple was brought down.

Those who rebel against God do not become wise but show a spiritual blindness that would be baffling if we did not know that it is Satan who blinds their eyes. "In whom the god of this world hath blinded the minds of them which believe not, lest the light of the glorious gospel of Christ, who is the image of God, should shine unto them" (2 Corinthians 4:4 KJV).

My challenge: Do not be deceived by our wicked enemy, Satan. Reject his lie. Pray that God may give you faith to see and receive the truth.

May 25/Day 145

Weeping and Shouting

Today's reading: Ezra 2:1-3:13

My selection: Ezra 3:13

The people could not distinguish the sound of the joyful shout from the sound of the people's weeping, for the people shouted with a great shout, and the sound was heard far away.

My reflections: When Cyrus the Persian conquered Babylon, he, though presumably not a believer, was moved by God to send the captives of Judah back to Jerusalem to rebuild the temple. The return was carried out under Zerubbabel. The returnees soon rebuilt the altar and began making sacrifices.

Not long afterward, they set about to rebuild the temple itself. When the temple foundation was laid the people lifted up their praises to God, but there were among them some old men who had seen the original temple. When they saw the new foundation, they wept. These elders wept because they realized that the new temple would be nothing in comparison to the old. [You can read Haggai 2 to find out how the Lord comforted these weeping senior saints.]

In this world, hope is always mixed with disappointment. At the rebuilding of the temple, some rejoiced and some wept. Both were right in their response because it was a hopeful day and yet a sad day. It was sin that brought down the first temple, a sad thing; but that new temple would one day see the Messiah come and declare to the Jews that He was the true temple of His people, a temple that would endure for eternity (John 2:18-22).

My challenge: The earthly temple in Jerusalem is gone, but that is all right. The true High Priest has entered into the heavenly temple with a perfect sacrifice for sin (Hebrews 9:24). Bring yourself, corrupted and hopelessly stained by sin, to Him and be forgiven. Maybe you, too, will weep and shout alternately.

May 26/Day 146

God's Sovereignty over Kings

Today's reading: Ezra 4:1-7:28

My selection: Ezra 6:22

They kept the Feast of Unleavened Bread seven days with joy, for the Lord had made them joyful and had turned the heart of the king of Assyria to them, so that he aided them in the work of the house of God, the God of Israel.

My reflections: Here is an example of the well-known proverb: "The king's heart is in the hand of the Lord, as the rivers of water: he turneth it whithersoever he will" (Proverbs 21:1 KJV).

My challenge: If we believe this, we should reflect our confidence through prayer for the king (or president) rather than complaining about him. Whether he knows it or not, he is God's servant for our good (Romans 13:4). God will deal with him if he fails to fulfill his mandate as servant.

Stop complaining. Start praying. God rules over the hearts of kings.

May 27/Day 147

The Importance of Marrying in the Lord

Today's reading: Ezra 8:1-10:44

My selection: Ezra 10:10-11

10 And Ezra the priest stood up and said to them, "You have broken faith and married foreign women, and so increased the guilt of Israel. 11 Now then make confession to the Lord, the God of your fathers and do his will. Separate yourselves from the peoples of the land and from the foreign wives."

My reflections: As Ezra led the captive people of Judah and Israel back to Jerusalem and to the restoration of worship of the true God, he discovered that many of them, even the priests, had taken foreign wives. He gathered them together in the midst of a heavy downpour and exhorted them to repent and separate themselves from their foreign wives to avert the wrath of God.

This prohibition of marrying foreigners did not include those who converted to faith in the God of Abraham, Isaac, and Jacob (e.g. Rahab and Ruth were included in the genealogy of Jesus Christ), but it did include pagan wives who would turn the hearts of their husbands away from the Lord. Solomon was a prime example of how this could happen (1 Kings 11). Nor were women of Israel free to marry pagan men.

The choice of a marriage partner largely determines the spiritual and theological direction of one's life. This is why so much emphasis is made on "marrying in the Lord" and not being "unequally yoked with unbelievers". [See 1 Corinthians 7; 2 Corinthians 6:14-7:1.] Certainly, many Christians have married unbelievers and have learned the bitter truth that this is a foolish decision which follows them all their lives. It is not an unforgiveable sin, but it is a dangerous road to take which makes it difficult to grow and serve the Lord and to raise godly children. It sometimes results in the unbeliever coming to faith, but this seems to be the exception rather than the rule. Often it results in the believing spouse either renouncing the faith or being restricted in his or her growth and service for Jesus Christ.

My challenge: If you have married an unbeliever, you must seek to win that one to the Lord (1 Peter 3:1-7). If he or she is willing to live with you, you must make the best of that marriage (1 Corinthians 7:12-16). If you are unmarried, pray for the grace to remain single unless and until God leads you to a godly spouse.

If you are married to a Christian and you are growing in love and knowledge of the Lord together, then give thanks to God for that. Be sure to encourage your spouse to seek God and to serve Him all the days of your life together.

May 28/Day 148

Exemplary Leadership

Today's reading: Nehemiah 1:1-4:23

My selection: Nehemiah 4:20

In the place where you hear the sound of the trumpet, rally to us there. Our God will fight for us.

My reflections: Nehemiah is one of the finest examples of a leader ever known. Here are three essential attributes for all leaders, which he modeled well:

1. Faith. He sought God's direction from the very beginning of his project. His prayers are mentioned several times. He believed God that the work would be done, and he instilled confidence in God in all who worked with him. In the face of frustrating work and fierce opposition he proclaimed, "Our God will fight for us."

2. Wisdom. He wisely and carefully took steps to get official permission from the Persian king, Artaxerxes, for his project. He gathered information secretly before announcing his plans to the people of Jerusalem. He got good intelligence on what his enemies were up to so that they could not surprise him. He organized the workers on the wall so that all the groups could progress simultaneously without getting in each other's' way. He armed and instructed the workers so that they could change roles from workers to soldiers, if needed, at a moment's notice. He developed a simple communication system and informed all those involved as to how it worked.

3. Courage. In the face of obstacles from the work and the enemies, he remained undaunted. His trust was in the Lord, but he worked with the understanding that God works through means,

often His people, to accomplish His plans. As the old saying goes, "Pray as if it all depends on God; work as if it all depends on you."

My challenge: Do you have a leadership responsibility in some sphere of your life? Are these three attributes evident to those who look to you for leadership? Take time to think about how faith, wisdom, and courage in your role as a leader will bring glory to God. After all, it is about His glory.

May 29/Day 149

Work Done with the Help of God

Today's reading: Nehemiah 5:1-7:72

My selection: Nehemiah 6:15-16

[15] So the wall was finished on the twenty-fifth day of the month Elul, in fifty-two days. [16] And when all our enemies heard of it, all the nations around us were afraid and fell greatly in their own esteem, for they perceived that this work had been accomplished with the help of our God.

My reflections: The wall was finished in 52 days. The enemies were stunned, afraid, and humbled. Not just because the people had worked so hard and so well, but because they perceived that this work had been accomplished with the help of their God.

There was no other way to explain this feat. None of the things the enemies had said were true. None of their opposition had been effective. God had been with His people.

Jesus told His disciples, "Let your light so shine before men, that they may see your good works, and glorify your Father which is in heaven" (Matthew 5:16 KJV). In the case of Nehemiah, even his enemies had to admit that God had helped them. Even his enemies had to, in a sense, give glory to God for the finished wall of Jerusalem.

My challenge: What seemingly impossible task has God called you to do? Are you trusting Him to overcome obstacles for the success of it? Is your desire that He be glorified in its accomplishment?

Approach your impossible task today in His strength, with His help, and for His glory.

May 30/Day 150

The (Often) Missing Element in Prayer

Today's reading: Nehemiah 7:73-10:39

My selection: Nehemiah 9:2

The Israelites separated themselves from all foreigners and stood and confessed their sins and the iniquities of their fathers.

My reflections: Here is a notable example of God's people confessing their sins corporately in worship before the Lord. Notice that they do not merely gloss over their sins but go into thorough detail about their own sins and the sins of their nation down through the years.

There is a well-known acrostic for prayer: A-C-T-S. It stands for Adoration, Confession, Thanksgiving, and Supplication. Yet as popular and widely known as this acrostic is, I wonder if there is a not a lack of serious confession of sin by believers today.

In public and private prayer, confession should not be hurried or minimized, but neither should specific requests for forgiveness and assurances of forgiveness based on the Word of God.

Old Testament believers knew that they needed to confess their sins and that their forgiveness depended on the Messiah who was still to come. How much better is our hope, no longer based on a future atonement but on the offering of Jesus Christ for the sins of His people.

My challenge: Be sure to take regular time to confess sin, ask forgiveness, and be reminded that "in [Jesus Christ] we have redemption through his blood, the forgiveness of sins, according to the riches of his grace" (Ephesians 1:7 KJV).

It gives God joy to forgive you for Christ's sake, fellow Christian, so may the joy of the Lord be your strength.

May 31/Day 151

Taking Time to Celebrate

Today's reading: Nehemiah 11:1-12:47

My selection: Nehemiah 12:43

They offered great sacrifices that day and rejoiced, for God had made them rejoice with great joy; the women and children also rejoiced. And the joy of Jerusalem was heard far away.

My reflections: Care was taken to dedicate the wall and to give thanks to the Lord for His strength and blessing which allowed the work to be completed. All of the people were invited, and many were given responsibilities for the sacrifices and the music. Men and women, boys and girls of all ages were included. This was a time of joy that came from God and was lifted up to God. What a happy moment this must have been as "the joy of Jerusalem was heard far away."

My challenge: It is wise and good to take time to celebrate the achievements accomplished by God's providence. God has built into our lives one day in seven for the purpose of giving thanks and worship to Him. Do you review His blessings and celebrate His goodness to you regularly?

Beware of rushing through life pursuing one goal after another with no thought of praising and thanking God. Stop and praise Him now for successful projects accomplished and goals achieved.

June 1/Day 152

Godly Living in a Pagan Society

Today's reading: Nehemiah 13:1-Esther 3:15

My selection: Esther 2:17

The king loved Esther more than all the women, and she won grace and favor in his sight more than all the virgins, so that he set the royal crown on her head and made her queen instead of Vashti.

My reflections: Esther handled herself wisely before the king and the court. She listened to the advice of her cousin/foster father, Mordecai, and of the king's eunuch. So, she stood out from all the other candidates for queen, winning grace and favor. This gave her credibility when she reported an attempted assassination of the king and when she had to appeal to the king for the lives of the Jews in the kingdom.

Esther shows the importance of living with wisdom and integrity in the midst of a hedonistic society. [See Esther 1:8.] It further shows that God rules sovereignly over all the kingdoms of the earth. None escape His judgment.

My challenge: Do you feel the pressure of life in a godless society? Do you wonder if it is worth the price to live with integrity and humility among people whose chief thought is personal fulfillment and pleasure? Peter admonishes us: "Having your conversation honest among the Gentiles: that, whereas they speak against you as evildoers, they may by your good works, which they shall behold, glorify God in the day of visitation" (1 Peter 2:12 KJV).

Remember Esther, an example of living with honorable conduct before the face of a God who rules even over pagan kingdoms. Tomorrow we will consider Mordecai, too.

June 2/Day 153

A Delayed Reward with Accrued Interest

Today's reading: Esther 4:1-9:17

My selection: Esther 6:3

And the king said, "What honor or distinction has been bestowed on Mordecai for this?" The king's young men who attended him said, "Nothing has been done for him."

My reflections: Much could be said about the obvious character of Mordecai and of Esther: his wisdom, her courage, etc. It may be less obvious to say that Mordecai's humility is seen in his apparent willingness to do the right thing, reporting the plot of the king's would-be assassins, without reward or recognition.

I do not know how much time had elapsed between Mordecai's reporting of the assassination plot and the king's sleepless night on which he realized that Mordecai had never been rewarded for his loyalty. Mordecai had made no appeal for reward or recognition. Because of that, the timing of the king's decision to have Haman honor Mordecai brought even greater joy to the Jews and an ominous sense of impending doom to Haman and his family. Indeed, the last public act of service of Haman was to lead his enemy, Mordecai, through the streets of the capitol on the king's horse, dressed in the king's robes and proclaiming, "Thus shall it be done to the man whom the king delighteth to honor" (Esther 6:9 KJV). That very night the wicked Haman would die on his own gallows.

My challenge: Has your faithful service been unrecognized and unrewarded? How have you responded to the slights you have received? Can you see how being faithful and loyal without recognition is still the right thing to do? Can you see how God may be reserving your recognition and reward for a particular moment when it will mean even more?

Mordecai exemplifies the commands and promises of Colossians 3:23-25 where we are commanded to work hard as if serving the Lord expecting only His reward in His time. Who knows? The reward may come with accrued interest.

June 3/Day 154

God's Purposes in Evil

Today's reading: Esther 9:18-Job 3:26

My selection: Job 1:12

The Lord said to Satan, "Behold, all that he has is in your hand. Only against him do not stretch out your hand." So Satan went out from the presence of the Lord.

My reflections: The case of Job illustrates a number of important truths about God, man and Satan.

1. God knows those who trust in Him. God knew Job by name.

2. God is glorified in those who trust Him. For God, Job was an example to be held up to Satan of a man who walked with Him.

3. Satan seeks to diminish God's glory by questioning the true motivation of believers.

4. God has power and authority to send undeserved testing into the life of the believer for His own secret purposes. The suffering Christian may ask "Why?" but, ultimately, God has no obligation to give all the desired answers. This should end many of the claims of the "health and wealth gospel."

5. Satan is limited by God in testing His people. No ill can befall the believer apart from God's permission.

6. For the mature believer, even the severest test of Satan cannot thwart his trust in God.

My challenge: Are you facing severe testing? Get comfort and encouragement from Job, knowing that, like him, if you trust in the Lord, He knows you and has a purpose to bring glory to Himself through your trials. That will also result in your glory when the end of this world comes.

June 4/Day 155

Eliphaz' Error

Today's reading: Job 4:1-7:21

My selection: Job 4:2

Remember: who that was innocent ever perished? Or where were the upright cut off?

My reflections: Eliphaz comes to comfort Job, but he is missing a vital truth. After mentioning Job's past virtuous life, he suggests that Job has now become impatient. Eliphaz has a simplistic way of looking at God's dealings with men: if you do good, you will be rewarded; if you do evil you will be punished with suffering. Therefore, if you are suffering, it must always be as a result of doing evil. In other words, the innocent never suffer. There is some fault in Job (maybe this impatience?) that is causing all his present suffering.

What is wrong with Eliphaz' analysis is that it is not true in the case of Job. He is not suffering for some failure; rather, he is suffering because he has been chosen by God to demonstrate to Satan that he trusts God, not for what he can get, but for who God is. He worships God from a pure heart, not for selfish gain.

Job models, on a small scale, a truth that will become clearer in the gospel that an upright man can suffer unjustly. The only truly innocent One, the Lord Jesus Christ, God Incarnate, would be beaten, ridiculed, and killed in the most evil and unjust act of history so that all who believe in Him should not perish but have eternal life.

My challenge: Are you trusting Jesus Christ for your acceptance before God? Your own works may be better than those of others, but they are insufficient to merit the forgiveness of the

Holy One. Do not make Eliphaz' error, thinking our good works can save us. Trust in Him who, though innocent, perished and who, though upright, was cut off. Trust in Him who, though He perished and was cut off, was raised from the dead and lives forever. [See 2 Corinthians 5:21.]

June 5/Day 156

Bildad's Faulty Solution

Today's reading: Job 8:1-10:22

My selection: Job 8:6

If you are pure and upright,
Surely then he will rouse himself for you
And restore your rightful habitation.

My reflections: Like Eliphaz, Bildad's view is simplistic and, since he has no knowledge of God's secret purposes, he makes assumptions which are incorrect. God is just. This is true as far as it goes, but it is not the only attribute of God nor is man capable of judging what is just to God. Bildad further reasons that suffering comes from God, who is just, so if one suffers, it is his own fault, and he needs to repent and seek mercy. The premise is true, but the conclusion is not, or at least not always, so. Not all suffering is a direct result of one's own sin. Jesus clarified this in John 9:2-3. God may have other purposes in suffering besides punishment for personal sin.

My challenge: We need to learn from Bildad's error. God leads us, so we know what to do, but He doesn't always explain to us everything we would like to know about the cause or purpose of our suffering. When we suffer we tend to ask "Why?" and apparently this is acceptable. God did not rebuke Job for asking "Why?" But do we also ask "Why?" when we are incredibly blessed or only when we suffer?

It is always wise to confess our known sins. It is always wise to give thanks and praise to God for blessings far beyond what we deserve. It is always wise to trust God when we suffer for no apparent reason. It is generally wise to remain silent in attempting to draw conclusions about God's hidden purposes in the providential circumstances of our lives and in the lives of others.

Avoid Bildad's faulty solution. Beware of trying to second-guess an infinite, wise, and sovereign God.

June 6/Day 157

Unswerving Hope

Today's reading: Job 11:1-14:22

My selection: Job 13:15

Though he slay me, I will hope in him; yet I will argue my ways to his face.

My reflections: Zophar weighs in last of the three would-be comforters of poor Job. He varies from the first two commentators only in the intensity of what he says. God is punishing Job less than his guilt deserves. On the other hand, if Job will just do the right thing he will experience unimaginable blessing.

Job again pushes back. His friends are not saying anything he doesn't know already. But he needs better answers. There is something missing in this whole discussion, and that is the wisdom of God.

So, Job, in 13:15, acknowledges that God can kill him and that He may kill him. Yet his hope is in the Lord. There is no one else to look to. Nevertheless, he will lay his case before God. Trust in God does not mean we understand all He is doing. Trust in God does not mean we will never cry out to Him for answers. Trust in God means that, even though He slays us, we will not forsake our hope in Him.

There is a parallel here with Peter's words to Jesus in John 6. After many of Jesus' former disciples had left Him, He asked the twelve, "Will ye also go away?" Peter replied, "Lord, to whom shall we go? Thou hast the words of eternal life. And we believe and are sure that thou art that Christ, the Son of the living God" (John 6:67-69 KJV).

My challenge: Settle it now: trust Him, hope in Him, though He slay you.

June 7/Day 158

Who's the Smartest?

Today's reading: Job 15:1-18:21

My selection: Job 15:9

What do you know that we do not know?
What do you understand that is not clear to us?

My reflections: The dialogue with Job now enters the second cycle, but the quality of the conversation does not improve. Eliphaz picks up on Job's comments in which he compares their wisdom and intelligence retorting (in essence) that "we are as smart as you are" and "we could teach your father a thing or two."

This sort of argument is generally fruitless as it tries to establish intellectual superiority in order to discredit every statement by the opponent. Job's friends stand together against him, so he is outnumbered. They take turns accosting him while he continues in pain and anguish.

At this point, the debaters have quit addressing the issue and started attacking their opponent. The original question of "Why is Job suffering?" has given way to "Who of us is the wisest?" It has become a battle of egos.

My challenge: Be humble in debate. Stick to the issue and avoid character attacks which show you have no argument. Make your words soft as you may have to eat them at any time.

Job: True Confidence or Naïve Denial?

Today's reading: Job 19:1-21:34

My selection: Job 21:7

Why do the wicked live, reach old age, and grow mighty in power?

My reflections: Should Job hold to his confidence that his Redeemer lives and that he, Job, will see Him at the last (19:25)?

Zophar says "No!" arguing that "the wicked suffer." If Job suffers, he must be wicked. Zophar thinks Job should not be so sure of his standing before God.

Job fights back that the wicked do not suffer, at least not always. It is difficult to conclude from observation that "crime doesn't pay." Too many seem to get away unscathed with great sin.

Is it worth it to obey God? Is there a consistent reward for being honest and holy? We could take a survey, but the results would not always be obvious. Unbelievers and atheists can be successful in love and war. Christians can lose at both.

Here is where faith in special revelation comes in. What we observe in this world (general revelation) is only part of the story. There does not seem to be a consistent correlation between godly living and success nor between sinful living and failure.

But this present visible world is not all that is or all that will be. In the Bible, God reveals some of His purposes and ultimate plans for mankind which fills in some crucial details. The wicked will not stand in the coming judgment even though in this world they may have seemingly succeeded. [See Psalm 1 & 73.]

In 2 Corinthians 5:10 (KJV) we read: "For we must all appear before the judgment seat of Christ; that every one may receive the things done in his body, according to that he hath done, whether it be good or bad."

Why do the wicked succeed? Answer: they don't, if you know what happens after death. Why may a righteous man suffer? Answer: he doesn't, if you know what happens after death.

My challenge: Job was right to hold confidently to his hope in a living Redeemer whom he would someday see. Are you confident of your Redeemer's saving you? Trust Him today.

June 9/Day 160

God's Purpose in Suffering

Today's reading: Job 22:1-25:6

My selection: Job 23:8-10

[8] "Behold, I go forward, but he is not there, and backward, but I do not perceive him; [9] on the left hand when he is working, I do not behold him; he turns to the right hand, but I do not see him. [10] But he knows the way that I take; when he has tried me, I shall come out as gold.

My reflections: Job's suffering covers loss in every area of his life: material possessions, bereavement of children, physical disease, and abandonment by wife and friends. What does he have left? Certainly, all he has is his faith in God.

But that is enough. When all else is gone Job trusts in the Lord.

In this passage Job shows that he is neither in denial nor in despair. He admits that he cannot see God. He doesn't understand what God is doing. But he does understand why God is doing it.

God is testing him, trying him, to produce a purer follower. God knows Job's life. He knows what is happening with Job and how Job is handling it. God has lost neither control of nor contact with the exemplary man whom He held up to Satan.

This theme is echoed loudly in the New Testament. The Apostle Peter speaks about the purposes of God in our suffering. [See 1 Peter 1:6-7.] God is glorified when His people praise Him in the midst of blessings and prosperity, but how much more He is glorified when His people praise Him in the midst of suffering and need!

My challenge: Praise God in the pain and suffering you experience today. He has a purpose and you will come forth as gold. You have God's word on that.

June 10/Day 161

First Rays of Light

Today's reading: Job 26:1-31:40

My selection: Job 26:14

Behold, these are but the outskirts of his ways,
and how small a whisper do we hear of him!
But the thunder of his power who can understand?

My reflections: So far in the dialogue, there has been no end of complaining and questioning God on Job's part. That is understandable, but fruitless. There has been no end of accusing Job and defending God on the part of his three friends. That is also understandable, though riddled with error.

Now Job begins to focus on the greatness of God. He is powerful and sovereign over creation. He has understanding, but we cannot understand Him. We only see the outskirts of His ways. We get a whisper from Him, but His power thunders and we don't understand it.

Job is beginning to head in the right direction. He is heading the conversation toward the fear of the Lord which is where we must always start if we would gain wisdom. "The fear of the Lord, that is wisdom," he says in Job 28:28 (KJV).

Job is beginning to sound like Paul: "O the depth of the riches both of the wisdom and knowledge of God! How unsearchable are his judgments, and his ways past finding out!" (Romans 11:33 KJV).

My challenge: If you need wisdom today, begin by recognizing the awesome (worthy of fear) God who rules the universe. Proclaim His greatness. Accept His right not to reveal all His judgments to you. Be at peace that all is well in heaven and He will make all things well for His people.

Remember to Extol His Work

Today's reading: Job 32:1-36:33

My selection: Job 36:24

Remember to extol his work, of which men have sung.

My reflections: Elihu, the youngster who sat quietly during this long dialogue, now speaks up. Although he indicts all the others, he seems to pick up on the final words of Job and helps to refocus attention on the greatness and majesty of God. When he is done, God speaks to Job.

In the selection here, Elihu reminds us of two important truths:

1. All mankind sees God's work, His creation. What He has done is before the eyes and ears of every person. Paul would later add that "they are without excuse" if they do not believe (Romans 1:18-20).

2. Although God is not completely known, we know enough to extol His work and we ought to do that. Again, Paul would observe that men fail to acknowledge God or give thanks to Him (Romans 1:21).

The gospel, not fully known to Elihu nor Job at the time of the writing of the Old Testament, tells us that God has revealed Himself truly in His Son. In the gospel, we know Him not only vaguely through His creation but also, as believers, personally through His Son, Jesus Christ, who has made known the Father (John 1:17-18).

My challenge: Despite the trials you face today, remember to praise God and extol Him for His work which includes not only the creation we see around us but the re-creation of all who are in Christ (2 Corinthians 5:17).

Sanctification: It's a Process

Today's reading: Job 37:1-40:24

My selection: Job 40:4-5

[4] *"Behold, I am of small account; what shall I answer you?*
I lay my hand on my mouth. [5] *I have spoken once, and I will not answer;*
twice, but I will proceed no further."

My reflections: Job lost everything in this world except his pride which was not revealed and removed until God confronted him. Does God seem stern with Job who has suffered so much? God knows every person and knows His own purposes to cleanse Job until he comes forth as gold (Job 23:8-10).

Like every other person in Scripture who comes face to face with God, Job is crushed. His self-righteousness drains out. He does not rail against God. He humbles himself before the Sovereign Creator of the universe.

The ultimate cure for pride is to see God face to face. All the suffering imaginable in this world cannot completely rid us of it.

As Scripture tells us, "Beloved, now are we the sons of God, and it doth not yet appear what we shall be: but we know that, when he shall appear, we shall be like him; for we shall see him as he is" 1 John 3:2 (KJV).

My challenge: If you are a believer, trusting in Jesus Christ for forgiveness of sins through His death on the cross, then your standing as God's child is secure. Your future final sanctification is assured though not yet complete. Press on to know Him. Hunger and thirst for righteousness. Remember He will complete His work in you. [See also: Matthew 5:6; Romans 8:29; 2 Corinthians 3:18; Philippians. 1:6; 3:21; 2 Peter 1:4.]

June 13/Day 164

The Blessed Man

Today's reading: Job 41:1-Psalm 7:17

My selection: Psalm 1:1

Blessed is the man who walks not in the counsel of the wicked,
Nor stands in the way of sinners, nor sits in the seat of scoffers;

My reflections: I admire the characteristics of the blessed man. He is free from peer pressure. He loves God's law so much that he meditates on it day and night. He is fruitful and prosperous in all he does.

But to whom is this referring? Who does all these things consistently?

Do you?

I don't.

Christ alone has fully obeyed the law of God. Christ alone has lived the perfect life. All the rest of us are more accurately described in vs. 4-5 of chapter 1.

Nevertheless, by faith, wicked men and women, boys and girls become new creations IN Christ and participate in His life. In Him believers are blessed too because His righteousness has been credited to us (1 Corinthians 1:30).

My challenge: Believer, you will not be cast out in the Day of Judgment. You will by grace through faith stand in the congregation of the only truly Righteous One, God the Son, the Lord Jesus Christ.

Strive to be like Him who delights in God's law but do not trust in your striving or despair in your failing. He kept the law perfectly in place of all His people. He saves all who come to Him in faith and repentance.

June 14/Day 165

No Hand Wringing, Please!

Today's reading: Psalm 8:1-15:5

My selection: Psalm 11:4

The Lord is in his holy temple;
The Lord's throne is in heaven;
His eyes see, his eyelids test, the children of man.

My reflections: It is not unusual to hear professing believers wailing about the evils of the world. "All is lost", they say. The youth are going down the drain. The family is lost. The politicians are corrupt. The media is biased in favor of evil. On and on.

There is some validity in these observations.

But wait!

Have we forgotten that God is in His holy temple? Have we forgotten that He is not sleeping, but if it seems his eyelids are closed it is only a way of testing men?

My challenge: Remember what God says. He reigns. He will bring judgment. Wait upon Him. Trust Him. Let your speech and thoughts today reflect that confidence.

June 15/Day 166

Danger and Delight

Today's reading: Psalm 16:1-19:14

My selection: Psalm 16:1-3

[1] Preserve me, O God, for in you I take refuge.
[2] I say to the Lord, "You are my Lord;
I have no good apart from you."
[3] as for the saints in the land, they are the excellent ones,
in whom is all my delight.

My reflections: There is a cliché going around currently, "It's all good." It sounds very cheery and optimistic, but doesn't it run counter to reality and Scripture?

David takes refuge in the Lord because all is not good. There are evil forces out there. They present danger to all who seek only the true and living God. Humanity is divided. There are the saints (vs. 3) and there are those who run after another god (vs. 4).

There is danger of direct opposition from those who are not saints. There is danger of being shaken in one's own resolve to follow after the Lord. David steels himself by holding the Lord always before Him, by keeping the Lord as his only source of good, and by reflecting on the pleasures to come in His presence.

My challenge: Do not be shaken. Take refuge in the Lord. Be built up by the fellowship of the saints. In the face of danger, delight in Him.

June 16/Day 167

Asking God Not to Remember

Today's reading: Psalm 20:1-25:22

My selection: Psalm 25:7

Remember not the sins of my youth or my transgressions;
according to your steadfast love remember me,
for the sake of your goodness, O Lord!

My reflections: David asked God not to remember the sins of his youth. Although we do not know David's age at the time of this Psalm, he was old enough to have enemies and old enough to feel that youth was behind him. He may have been a middle-aged adult or an old man, but he had not forgotten the sins of his youth. They still troubled him. They weighed on him like a heavy load which he had carried for years, maybe decades.

So, he asks God *not* to remember the things that he (David) *cannot* forget.

Perhaps you too are troubled by the memory of the sins of your youth. Perhaps you have carried the weight of guilt for too long. Have you asked God specifically not to remember them against you?

David appealed to God on the basis of God's mercy and steadfast love, not on the basis of his own good works or improved track record. God's love and mercy was turned into action when He sent His Son, the Lord Jesus Christ, to bear the sins of all who would trust in Him.

My challenge: Lay down the burden of your youthful sins at the cross. That is where the Lamb of God paid the penalty for those sins, my brother or sister in Christ. Trust Him not to remember. Never think of those sins again apart from the memory of the Son of God suffering and paying the price to purchase your forgiveness.

June 17/Day 168

One Thing

Today's reading: Psalm 26:1-31:2

My selection: Psalm 27:4

One thing have I asked of the Lord,
that will I seek after: that I may dwell in the house of the Lord
all the days of my life, to gaze upon the beauty of the Lord
and to inquire in his temple.

My reflections: If you could ask for one thing from the Lord, what would it be?

David asked to dwell in the house of the Lord all the days of his life, to gaze upon the beauty of the Lord and to inquire in His temple. While this sounds like several things, we should understand this to be one composite thing involving a lifestyle of worship and service to God.

David understood several important things in this prayer:

1. The presence of the Lord is a gift of His grace. David did not presume that God would grant him this desire but asked for it.

2. The Lord is beautiful. To gaze upon Him is the most satisfying and awesome thing a human can experience.

3. Human nature is unstable without God's help. David asked the Lord to grant him the grace to remain constant all the days of his life.

My challenge: The greatest thing in life is to know God, the essence of eternal life (John 17:3). Let it be your single overarching goal to the end.

June 18/Day 169

Why the Whole World Must Fear the Lord

Today's reading: Psalm 32:1-35:28

My selection: Psalm 33:8

Let all the earth fear the Lord;
let all the inhabitants of the world stand in awe of him!

My reflections: When God judged the people at Babel, He laid the foundations for a world divided by languages and tribes. [See Genesis 11.] In foolish ignorance, the nations that resulted typically created their own deities and theologies. They conceived of their gods as territorial (gods of the plains, gods of the hills) or departmental (gods of fertility, gods of weather, etc.).

The God of Israel revealed Himself as the God of all creation and of all the nations. He made everything and everyone. The whole earth is called to stand in awe of Him who is the Creator of all.

He is also the God of Providence. His plans cannot be thwarted. He actively rules over everything and everyone. Therefore, He has ultimate control over who wins wars, elections, and even the lottery. [See Proverbs 16:33.]

He fulfills His eternal decrees and blesses the nation whose God is the Lord. He unites both Jews and Gentiles in one people, His Church (Ephesians 2-3). Meanwhile, they live in the midst of the nations of this world, testifying to His gospel, and calling those who will to believe.

My challenge: Are you confident that His plans cannot fail? Are you confident that the nations who seek to recreate Babel in a pagan world unity will be frustrated in the end? Fear God who reigns. Stand in awe of Him.

June 19/Day 170

God's Arrows

Today's reading: Psalm 36:1-39:13

My selection: Psalm 38:1-2

[1] O Lord, rebuke me not in your anger,
nor discipline me in your wrath!
[2] For your arrows have sunk into me,
and your hand has come down on me.

My reflections: David is in agony. He is sick and overwhelmed with grief, but he does not ask "Why?"

He knows why.

He has sinned. God is disciplining him for his sin. David acknowledges his iniquity. He understands the Lord's indignation. He does not shift the blame. He does not make excuses. He asks for mercy. He does not resent or resist the Lord's discipline. He merely asks that the full weight of God's just anger and wrath not come down upon him.

The godly man or woman receives the discipline of God. He does not waste time looking for excuses and scapegoats. He seeks the mercy and grace of the One who has sent the discipline.

Hebrews 12:5-11 reminds us that painful discipline from the Lord shows that He is treating us as sons (or daughters). His correction proves His love because although He receives us as we are He does not leave us as we were.

My challenge: Has God's hand been heavy upon you? Give thanks for His love. Confess known sin. Seek His wisdom to understand the intent of His discipline.

June 20/Day 171

Full Circle

Today's reading: Psalm 40:1-45:17

My selection: Psalm 40:1-3

[1] I waited patiently for the Lord; he inclined to me and heard my cry.
[2] He drew me up from the pit of destruction, out of the miry bog,
and set my feet upon a rock, making my steps secure.
[3] He put a new song in my mouth, a song of praise to our God.
Many will see and fear, and put their trust in the Lord.

My reflections: The Psalmist, in a few lines, describes the process of going from the pit of destruction, through patient prayer, deliverance, security, praise and, finally, fruitful testimony.

All this does not often occur in rapid succession. These are titles of, what are usually, very long chapters. Yet it is good to look back and see how faithful God is to His children who are in despair.

My experience is that there is almost always some area of my life that could be described by one of these stages in this spiritual cycle from despair to fruitfulness. Perhaps, in different areas, I am in different stages simultaneously. Marriage is great. Career is starting to get better. An important relationship is in crisis, etc.

My challenge: Wherever you are on the spectrum, God is there. Keep trusting. Keep crying out to Him, but don't forget to sing the new song when He sets you upon a rock.

Don't Just Do Something; Stand There!

Today's reading: Psalm 46:1-50:23

My selection: Psalm 46:10

Be still, and know that I am God: I will be exalted among the heathen, I will be exalted in the earth.

My reflections: In the midst of trouble, such as wars or floods, our natural human default position is to forget who God is and to be overcome by fear. We easily lose sight of the fact that God dwells in a stable, unmovable place. As nations rage and kingdoms totter, His voice melts the earth. He brings wars to cease.

We easily forget that He is with us.

Instead of frantically running in all directions, God tells us to *be still, and know that I am God.* He still rules over all. The trouble around us is just another opportunity for Him to be exalted among the nations. It is just another opportunity for us to re-learn that the Lord of hosts is with us. The God of Jacob is our fortress.

My challenge: Think about the peaceful calm that reigns in heaven around the throne of God. Consider how God is present in the turmoil of your life. Be still. Let Him be exalted in your heart, mind, and words.

Confession of Sin to God

Today's reading: Psalm 51:1-57:11

My selection: Psalm 51:1-2

[1] Have mercy on me, O God,
according to your steadfast love;
according to your abundant mercy
blot out my transgressions.
[2] Wash me thoroughly from my iniquity,
and cleanse me from my sin!

My reflections: If David committed a series of most despicable sins, he models here a most thorough response to his guilt. This response includes:

1. Recognition of the heinousness of his sin. His sin resulted in the destruction of a marriage, the murder of a husband, lies, cover-up, and the death of a baby. Above this, David sees that his sin has been against a Holy God. No excuses. No blame shifting. He calls it what it is: sin and evil against God and before God (Psalm 51:4).

2. Request for undeserved forgiveness, cleansing, and restoration. David asks for mercy, instead of what he deserves, that the Lord restore to him the joy of his salvation and not take from him His Holy Spirit.

3. Anticipation of future service to God. David commits to use his restored position to serve God fully. Those who have experienced great forgiveness and cleansing from sin are most enthusiastic in proclaiming the gospel. [See Luke 7:47; Mark 5:20.]

My challenge: Do you confess sin as thoroughly as David? Let his confession be a model for you in seeking to go from sin and guilt to restoration and service.

Spiritual Drought: Getting Through It

Today's reading: Psalm 58:1-64:10

My selection: Psalm 63:1-3

[1] O God, you are my God; earnestly I seek you;
my soul thirsts for you;
my flesh faints for you,
as in a dry and weary land where there is no water.
[2] So I have looked upon you in the sanctuary,
beholding your power and glory.
[3] Because your steadfast love is better than life,
my lips will praise you.

My reflections: David seems to refer here to a period of spiritual dryness. His circumstances were difficult, assuming this may have been set in the time of his flight from King Saul when he was in the wilderness of Judah. [See the title of the Psalm.] Difficult and stressful circumstances can certainly rob one of time to pray and meditate on God's word resulting in spiritual drought.

What does David do in response to this condition?

1. He recognizes his spiritual dryness. He is perceptive enough to know that this is neither normal nor acceptable. He wants to bask in God's presence every day (Psalm 27:4). That is not happening.

2. He calls out to God. He expresses his longing for God in prayer. James 4:8 says, "Draw nigh to God, and he will draw nigh to you."

3. He goes to the sanctuary and looks upon the Lord, beholding His power and glory. He does not avoid the place where God's people come to worship Him. Rather he goes to the place God has

designated for His people to worship and find reconciliation with Him.

4. He praises God and commits himself to continue doing that as long as he lives.

My challenge: If you are in a time of spiritual drought, be glad that you are able to detect that. Retrace David's steps whenever you seek to be revived in heart and refreshed in soul.

One Day at a Time

Today's reading: Psalm 65:1-68:35

My selection: Psalm 68:19

Blessed be the Lord, who daily bears us up; God is our salvation.

My reflections: God's faithful support comes to us day by day. Just as His mercies are new every morning (Lamentations 3:22) so is His strength which bears us up. He is our salvation. He does not give us a lifetime of grace in advance but daily bears us up. Therefore, it is necessary to come daily to Him for fresh strength. It is necessary to be renewed daily in our minds to think and act in godly ways.

My challenge: As you see His daily faithfulness, recognize with the Psalmist that God daily bears you up. He deserves all praise. I love to sing the words of the old hymn:

Strength for today and bright hope for tomorrow
Blessings all mine with ten thousand beside
Great is Thy faithfulness, great is Thy faithfulness
Morning by morning new mercies I see
All I have needed Thy hand hath provided
Great is Thy faithfulness, Lord, unto me. (Thomas O. Chisholm 1866-1960)

June 25/Day 176

Purpose in Old Age; A Purpose for Old Age

Today's reading: Psalm 69:1-72:20

My selection: Psalm 71:17-18

17 O God, from my youth you have taught me,
and I still proclaim your wondrous deeds.
18 So even to old age and gray hairs,
O God, do not forsake me,
until I proclaim your might to another generation,
your power to all those to come.

My reflections: Elderly folks are sometimes heard to express a sense of uselessness in this world. Their physical abilities are increasingly limited. Their interests in various activities may be lessened. Life can seem to be a mere matter of survival. What is there to live for?

Here the psalmist rejoices in God's faithfulness to him over the years of his life. He sets as his goal to proclaim the wondrous deeds of the Lord to another generation. Only the elderly can have the perspective that comes with having lived for many decades. One may read the history of a bygone era, but there is a special view of history that comes through the eyewitness accounts of our elderly relatives and friends.

My challenge: If you are elderly, are you taking opportunities to pass on to another generation the wondrous deeds and might of God that you have experienced? If you are a younger person, are you making an effort to glean from the wisdom and personal experience of a lifetime of faith that is stored in the minds of the senior saints in your life?

Take advantage of the opportunity to grow in the Lord by interacting with someone at least 20 years older or younger than you. If you are my age, you will find it increasingly difficult to even find people 20 years your senior.

June 26/Day 177

How the Powerful Rise and Fall

Today's reading: Psalm 73:1-77:20

My selection: Psalm 75:6-7

6 For not from the east or from the west
and not from the wilderness comes lifting up,
7 but it is God who executes judgment,
putting down one and lifting up another.

My reflections: Undoubtedly, the topic of political power and social influence is never far from the lips of many of us. The media loves a good scandal involving high profile people in politics, religion, the arts, etc. We wonder how people with such feet of clay manage to gain so much prestige and power. We are tempted to think the world is out of control.

Here we are reminded that God is in control of those who think they are in control. Ultimately, it is God who oversees the rise and fall of men. We vote but it is God who determines who is ultimately elected.

My challenge: Are you stressed about who gets elected as our leaders? They are the ones God wants in place even though they may appear to be serving an agenda contrary to His. No one gets a position without God's permission.

Trust Him. Pray for your leaders. Like us, they will one day have to answer to the Judge of all the earth for their management of what He entrusted to them.

June 27/Day 178

National Hero

Today's reading: Psalm 78:1-79:13

My selection: Psalm 78:5

He established a testimony in Jacob
and appointed a law in Israel,
which he commanded our fathers
to teach to their children.

My reflections: National histories typically have national heroes and villains. In US history, the former have generally been men like George Washington, Abraham Lincoln, and Martin Luther King. The latter include Benedict Arnold, John Wilkes Booth, and Lee Harvey Oswald.

Israel is different. Their national hero is God. He is the only One who is always perfect, just, wise, powerful, and gracious. Of course, the history of Israel has its human heroes, too, but they are painted as very human and their depravity seeps out in the story. Noah got drunk and exposed himself. Abraham lied. Moses was punished for anger and for dishonoring the Lord. David committed adultery and tried to cover it up with murder.

God is the true hero of Israel's history and, in reality, of all human history. The call goes out to all mankind, "Look unto me, and be ye saved, all the ends of the earth: for I am God, and there is none else" (Isaiah 45:22 KJV).

My challenge: God is worthy of the worship of every person on earth. In Him and Him alone, there is salvation. Ultimately, everyone will recognize Him. Those who have turned to Him will be saved. These will come from the ends of the earth. Praise Him for His coming glory. May it be soon. If you have not turned in faith to Him, today is the day of salvation.

June 28/Day 179

What Matters?

Today's reading: Psalm 80:1-85:13

My selection: Psalm 84:10

For a day in your courts is better
than a thousand elsewhere.
I would rather be a doorkeeper in the house of my God
than dwell in the tents of wickedness.

My reflections: So, what really does matter? According to this psalm, what matters is to be in God's presence and to serve Him in even the most humble way. It is enough to be near the Lord and to have the lowest position in His house. Why? Because in this there is blessing which eliminates every other longing.

How are we likely to miss this truth? Typically, we seek greatness in the wrong things, that which is temporal or that which is false or both. Too often, the ladders we climb are leaning against the wrong walls.

My challenge: Seek what matters, to be at peace with God through Jesus Christ and to serve Him in your calling without regard for personal glory and honor. It is enough. It is more than enough. It matters. It is all that matters.

June 29/Day 180

Clear-minded and Single-hearted

Today's reading: Psalm 86:1-89:52

My selection: Psalm 86:11

Teach me your way, O Lord,
that I may walk in your truth;
unite my heart to fear your name.

My reflections: Two potential problems affect the psalmist here. He is aware of them both and he prays for the Lord's assistance that he not be tripped up by either of them.

1. Ignorance of God's way.

2. Ambivalence that results in a lack of fear of the name of the Lord.

To walk in truth before God depends on knowing His way. The Scriptures give us clear light to know His way and for that we can be very thankful. But knowledge of the Bible alone is not enough. The believer, who knows himself, realizes he also needs a heart that is unwavering and undivided so that he will not stray from the fear of God.

My challenge: This is my prayer today: "Lord, help me to know your word and to be watchful of my heart that I not grow complacent or presumptuous but walk in truth and in fear before you."

Be faithful to study God's word. Be vigilant of your heart.

Where to Turn for Consolation

Today's reading: Psalm 90:1-95:11

My selection: Psalm 94:19

When the cares of my heart are many,
your consolations cheer my soul.

My reflections: Grief, pain, sadness, and confusion weigh down every human heart at some point. Suffering is the lot of all in this fallen world.

What distinguishes the Christian is how he handles that suffering, the cares that weigh down his heart. The psalmist sets an example of finding consolation from the Lord.

How would he do that? He remembers that God is Judge and He will avenge His people. Suffering is part of God's discipline of His children, so pain is not useless and random. The Psalmist thinks of God's love toward him. All of this is revealed in God's word and consoles the beleaguered writer.

As Christians living in the light of the new covenant made with us by our Lord Jesus Christ, we have great consolation through what is traditionally called the ordinary means of grace: prayer, God's Word (especially the preaching of it) and the sacraments (baptism and the Lord's Supper). These imply personal activities, family activities, and congregational activities.

My challenge: What cares weigh upon your heart today? Seek the Lord's consolations. Do not neglect the means of grace. May your soul be cheered in Him.

July 1/Day 182

God Unchanging

Today's reading: Psalm 96:1-102:28

My selection: Psalm 102:27-28

[27] *You are the same, and your years have no end.*
[28] *The children of your servants shall dwell secure;*
Their offspring shall be established before you.

My reflections: Good news! God the Creator is unchanging and unchangeable. His works will perish, but He will not. He is eternal. He is perfect. Because He is perfect, He cannot become more perfect. Nor can He become less perfect. He never changes. His purposes, decrees, and promises endure forever.

The other good news for the believer is that God's servants dwell secure. They will outlast even God's creation. We err if we place our trust in the creation and not the Creator. We err if we do not understand that His works, majestic as they are, point to Him not to themselves.

My challenge: Praise God for His eternal, perfect, unchangeable existence. Trust in Him, not in the world or the things of the world, although He has made them. Know that in Him you dwell secure, forever.

Biblical Principles of Worship

Today's reading: Psalm 103:1-105:45

My selection: Psalm 103:1

Bless the Lord, O my soul,
and all that is within me,
bless his holy name!

My reflections: Whether corporate or private, our worship, if it is to be biblical, must reflect these principles:

The object of worship is the Lord. He is to be central in our words and hearts.

Worship must be sincere. We are called to bless Him with all that is within us. No double-mindedness here.

Worship must focus on God's blessings to us. Healing, security, satisfaction, and renewal are all part of His blessings and are to be found in Him

Forgiveness is the foundational blessing of God to His people. Our relationship is based on His gracious forgiveness to those who come to Him through Jesus Christ, the Lamb of God and the High Priest who gave Himself as the once-for-all offering for sin.

My challenge: God's power and grace touch every area of our lives. Be sure your worship reflects an awareness of the principles of worship found here. Bless the Lord, today.

July 3/Day 184

Speak up!

Today's reading: Psalm 106:1-107:43

My selection: Psalm 107:2

Let the redeemed of the Lord say so,
Whom he has redeemed from trouble.

My reflections: God's shows redeeming grace in the lives of His people who are in all kinds of trouble:

- Wandering homeless in the desert
- Dying in prison dungeons
- Sick on the verge of death
- Facing shipwreck on stormy seas

He delivers His own who call to Him and those He delivers are called to give Him thanks.

My challenge: How has God delivered you? Do your thankful words match (or seek to match) His great power, mercy and grace? Thankless people are on the road to idolatry (Romans 1:21). If you have been redeemed, say so!

July 4/Day 185

Science, History, and Worship

Today's reading: Psalm 108:1-114:8

My selection: Psalm 111:2

Great are the works of the Lord,
studied by all who delight in them.

My reflections: Here the Psalmist validates the study of science (the works of God) and history (remembering His wondrous works). There is no inherent conflict between faith and the study of the physical world. Belief in the God of the Bible does not conflict with a study of the events of the past. These disciplines are often studied in a secular setting without any acknowledgement of a Sovereign Eternal God, but this will not be the approach of the Christian scientist or historian. The believer who studies needs to understand that the Lord is the One who has created all things and sustains them by His providence. The follower of Christ who studies history must remember that all things come from God and are for Him and it is His hand that is guiding human history.

My challenge: Do you delight in God's works either as a scientist or an historian? As you study, praise Him for the wonders of what He has made and what He has done throughout human history.

July 5/Day 186

Entering the Gates of Righteousness

Today's reading: Psalm 115:1-118:29

My selection: Psalm 118:19

Open to me the gates of righteousness,
that I may enter through them
and give thanks to the Lord.

My reflections: The Psalmist prays for entrance through the gates of righteousness. He got his answer and was granted salvation. Here we see a clear reference to Jesus Christ, the stone that the builders rejected who would become the cornerstone. The day of salvation has come, a day which the Lord has made, worthy of all rejoicing.

My challenge: Enter the gates of righteousness through the One who is "the way, the truth and the life" (John 14:6 KJV). He was rejected by those who built the temple but not by the God of the temple. In Him alone we have salvation. [See also Matthew 21:42; 1 Peter 2:4-7.]

July 6/Day 187

Answering the Taunter

Today's reading: Psalm 119:1-85

My selection: Psalm 119:41-42

41 Let your steadfast love come to me, O Lord,
your salvation according to your promise;
42 then shall I have an answer for him who taunts me,
for I trust in your word.

My reflections: The Psalmist has put all his hope in the Lord. Practically speaking, this means diligent study of God's Word and daily discipline to obey His commands. For this, he has been taunted by a skeptic who does not believe and sees all this effort as foolish. But it is undeniable: the writer has plainly not been delivered from all his problems. The taunter takes opportunity to heap ridicule upon him for believing in vain.

My challenge: One of the most painful experiences for a Christian is to be in trouble and then to be mocked for having trusted in God. If you are in this situation, do as the Psalmist does here and call upon God to let His steadfast love come to you, bringing salvation according to His promise. Deliverance may not be immediate. Your faith may well be tested, but you will be in company with Job who said, "Though he slay me, yet will I trust in him" (Job 13:15 KJV).

By the way, it is easier to prove that faith is real in a time of adversity than in a time of prosperity. It may not shut up the skeptic, but, I suspect, it will give him pause.

July 7/Day 188

God's Sovereignty

Today's reading: Psalm 119:86-176

My selection: Psalm 119:90-91

[90] Your faithfulness endures to all generations;
you have established the earth, and it stands fast.
[91] By your appointment they stand this day,
for all things are your servants.

My reflections: What does it mean that God is sovereign, that He rules over all? Here we get some insight on the matter.

1. It means His word cannot be thwarted. What He says stands.

2. It means that His faithfulness is unchanging down through the years of time, from generation to generation.

3. It means that the earth endures, and we count on the continuation of the cycles of days, seasons, and years without uncertainty.

4. It means that everything serves God's purposes. God ultimately works it all together for His glory and the good of His people.

My challenge: Do you praise Him for His sovereign rule over all things today? Are you confident in His rule and purposes? Trust Him. Praise Him. He is ruling over the things out of your control which include the things you mistakenly think are in your control.

July 8/Day 189

Handling Guilt and Grief

Today's reading: Psalm 120:1-131:3

My selection: Psalm 130:1-2

[1] Out of the depths I cry to you, O Lord!
[2] O Lord, hear my voice!
Let your ears be attentive
to the voice of my pleas for mercy!

My reflections: In a memorable performance, Mel Gibson, portraying Lt. Col. Hal Moore in the movie "We Were Soldiers", quotes this psalm as he says goodbye to his wife and children and leaves for the front-lines of the Viet Nam war in 1965. You do not have to be a combat soldier, though, to feel the pain of despair and weight of guilt that comes to the human soul at some point or another in life.

How do you handle grief and guilt?

As always, the psalmist points us to God and does three things

Acknowledgement. He calls to the Lord acknowledging his state of despair.

Reminder. He reminds himself of the Lord's forgiveness which is meant not to make us presumptuous of His mercy but actually increase our fear, reverence, and awe of Him.

Commitment. He commits himself to wait on the Lord and hope in the Lord while calling all Israel to do the same.

My challenge: Acknowledgement. Reminder. Commitment. This is the biblical formula for dealing with the despair we so often experience through overwhelming circumstances and the weight of our own sin. Repeat as needed.

May He redeem you from all your iniquities, for with the Lord is steadfast love.

July 9/Day 190

You Can't Leave Work Early

Today's reading: Psalm 132:1-138:8

My selection: Psalm 138:8

The Lord will fulfill his purpose for me; your steadfast love, O Lord, endures forever. Do not forsake the work of your hands.

My reflections: It is not uncommon to hear people say, "I won't die till my work here is done." Unlike so many clichés of dubious veracity, this one actually is true, as this passage shows.

We are more likely to think about our mortality when we are in the midst of trouble. When we, Christians, think of our mortality we are likely to comfort ourselves in the knowledge of God's sovereign control over our life and death. We are likely to re-focus our attention on our purpose and redouble our efforts to line up with what we understand that to be.

Our purpose is given to us by God. It is his purpose for me not my purpose for myself. It is the work of his hands, so He fulfills it in and through us. This does not mean we do nothing. It does mean that the purpose for which He made us will be completed. He guarantees that. [See Philippians 1:6; 2:12-13.]

My challenge: If you are walking in the midst of trouble today, know that nothing can thwart God's purpose for you. He will fulfill it before He takes you home. It's also okay to ask Him to keep working in and through you. Be confident. Be blessed today in taking a step closer to the final fulfillment of God's purpose for you here.

You can't leave work early. God guarantees it.

July 10/Day 191

God's Knowledge

Today's reading: Psalm 139:1-144:15

My selection: Psalm 139:6

Such knowledge is too wonderful for me;
it is high; I cannot attain it.

My reflections: In the Westminster Confession of Faith (Chapter 2) we read "[God's] knowledge is infinite, infallible, and independent upon the creature, so as nothing is to Him contingent, or uncertain." I find it comforting to know that God cannot be surprised by anything and cannot learn anything He did not already know. In today's reading, we see how this general characteristic of God extends to us personally.

God knows our every move, our thoughts, and our words before we say them. We are not robots, but He does exercise His control over us, providentially allowing or preventing the steps we would take and the decisions we would make. We are free (sort of) and responsible, but we are not alone, and we do not function in a vacuum. Like David here, who found these thoughts "high", we certainly do not always understand God's purposes for allowing or preventing our proposed paths, but many of us recognize His care and goodness in their outcomes.

My challenge: Rejoice today in His complete knowledge of you. Walk before Him confidently but wisely.

July 11/Day 192

God's Presence

Today's reading: Psalm 145:1-Proverbs 1:7

My selection: Psalm 145:18

The Lord is near to all who call on him,
to all who call on him in truth.

My reflections: What a comforting promise! There are no restrictions as to when we may call, where we may call, or why we may call. We may call night or day. We may call in sickness or health. We may call whether devastated by grief or overflowing with joy. We may call at church, at home, at work, or in travel.

There is one qualification given: we must call in truth. We may not call with insincerity (James 1:5-8). We may not call with doubt. But when we call in truth we have His promise to be near to us.

Should we expect instant relief from every problem? No, it does not say all our problems will immediately disappear. It does say the Lord will be near.

My challenge: In the midst of great suffering, overwhelming grief, an uncertain future, or perplexing decisions, is His presence enough? Can you endure, knowing He is with you? James gave a similar promise in his epistle (James 4:8 KJV): "Draw nigh to God, and he will draw nigh to you." Call to Him. Draw near to Him. Know His presence. It is enough to have Him near.

July 12/Day 193

Resisting Our Default Position

Today's reading: Proverbs 1:8-3:35

My selection: Proverbs 3:3

Let not steadfast love and faithfulness forsake you; bind them around your neck; write them on the tablet of your heart.

My reflections: The tone of Proverbs is that of warnings and promises. We are called to seek wisdom and to avoid folly. We are promised blessings if we do the former and consequences if we don't do the latter. A good life is not that complicated, but neither is it easy. We forget the way of wisdom too often in the midst of pressure. Our default position as recovering sinners is that of going with the flow. It assures acceptance by society. It feels good to our flesh.

But for Christians, our goal is not acceptance by society or comfort for our flesh. Our goal is to glorify God. There is enjoyment in that goal, but we must first escape from the seduction of the world, the flesh, and the devil.

This is why we must resist the tendency to lose sight of steadfast love and faithfulness. These qualities have to be tied around our necks because they slip away from us when they are not. Yet when we do keep them with us, they result in favor and good success before God and man.

My challenge: Resist your default position. Pray that steadfast love and faithfulness may be with you today. Seek favor with God and with the people who matter, those who also seek His favor.

July 13/Day 194

Things God Hates

Today's reading: Proverbs 4:1-6:35

My selection: Proverbs 6:16

There are six things that the Lord hates, seven that are an abomination to him.

My reflections: It is easy to see how despicable are every one of the sins listed here (Proverbs 6:16-19). These are not merely outward sins but inward as well. Take, for example, haughty eyes and the sowing of discord among brothers. These are not just the gross sins of murder and lying under oath, but also the more subtle sins of pride and of intentionally creating conflict.

Discord among brothers is sown by gossip, that is, passing along information whether true or false, for the purpose of turning one person against another. Discord is sown by the failure to overlook a fault and by the failure to forgive others. Discord is sown by plotting against another and by lying about another.

My challenge: What can you do to sow harmony rather than discord among brothers? Seek to live in peace with others (Romans 12:18). Seek to be a peacemaker (James 3:18). Hate what God hates; but, beware, these sins lurk in you and me. Only in Christ can we be forgiven, made new creatures, and set on a path that, in glory, will result in our complete transformation into His likeness. Meanwhile, pursue growth in holiness.

The Daily Pursuit of Wisdom

Today's reading: Proverbs 7:1-9:18

My selection: Proverbs 8:34

Blessed is the one who listens to me,
watching daily at my gates,
waiting beside my doors.

My reflections: Wisdom speaks urging the simple to come to her rather than to be seduced by folly. Wisdom promises life and favor from the Lord and warns of injury and death on the alternate path.

All this is plain and easy to understand. Yet the daily discipline of seeking wisdom does not come naturally. It requires turning away from the sirens that beckon us to folly in our culture and in our own hearts.

My challenge: Do not expect to choose naturally and automatically the path of wisdom. It is to be found in regular daily prayer and Bible study which cultivates a fear of God and hatred for evil (Proverbs 8:13).

Make it a priority to seek wisdom daily. Slow down. Take time. Listen. Watch. Wait. You will be blessed. Remember: in Christ "are hid all the treasures of wisdom and knowledge" (Colossians 2:3 KJV).

July 15/Day 196

The Other Meaning of Black Friday

Today's reading: Proverbs 10:1-12:28

My selection: Proverbs 12:9

Better to be lowly and have a servant than to play the great man and lack bread.

My reflections: There is a significant amount of pressure on people in our society to flaunt their wealth or, as this verse says, *play the great man.* With the accessibility of instant loans through credit cards, one may thoughtlessly indulge the urge to buy impulsively incurring enslaving debt.

Fools are caught in the snare of trying to impress others with what they have while in actuality they end up without even enough to eat.

"Black Friday" will become a dark day when the Visa bill comes due.

My challenge: Are you living in a manner which is within, or even below, your means? Are you resisting the pressure to always have the latest and greatest new product or fashion merely to impress others? Are you teaching this principle to your children or contradicting it by teaching them that Christmas means going into debt so that we will receive as much or more than everyone else?

Live within your means. Be a giver, not an impress-er. Walk before God in integrity. It is His opinion, not that of a materialistic society, that counts.

July 16/Day 197

Handling Fools

Today's reading: Proverbs 13:1-15:33

My selection: Proverbs 14:7

Leave the presence of a fool, for there you do not meet words of knowledge.

My reflections: The Proverbs give instructions on how to handle dangerous people, those who are angry, devious, seductive, etc. Here is an example of instruction concerning how to handle a fool.

Walk away.

How can you tell if someone is a fool? The Proverbs give many characteristics of a fool. Without going further than chapters 13-15 (today's reading), we see several telltale signs of a fool:

The fool brags about his own foolishness (13:16).

The fool is drawn to evil (13:19).

The fool gets his friends into trouble (13:20).

The fool gets himself in trouble by his big mouth (14:3).

The fool is deceived and does not see the connection between his folly and its consequences (14:8).

The fool does not recognize his need for God's forgiveness (14:9).

The fool is reckless and careless (14:16).

The fool hates his father's instruction (15:5).

My challenge: Beware of the fool. He will not hear your wise advice. He will bring you down to his level if you continue in his company. Walk away.

Friendship that Sticks

Today's reading: Proverbs 16:1-18:24

My selection: Proverbs 18:24

A man of many companions may come to ruin,
but there is a friend who sticks closer than a brother.

My reflections: In this age of Facebook and other social media, many jokes are made about internet friendships. One cartoon shows two people talking in a funeral service. The coffin is sitting in front but, except for the two people, the place is empty. One says to the other: "He had 2000 friends on Facebook. I can't understand why so few came for his funeral."

Sad but true. We may have become content with many superficial relationships in place of a few real ones. The problem is not a new one. The warning is given here. It is possible to have many buddies, when there's a party, but no real friends.

A parallel passage says: "A friend loveth at all times, and a brother is born for adversity" (Proverbs 17:17 KJV).

My challenge: Beware of fair-weather friends. Do not count on them. On the contrary, be a friend and a brother who truly loves in the good and the bad times. Who needs you to stick close today? Who is your closer-than-a-brother friend? May you know the One who said, "I have called you friends" and who laid down His life for His friends (John 15:13-15 KJV).

July 18/Day 199

The Glory of Overlooking an Offense

Today's reading: Proverbs 19:1-21:31

My selection: Proverbs 19:11

Good sense makes one slow to anger,
and it is his glory to overlook an offense.

My reflections: A hothead (one quick to explode at the first sign of provocation) does not demonstrate good sense. In fact, one who restrains his anger and even overlooks an offense is seen as a glorious person.

My father, who served as a sergeant in the US Army in WWII, said you could usually tell an officer's rank by his attitude. The higher the rank, the more humble the attitude. They were not the captains, majors, colonels, and generals who were blowing their tops, but the second lieutenants, the lowest-ranked officers. The enlisted men, consequently, often admired the higher-ranking officers but resented the arrogance of the lower ranking ones.

My challenge: Do you overlook offenses committed toward you? Do you restrain your anger? James repeated this principle in his epistle: "Wherefore, my beloved brethren, let every man be swift to hear, slow to speak, slow to wrath. For the wrath of man worketh not the righteousness of God" (James 1:19-20 KJV).

Show good sense. Let God's glory shine from your life; seek to overlook offenses as much as possible.

July 19/Day 200

The Way to Riches, Honor, and Life

Today's reading: Proverbs 22:1-24:34

My selection: Proverbs 22:4

The reward for humility and fear of the Lord is riches and honor and life.

My reflections: Throughout the Proverbs there are examples of the principle of cause and effect. Do "A", and "B" will result. Don't do "C", and "D" will be the consequence. There may be random cases in which the expected effect does not follow but these cause and effect relationships are quite consistent. The exception proves the rule.

In the case of this proverb, it stands in contrast to what is often being taught today under the banner of "the prosperity gospel." Neither humility nor the fear of the Lord is being promoted. On the contrary, it is self-confidence, even pride in oneself, that is preached. They say, "God is not to be feared as He is only love and wants you to be happy and successful. Expect a miracle! You have a right to it."

This message has wide appeal because most of us want riches, and honor, and life. The question is "How do we seek them?" According to this passage, it is not obtained through selfishness and arrogance. Humility and the fear of the Lord go hand in hand and lead to the desired good life. True humility is to fear the Lord, to bow reverently before Him each day and offer oneself as His servant and worshiper. That sort of attitude reflects a proper fear of the Lord and leads to riches, and honor, and life. But to the one who is humble and fears the Lord, I suspect that the riches, honor, and life, available in this world, do not matter much. The humble God-fearer finds true riches, and honor, and life in Christ alone.

My challenge: Walk in humility and in the fear of the Lord, today, tomorrow, and the next day. Eventually, you may see riches, and honor, and life in this world, but, through Christ, you certainly will in the next.

July 20/Day 201

Hard Things

Today's reading: Proverbs 25:1-27:27

My selection: Proverbs 27:5-7

5 Better is open rebuke
than hidden love.
6 Faithful are the wounds of a friend;
profuse are the kisses of an enemy.
7 One who is full loathes honey,
but to one who is hungry everything bitter is sweet.

My reflections: Here are some things which are hard to do:

Wound a friend for their own good.

Eat something delicious when you are full.

Eat something bitter.

These all point to the fact that growth in faith and godliness is often hindered because it is hard to do the things which result in faith and godliness in one another. We either will not administer loving correction to others or we will not accept correction delivered in love by a friend.

My challenge: How may we overcome our resistance to do the hard things? Stay hungry to learn and to grow. Accept with gratitude the bitterness of a rebuke. Reprove a friend when appropriate. Do not fear losing a friend, rather, fear being unfaithful before God.

July 21/Day 202

A Warning Against Stereotyping

Today's reading: Proverbs 28:1-30:33

My selection: Proverbs 28:6

Better is a poor man who walks in his integrity
than a rich man who is crooked in his ways.

My reflections: There are numerous proverbs which mention wise men and fools, honest men and wicked men, and rich men and poor men. It is important to note that the wise and honest are not always rich nor are they always poor. The fool and the evil man may be either wealthy or needy.

There is always a danger of oversimplifying these categories and lumping the poor with the sluggard or the wealthy with the diligent. A poor man may be wise (28:11). A rich man may be a sluggard (28:19). However, the wise, poor man and the foolish, rich man will probably not remain so for long, but, all things being equal, they will tend to switch places as far as material assets are concerned.

It is erroneous to see all the poor as oppressed or all the rich as wise and diligent. Beware of the stereotypes. Beware of neglecting those who are truly needy or despising and overtaxing those who have worked hard to wisely build wealth.

My challenge: If you are wealthy, pray that God would give you wisdom to identify those who deserve help and grace to be generous with them. If you are needy, pray that God would give you grace and strength to be as wise and diligent as possible in your circumstances and that He would providentially meet all of your needs.

An Excellent Wife; A Grateful Husband

Today's reading: Proverbs 31:1-Ecclesiastes 2:26

My selection: Proverbs 31:10-11

10 *An excellent wife who can find?*
She is far more precious than jewels.
11 *The heart of her husband trusts in her,*
and he will have no lack of gain.

My reflections: I am fairly certain that a vast number of wives who read this chapter do not feel adequate to meet the standards of this multi-talented, consistently-disciplined super woman. Probably there never has been any single woman who completely fulfilled this description day in and day out over the course of a lifetime.

My challenge: Depending on your personality, wives, you will either be challenged or frustrated by Proverbs 31. Let it not frustrate you. As a believer in Jesus Christ, you are accepted in Him despite your imperfections. "There is therefore now no condemnation to them which are in Christ Jesus, who walk not after the flesh, but after the Spirit" (Romans 8:1 KJV). "It is of the Lord's mercies that we are not consumed, because his compassions fail not. They are new every morning: great is thy faithfulness" (Lamentations 3:22-23 KJV). Do let Proverbs 31 challenge you in a healthy way. You have His Spirit to produce fruit beyond your own ability (John 15; Galatians 5).

I am also quite sure that many of us, husbands, who read this passage, need to show greater honor toward our wives. Let us not use this passage as a basis for finding fault with our wives, but as a reminder of all that they do to make our lives and homes a taste of heaven. After all, the woman described here has a husband who is wise and influential in his community and that may not fully describe us either (vs. 23). Let this passage remind us that our wives deserve praise, probably more than we currently give them. Remember "a woman that feareth the Lord, she shall be praised" (Proverbs 31:30 KJV).

July 23/Day 204

Disillusionment with Heroes

Today's reading: Ecclesiastes 3:1-6:12

My selection: Ecclesiastes 3:16

Moreover, I saw under the sun that in the place of justice, even there was wickedness, and in the place of righteousness, even there was wickedness.

My reflections: The writer of Ecclesiastes, probably King Solomon, suffered from disillusionment. He no longer believed that familiar cliché "humans are basically good." He began to see men as no more than beasts. This is partly true, because, like beasts, men die. But unlike beasts, men and women face the judgment of God.

Controversy rages today among historians and biographers over how we should view our so-called national heroes like Thomas Jefferson. Was he a great, wise, noble founding father or a despicable, immoral, exploiting slave owner? Should we admire him or denounce him? As Christians, we can neither idolize any human figure nor completely disregard God's providence working through fallen human beings to bring about His purposes. Jefferson was more evil than many of us previously realized, but also one whom God, in His providence, used to complete His purposes in establishing our nation.

My challenge: God will ultimately judge every person. Meanwhile, we may not excuse ourselves by hiding behind someone we deem worse than us. Each of us is given a talent to use wisely for His glory. Use it well today. Jefferson could not hide, and neither can we. The real "hero" in human history is the God-Man, Jesus Christ, in Whom there is redemption from sin and guilt for all who believe in Him (Ephesians 1:3-14).

Overlooking a Curse; Forgiving an Offender

Today's reading: Ecclesiastes 7:1-10:20

My selection: Ecclesiastes 7:21-22

[21] Do not take to heart all the things that people say, lest you hear your servant cursing you. [22] Your heart knows that many times you yourself have cursed others.

My reflections: Solomon says one should not be too concerned about the random comments of people. If you listen long enough you will hear the most bizarre things. Someone, who should honor you, will instead curse you. But wait, says the wise king, you have done this, too.

The point Solomon is making is that you should ignore much of what is being said about you, because you need others to ignore some of the things you have said about them.

In the gospel of Jesus Christ, we learn that God does not merely overlook sins, but He forgives sinners who repent and trust in Jesus Christ's atonement for sin. The Lord amplified this concept of forgiveness in His parable of the unforgiving servant (Matthew 18:21-35). One who is forgiven ought to show forgiveness. Forgiveness should promote more forgiveness. To overlook offenses is good but to forgive them is godly.

My challenge: Beware of taking to heart all you hear. Remember: only a fool will allow anger to rest in his heart (Ecclesiastes 7:9 KJV). Overlook. Forgive as you have been forgiven.

July 25/Day 206

Enduring Love

Today's reading: Ecclesiastes 11:1-Song of Solomon 8:14

My selection: Song of Solomon 8:6

Set me as a seal upon your heart, as a seal upon your arm,
for love is strong as death, jealousy is fierce as the grave.
Its flashes are flashes of fire, the very flame of the Lord.

My reflections: True love between a husband and wife must endure a lifetime of trials and stresses, many waters and even floods. Will it last? That is the question many a young person has asked standing at the threshold of adult life.

Experience shows that sometimes the seemingly endless love of youth endures the trials of life and sometimes it does not. What is the difference? Mere physical attraction is not enough. The strength and beauty of youth fades away with time. Ecclesiastes 12 paints a dramatic portrait of the body wearing down and desire failing. Will your love last when age and illness ravages your bodies?

Commitment is the difference. The bride says, "Set me as a seal upon your heart, as a seal upon your arm." She is right to require this. Only this kind of permanent seal that affects both the heart and the body will endure until death breaks it.

My challenge: If you are in love, are you committed? Can you say, "I have set you as a seal upon my heart, as a seal upon my arm"--that is, "My heart is yours, my body is yours"? Will your love endure the flood waters that are sure to come? Do not enter into marriage without that commitment. If you are already-married, search your heart and determine to make this kind of commitment to your spouse often.

July 26/Day 207

Complete Cleansing

Today's reading: Isaiah 1:1-4:6

My selection: Isaiah 1:18

"Come now, let us reason together," says the Lord:
though your sins are like scarlet,
they shall be as white as snow;
though they are red like crimson,
they shall become like wool."

My reflections: The Lord, through His prophet Isaiah, has begun to enumerate the sins of Judah and Jerusalem. They have not just forgotten God, they despise Him. As a consequence, they are oppressed and overrun. They are about to be obliterated as a people. Their sacrifices are an offense to God, because they continue in empty rituals while they commit injustice and oppression against helpless widows and orphans.

But God calls them to come to Him and to be cleansed of their sin. Judgment looms, but there is still hope. All is not lost because the Lord is able to cleanse the most sin-stained person.

My challenge: Does the stain of your sin seem impossible to remove? In Christ, the most wicked are transformed and purified. God delights in saving repentant sinners. Do not think you are beyond the power of His grace. As the old hymn goes, "His blood can make the foulest clean, His blood availed for me." (by Charles Wesley "O, For a Thousand Tongues to Sing")

July 27/Day 208

Isaiah Responds to a Vision

Today's reading: Isaiah 5:1-8:22

My selection: Isaiah 6:1

In the year that King Uzziah died I saw the Lord sitting upon a throne, high and lifted up; and the train of his robe filled the temple.

My reflections: With these words, Isaiah begins his account of his vision of God. It stands along with John's vision of the Lord in Revelation 1:9-20 as one of the most awesome, overwhelming experiences ever recorded.

It is good to reflect on who God is seen to be here: sovereign, exalted, majestic, holy. He is being worshiped by the angels. No sooner does this vision sink into Isaiah, but he responds with a sense of his own sinfulness. He cries out in shame and repentance. Mercifully, one of the seraphim cleanses him and assures him of forgiveness and atonement.

After this, Isaiah is ready to respond to the call for service to the Lord.

The God of the Bible, the God of Abraham, Isaac, and Jacob reveals Himself in holiness but also in mercy. It is necessary to grasp something of this holiness, to respond with brokenness and repentance and to accept His cleansing and atonement. Before service for God, there must be cleansing by God. Before there is cleansing by God, there must be repentance before Him that springs from a sense of His holiness and our sinfulness.

My challenge: Worship God who is holy. Seek His cleansing. Eagerly embrace His calling for you.

July 28/Day 209

The Kingdom We Long For

Today's reading: Isaiah 9:1-12:6

My selection: Isaiah 11:9

They shall not hurt or destroy in all my holy mountain; for the earth shall be full of the knowledge of the Lord as the waters cover the sea.

My reflections: At the time Isaiah was writing, Judah faced imminent captivity, but, woven through his prophecy, there are hopeful promises of a glorious kingdom to come. In the context here, we read of peacefulness and safety. Snakes don't bite, and bears don't kill. Lions are pets for little children. Best of all, the knowledge of the Lord fills the earth as completely as the waters cover the sea.

In a world like that, there will be wisdom and righteousness. There will be no sin. God's rule will be recognized and respected. There will be no end to that kingdom for there will be no end of His government (Isaiah 9:6-7).

My challenge: Does that not give even more meaning to the prayer that Jesus Christ taught His disciples, "Thy kingdom come, Thy will be done in earth as it is in heaven"? (Matthew 6:7-13 KJV).

Pray it now. Pray it until the Kingdom comes. It has come in part and it is coming fully.

July 29/Day 210

Sin Unmasked

Today's reading: Isaiah 13:1-17:14

My selection: Isaiah 14:13,15

13 You said in your heart,
I will ascend to heaven;
above the stars of God
I will set my throne on high;
I will sit on the mount of assembly
in the far reaches of the north;
15 But you are brought down to Sheol,
to the far reaches of the pit.

My reflections: Here Isaiah gives us a vivid and poetic description of the attitude which lies at the heart of all human sin, the desire to be lifted up above the stars of God and to be like the Most High. It was what made the serpent's appeal to Eve so attractive. "You will be like God," he told her. She thought about it. She took the forbidden fruit. She ate it. She gave it to her husband. He ate it. (Genesis 3:4-6)

Do you think of sins as merely mistakes? "No one is perfect," and "Boys will be boys", they say. No, it is not essential and natural to humanity in its original state to seek to become like God nor to seek to supplant God. It is essential to humanity, as originally created, to worship, serve, and enjoy God. But we are fallen, sinful, and not in our original state. At the heart of sin is a desire to be lifted up above God, to be God. Isaiah prophesies of the utter destruction that will come to the one who lifts himself up. He will be brought down to Sheol. He sought to sit in the far reaches of the north, but he will be brought down to the far reaches of the pit.

And so will you and I, unless we are re-created by grace through faith in Jesus Christ.

My challenge: Learn from Isaiah. He has unmasked the truth about sin. Do not dismiss sin as simple, human error. It is far worse than that. Pray that you may grasp how truly ugly and rebellious sin is. Flee, like a fatal disease, from every thought of pride and self-exaltation. Call upon God through His Son to grant you His Spirit so that you may believe in Him and repent of your rejection of Him as God. Walk before God, contented to be what He has made you in Christ, a new creature after His image to reflect His glory (2 Corinthians 5:17).

July 30/Day 211

Seeing God's Wise Providence

Today's reading: Isaiah 18:1-22:25

My selection: Isaiah 22:9-11

9 You saw that the breaches of the city of David were many. You collected the waters of the lower pool, 10 and you counted the houses of Jerusalem, and you broke down the houses to fortify the wall. 11 You made a reservoir between the two walls for the water of the old pool. But you did not look to him who did it, or see him who planned it long ago.

My reflections: At a time when Jerusalem was vulnerable to attack, the leaders were careful to prepare for a possible siege. They closed up breaches and prepared a source of water. There was nothing wrong with that in itself. But Isaiah tells them they did all this without either looking to God or understanding His wisdom in giving them certain topographical features which made the defense of the city possible. In other words, they worked hard but ignored God in the process. They trusted their weapons and their own efforts. They neither prayed to God nor praised Him for their success.

My challenge: How many minute details in your life have been put there by God for His purposes and yet are overlooked? Today, look for evidence of His wise providence in giving you exactly what you need for your good and His glory. Then praise Him for that providence.

July 31/Day 212

Perfect Peace

Today's reading: Isaiah 23:1-27:13

My selection: Isaiah 26:3

You keep him in perfect peace
whose mind is stayed on you,
because he trusts in you.

My reflections: The ultimate victory of the Lord God will be complete. Throughout this section, this victory is described in amazing and glorious ways. He will rule and His righteous people will be delivered. Death will be destroyed forever. All tears will be wiped away. God's great enemy will be vanquished.

Meanwhile, His people are called to keep their minds stayed on Him, to trust in Him. To the one who does this He promises to "keep him in perfect peace."

Lack of peace reflects lack of trust in the Lord. Worry and anxiety are not fruit of the Spirit; peace is. Could it be that the believer's most powerful tool for witnessing is peace?

My challenge: Does peace characterize your life? Take time to refocus your trust on Him today. Seek to be at peace through Him. Jesus said, "Peace I leave with you, my peace I give unto you: not as the world giveth, give I unto you. Let not your heart be troubled, neither let it be afraid" (John 14:27 KJV).

August 1/Day 213

Frantic Flight or Quiet Trust?

Today's reading: Isaiah 28:1-30:33

My selection: Isaiah 30:15-16

15 For thus said the Lord God, the Holy One of Israel,
"In returning and rest you shall be saved;
in quietness and in trust shall be your strength."
But you were unwilling, 16 and you said,
"No! We will flee upon horses";
therefore you shall flee away;
and, "We will ride upon swift steeds";
therefore your pursuers shall be swift.

My reflections: In chapters 28-30, Isaiah gives a litany of the evils of the people of Israel and Judah. God has been merciful to them. He has promised them salvation and strength conditioned upon their returning to Him, but they stubbornly want to fix their own problems. They will get their own horses to escape their enemies. But it won't work. They will be devastated by minimal opposition. They will be left abandoned and alone (Isaiah 30:17).

The promise is still true that salvation is found in coming to Christ who gives rest and strength. "Come unto me, all ye that labour and are heavy laden, and I will give you rest. Take my yoke upon you, and learn of me; for I am meek and lowly in heart: and ye shall find rest unto your souls. For my yoke is easy, and my burden is light" (Matthew 11:28-30 KJV).

My challenge: Where do you find salvation and strength today, in frantic self-effort or in quiet trust in the Lord? Trust in the One whom God has laid for the foundation and cornerstone, the Lord Jesus Christ. He is Savior and Lord who alone can save all who trust in Him. [Isaiah 28:16; Acts 4:11.]

Fools, Scoundrels, and Nobles

Today's reading: Isaiah 31:1-35:10

My selection: Isaiah 32:5

The fool will no more be called noble,
nor the scoundrel said to be honorable.

My reflections: Here is a picture of the kingdom to come, in which fools and scoundrels are shown up for what they are and the nobleman is honored. One of the characteristics of the fool is that his heart is busy "to utter error against the Lord" (Isaiah 32:6 KJV). He thinks himself to be a wise and accurate theologian, but instead he speaks folly, including folly about God. What a dangerous person is the fool! He misleads about things that matter, that is, about God, His word, and His truth. The fool is a blind man giving directions to other blind men. All who follow the fool go over the cliff.

The scoundrel, if anything, is worse. His intentions are destruction. He knows that he is bringing destruction on others with his schemes and injustice. In that future kingdom, the fools and scoundrels will no longer be honored and respected. The true nobility will reign.

My challenge: If you are a believer, are you careful to be sure your theology is accurate according to Scripture? Do not be a deluded fool or an evil schemer. Beware of following such. Seek to know, believe, and teach accurately the Word of God, the truth about God, and the promises and commands of God.

Beware of Mocking God

Today's reading: Isaiah 36:1-38:22

My selection: Isaiah 37:23

Whom have you mocked and reviled?
Against whom have you raised your voice
and lifted your eyes to the heights?
Against the Holy One of Israel!

My reflections: It is no small thing to mock the Lord. Sennacherib, king of Assyria, learned this the hard way. He foolishly prided himself in his military victories. He not only failed to give God the glory, but he even bragged that Judah's God could not save them. Before long, Sennacherib's army was distracted with another skirmish forcing a suspension of his aggression against Judah. This was followed by the king's assassination at the hands of his own sons while worshiping his idols.

God does not allow His name to be discredited. He will bring judgment, thorough and soon.

My challenge: Fear God. Sennacherib did not and paid for it.

August 4/Day 216

The Glory of God

Today's reading: Isaiah 39:1-42:17

My selection: Isaiah 42:8

I am the Lord; that is my name; my glory I give to no other, nor my praise to carved idols.

My reflections: Hezekiah, a king who had previously done many good things, foolishly sought to impress the visitors who came to him from Babylon (Isaiah 39). In so doing, he brought the judgment of God on his family and on Judah. The wealth and weaponry that he had shown off would be taken to Babylon along with his sons who would become the neutered servants of a foreign king. Hezekiah showed that his main concern was his own peace and security not the legacy he was leaving to his family and kingdom.

The world needs a better king than Hezekiah, one who will bring justice and be concerned, not with his own glory, but with the glory of God. Isaiah tells us that the true Servant King has been chosen and will establish real justice in the earth. We now know Him, the Lord Jesus Christ.

In His first coming, He perfectly kept God's law and was sacrificed for the sin of all who would believe in Him. He will come again to fulfill God's covenant with Abraham that in him all the families of the earth shall be blessed (Genesis 12:3).

My challenge: The end of all things is the glory of God. Do not be a Hezekiah seeking your own glory. Lift up Jesus Christ and give God the glory for His sovereign rule over the earth, for His goodness today, and for His coming perfect justice.

Why Some Do Not Believe

Today's reading: Isaiah 42:18-45:25

My selection: Isaiah 44:18

They know not, nor do they discern, for he has shut their eyes, so that they cannot see, and their hearts, so that they cannot understand.

My reflections: To worshipers of the Triune God of the Bible, it is ludicrous for anyone to take a piece of wood, use part of it for a fire to cook food and get warm and the rest of it to craft an idol to worship. "Why don't they get this?" we ask. Why can't they see the total irrationality of this practice and this belief? The reason, Isaiah tells us, is that God has shut their eyes and hearts so that they cannot see nor understand what should be obvious.

Does the thought that God blinds the eyes of idolaters seem unfair?

The Bible teaches that one must be born again (John 3:1-15) in order to see the kingdom of heaven. This is the work of the Holy Spirit called "regeneration." The preaching of the gospel is essential for lost people to be saved, but unless God, by His Holy Spirit, opens the blind eyes and closed hearts no amount of pleading and arguing and explaining and preaching will penetrate the dark soul.

But God does open blind eyes and closed hearts. He does regenerate people, by His Spirit, enabling them to believe the gospel and repent of their sin. Every day, in every continent, men and women, boys and girls are converted. It happened in first-century Thessalonica (1 Thessalonians 1:9-10). It happens today.

My challenge: Pray that God's Spirit will work in your family, community, and nation. God is able. He hears prayer. Keep proclaiming the gospel of Jesus Christ, but do not despair if the response is less than overwhelming. The problem does not lie in the message but in the hearer. God saves idol worshipers. Trust Him. Proclaim Christ. Leave the results with God.

None Like God

Today's reading: Isaiah 46:1-50:11

My selection: Isaiah 46:9-11

[9] *I am God, and there is none like me,*
[10] *declaring the end from the beginning*
and from ancient times things not yet done,
saying, 'My counsel shall stand,
and I will accomplish all my purpose.

My reflections: God's rule extends over all the earth. God's rule extends over man, beasts, and birds. God's rule means He accomplishes what He proposes. God's rule includes the complete fulfillment of His purposes.

My challenge: How are we to respond? "Remember this, and shew yourselves men" (Isaiah 46:8 KJV). Do not be blown around by the momentary, apparent triumph of evil. Do not be lured astray by other gods who seem to be in control. Fear and obey God alone. Trust and rely on Him. "Who is among you that feareth the Lord, that obeyeth the voice of his servant, that walketh in darkness, and hath no light? let him trust in the name of the Lord, and stay upon his God" (Isaiah 50:10 KJV). He alone is God. There is none like Him.

The Messiah's Anguish and Satisfaction

Today's reading: Isaiah 51:1-56:8

My selection: Isaiah 53:11

Out of the anguish of his soul he shall see and be satisfied;
by his knowledge shall the righteous one, my servant,
make many to be accounted righteous,
and he shall bear their iniquities.

My reflections: Christians understand this to be a clear reference to Jesus Christ, the promised Messiah of Israel. It speaks of the fulfilling of His work of atonement and salvation for His people.

1. He bore the iniquity of His people. Our sin was imputed, or charged, to Him. He endured our just punishment which brought anguish to His soul.

2. He made many to be accounted righteous. His righteousness is imputed, or credited, to His people. Christ Jesus is "wisdom, and righteousness, and sanctification, and redemption" of all who believe in Him (1 Corinthians 1:30 KJV).

3. He was satisfied with what He accomplished through the anguish of His soul on the cross.

My challenge: Are you one of His offspring? By natural birth, you are Satan's offspring. Only by new birth can you see the Kingdom of God and be among His offspring (John 3:3). Believe. Repent. Rejoice. Be amazed.

August 8/Day 220

Who Has Peace and Rest in Death?

Today's reading: Isaiah 56:9-60:22

My selection: Isaiah 57:1-2

1 *The righteous man perishes, and no one lays it to heart;*
devout men are taken away,
while no one understands.
For the righteous man is taken away from calamity;
2 *he enters into peace;*
they rest in their beds
who walk in their uprightness.

My reflections: Here is reassurance that the life to come is one of peace for the righteous man or woman. His (or her) death may be ignored or misunderstood to be a tragedy, but for the one who is counted righteous he is delivered from calamity, enters into peace, and rests on his bed (Isaiah 53:11).

My challenge: Be saddened by the death of a loved one, but at the same time, be comforted when you have every reason to believe that the deceased is counted righteous in Christ. Do not despair for the one who has entered into peace and rest. You too, if you believe in Him, will one day be welcomed into the peace and rest of God.

The Glories of the New Jerusalem

Today's reading: Isaiah 61:1-65:25

My selection: Isaiah 65:23

They shall not labor in vain
or bear children for calamity,
for they shall be the offspring of the blessed of the Lord,
and their descendants with them.

My reflections: Here Isaiah describes some of the glories that God will create in the new heavens and earth, or the New Jerusalem: vitality, prosperity, and security. That new world will be a joy and her people will be a source of gladness (65:18). They will labor productively. They will be the offspring of the "blessed of the Lord," Jesus Christ. Their children, too, will be His descendants. Thus, families will be united in Him. God will answer them before they call (65:24). They will lack nothing from God's hand.

What a glorious picture of God's tender mercies and loving plans for His people!

My challenge: Does your heart long for the promised New Jerusalem? Do you long for your loved ones to be united around Christ? Trust Him to bring this all about in His time and in His way. He is able to fulfill His every promise. You are a pilgrim in this land. Do not be too attached to it.

Judah Indicted

Today's reading: Isaiah 66:1-Jeremiah 3:5

My selection: Jeremiah 1:16

And I will declare my judgments against them, for all their evil in forsaking me. They have made offerings to other gods and worshiped the works of their own hands.

My reflections: The analogy God uses in charging Judah is that of an adulterous wife. Both Israel and Judah had forsaken their vows of faithfulness and had worshiped other gods. As a consequence, Israel was in captivity under Assyria, and Judah would be next to fall under Babylonia.

How foolish is spiritual adultery, aka, idolatry! Although God, the Creator and Sustainer of heaven and earth, graciously provides life and blessings, He is not worshiped or even thanked, but spurned and replaced with material things. Truly there is no logical or reasonable explanation for sin. It is always foolish. It seems wise, but it is evil and foolish.

My challenge: To counteract the tendency to worship other gods, give thanks to the true God, the God of the Bible revealed as Father, Son, and Holy Spirit. Thankfulness to the true God is the antidote for idolatry (Romans 1:21).

August 11/Day 223

Expertise in Evil

Today's reading: Jeremiah 3:6-5:31

My selection: Jeremiah 4:22

For my people are foolish;
they know me not;
they are stupid children;
they have no understanding.
They are "wise"—in doing evil!
But how to do good they know not.

My reflections: Jeremiah continues his indictment of Judah and Israel. They are foolish and stupid. They lack understanding in everything, except in how to do evil, which they have perfected. Later, he will say they are greedy, fraudulent, self-deceived, hardened, bold, and unashamed sinners. For this, judgment is about to fall.

My challenge: Are you alert to the danger that sin can easily blind your eyes? Do you fear God and give Him the praise due His name today? Give heartfelt praise and thanks for His wisdom in creation and providence. Guard your heart against bitterness toward Him and greed and envy toward others. Remember, "the fear of the Lord is the beginning of wisdom: and the knowledge of the holy is understanding" (Proverbs 9:10 KJV).

August 12/Day 224

Jeremiah's Grief

Today's reading: Jeremiah 6:1-8:22

My selection: Jeremiah 8:18

My joy is gone; grief is upon me;
my heart is sick within me

My reflections: The measure of a godly man can be seen in his response to sin and evil in the world. Paul said that love "Rejoiceth not in iniquity, but rejoiceth in the truth" (1 Corinthians 13:6 KJV).

Too often the response to sin and evil in others is to assume a holier-than-thou attitude. Sadly, it is not difficult for me to condemn as if I were exempt from any condemnation. But the sin and evil in our society and, even in our churches, will surely bring judgment; and it should bring us grief because those unbelievers whom we love will not escape even if we are found righteous in Christ.

My challenge: What is your response to the godlessness and corruption around us? Do you weep and grieve as Jeremiah did or assume a prideful, haughty attitude? Remember Jesus came to call sinners to repentance. Only repentant sinners are saved. Weep and pray for those who have not yet repented and believed.

What Delights God

Today's reading: Jeremiah 9:1-11:23

My selection: Jeremiah 9:23, 24

[23] Thus says the Lord: "Let not the wise man boast in his wisdom, let not the mighty man boast in his might, let not the rich man boast in his riches, [24] but let him who boasts boast in this, that he understands and knows me, that I am the Lord who practices steadfast love, justice, and righteousness in the earth. For in these things I delight, declares the Lord."

My reflections: People compare themselves to others based on intelligence, power, and wealth. In every category, God exceeds every person. He tells us the greatest thing about any man or woman is his or her knowledge of God, a knowledge that comes through His Word and His Spirit. There is nothing inherently wrong with being intelligent, wealthy, or powerful, but these characteristics can never be the basis for a Biblical value system. The important quality in the Kingdom of God is the true knowledge of God.

God has revealed Himself in Scripture as One of steadfast love, justice, and righteousness. He is not a mushy, cosmic cupcake, all-loving and without justice and righteousness. Neither is He some great divine accountant keeping track of good and bad deeds and administering merciless retribution for any missteps. He is holy but gracious. We cannot be good enough to merit His love, but by faith in the perfect offering of His Son for our sins, we are reconciled to Him. As we boast in the knowledge of Him, He is delighted.

My challenge: Make knowledge of God your highest and greatest value. Be spurred on as you meet others who know God in truth. Seek to know Him better through His Word by faithful preaching and personal study.

August 14/Day 226

Flourishing in a Difficult Ministry

Today's reading: Jeremiah 12:1-15:21

My selection: Jeremiah 15:16

Your words were found, and I ate them,
and your words became to me a joy
and the delight of my heart,
for I am called by your name,
O Lord, God of hosts.

My reflections: Jeremiah's ministry was a most difficult one. His message was not encouraging, but one of impending judgment. His hearers were not only unreceptive but were hostile and sometimes violent towards him.

But he understood he was the Lord's, called by the name of the God of Israel. His identity was lost in his God. For that reason, he took delight in the Word of God. It became a joy and delight to him in the midst of oppression. He did not merely survive, but flourished, in the hardest of circumstances.

My challenge: In the midst of the trials of your calling, do you ingest God's word (spiritually speaking)? Do you find delight in it? Is it the joy of your heart? Is your identity wrapped up in Him?

Pray that you may answer "yes" to these questions. Pray that you may flourish in a difficult place.

August 15/Day 227

God's Justice and the Human Heart

Today's reading: Jeremiah 16:1-19:15

My selection: Jeremiah 17:9-10

9 The heart is deceitful above all things,
and desperately sick;
who can understand it?
10 I the Lord search the heart
and test the mind,
to give every man according to his ways,
according to the fruit of his deeds.

My reflections: Here is a classic statement of the natural condition of the human heart in a fallen world. It is *deceitful above all things.* Who is deceived by the heart? We are. We are deceived by our own hearts, and we are deceived by each other's' hearts. We are convinced that our motives are always (or almost always) noble. We fail to see that the consequences of our sin and the fruit of our selfishness do not satisfy.

The only One who understands our hearts is the Lord. He searches and knows hearts and minds, and He rewards or punishes accordingly. God's judgment is just because it is based on truth, not the deceptiveness of the heart. One day, "God shall judge the secrets of men by Jesus Christ according to [Paul's] gospel" (Romans 2:16 KJV).

Is there any hope for man whose heart is deceitful? Yes, for the man is blessed who trusts and hopes in the Lord (Jeremiah 17:7 KJV).

My challenge: Give up blind trust in human ability and nobility, your own and that of others. Trust in the Lord, in His word and His will. Trust Him and obey Him. Blessing is promised.

August 16/Day 228

Lying Prophets

Today's reading: Jeremiah 20:1-23:32

My selection: Jeremiah 23:16

Thus says the Lord of hosts: "Do not listen to the words of the prophets who prophesy to you, filling you with vain hopes. They speak visions of their own minds, not from the mouth of the Lord.

My reflections: The false and presumptuous prophets of Judah told the people that they could follow their own hearts with impunity. "No disaster will come upon you," they confidently proclaimed. God, through the faithful prophet Jeremiah, told them to ignore these messages and messengers.

How similar to the many health and wealth preachers of our day! They typically give no warning about God's holy wrath against sin, no warning about judgment to come. One of them has said there is no need to proclaim this negative message, that people are well aware that they have sinned and failed God. Really? That was not true in Jeremiah's day, and I do not believe it is true in ours. The human heart is deceitful, telling us we are OK when we stand under impending judgment. [See yesterday's reading on Jeremiah 17:9-10.]

My challenge: Are you trusting in lying prophets? Ignore them. Hear the truth of God's word. Pay attention to His commands for justice and holiness lest you fall under His judgment. Make confession of sin a regular practice.

August 17/Day 229

Encouraging a Jeremiah

Today's reading: Jeremiah 23:33-26:24

My selection: Jeremiah 26:16

Then the officials and all the people said to the priests and the prophets, "This man does not deserve the sentence of death, for he has spoken to us in the name of the Lord our God."

My reflections: How ironic that the religious leaders opposed the word of God from Jeremiah while the public officials and general population feared bringing the judgment of God on themselves.

How about today? Too often the church in western society tries to be cool, edgy, and popular while ignoring the pending judgment of God. But does anyone fear God's judgment amongst our civic leaders?

My challenge: Hear the faithful preachers of God's word who care not for political correctness or personal popularity. If you know a Jeremiah, encourage him today.

August 18/Day 230

Making the Most of Your Suffering

Today's reading: Jeremiah 27:1-29:32

My selection: Jeremiah 29:7

But seek the welfare of the city where I have sent you into exile, and pray to the Lord on its behalf, for in its welfare you will find your welfare.

My reflections: God's will for His people may lead through very dark valleys, tears, trials, and a very miserable exile. Judah was, by God's will, in exile in Babylon. They were where they were supposed to be, as uncomfortable as it was. God commanded them to pray for their captors and to be a blessing to the nation that had overcome them. Ultimately, they would be blessed, too, and would return to their land.

My challenge: You may not like the place you are in right now but seek to promote good and to be a benefit in your current setting. If you are God's, He has your good planned and it will not be thwarted (29:11).

The New Covenant

Today's reading: Jeremiah 30:1-31:40

My selection: Jeremiah 31:33-34

[33] "But this is the covenant that I will make with the house of Israel after those days, declares the Lord: I will put my law within them, and I will write it on their hearts. And I will be their God, and they shall be my people. [34] And no longer shall each one teach his neighbor and each his brother, saying, 'Know the Lord,' for they shall all know me, from the least of them to the greatest, declares the Lord. For I will forgive their iniquity, and I will remember their sin no more."'

My reflections: God promised to make a new covenant with His people. That new covenant would bring deliverance, not just from political slavery in Egypt as in the old covenant, but from spiritual slavery to sin and guilt. Under the new covenant, God's people would be changed on the inside. The law would be in their hearts. God would be their God. They would be His own people. They would know Him. He would forgive them.

All this was fulfilled in Jesus Christ. In Him, we are new covenant people. We stand before Him. He gives us His Spirit to live in us. Although we are not yet perfect, a new era has begun, an era which will culminate upon Christ's return (Philippians 1:6).

My challenge: Be encouraged today in God's new covenant, if you are His. You are forgiven, adopted, and sanctified before Him. Bear the fruit of confident joy in Him.

Great and Hidden Things

Today's reading: Jeremiah 32:1-34:7

My selection: Jeremiah 33:3

Call to me and I will answer you, and will tell you great and hidden things that you have not known."

My reflections: Jeremiah, locked up as a troublemaker in a city under siege, received revelations from God, the Creator and Sustainer of the earth, as to what He would do. God delighted to reassure His prophet who was suffering for His sake in the midst of a "hopeless" situation. What God showed him was astounding.

God was going to send a "righteous branch" from the line of David who would rule justly and establish Judah and Jerusalem. We, Christians, take this to refer to Jesus Christ whose kingdom has already come and begun. It will be fully established at His return.

My challenge: Like Jeremiah, we live in an in-between time with suffering now but a great hopeful future in which the Son of God, Jesus Christ, will rule perfectly. Be hopeful in His promises. Look to Him and His Word which tells us great and hidden things we would never have known.

Zedekiah's Manipulating Ways

Today's reading: Jeremiah 34:8-37:21

My selection: Jeremiah 37:3

King Zedekiah sent Jehucal the son of Shelemiah, and Zephaniah the priest, the son of Maaseiah, to Jeremiah the prophet, saying, "Please pray for us to the Lord our God."

My reflections: King Zedekiah did not listen to Jeremiah, but he did attempt to use Jeremiah. He asked for prayer. Jeremiah went to the Lord and got a message for the king that the army of the Chaldeans would withdraw but they would return and burn Jerusalem. Jeremiah was fearless in confronting Zedekiah, and Zedekiah protected Jeremiah from some of the possible consequences of his unpopular message.

God will not be used by anyone. Zedekiah thought he could get God's help without a commitment to obedience on his part. Ultimately, Jeremiah's words were proven true.

My challenge: Be faithful to the Lord in the face of strong opposition. Declare His truth though it cost you pain and suffering.

August 22/Day 234

Diary of a Wimpy King

Today's reading: Jeremiah 38:1-41:15

My selection: Jeremiah 38:5

King Zedekiah said, "Behold, he is in your hands, for the king can do nothing against you."

My reflections: Zedekiah is the poster boy for the weak leader, one who will not take a stand on principles as he tries just to get along with everyone. He would not defend Jeremiah from his enemies, but later he secretly consulted Jeremiah and tried to hide his sympathies from the public. In the end, Zedekiah saved neither the kingdom nor himself (39:1 ff). He stands in stark contrast to Jeremiah who listened to the Lord and fearlessly proclaimed the truth.

Both Zedekiah and Jeremiah were given responsibilities. Both suffered as a result of the circumstances of their time. But Jeremiah suffered for doing what was right, boldly announcing what God had revealed and prescribing the best course of action. Zedekiah was wishy-washy, always trying to avoid problems, suffering, and confrontations. He failed to make hard decisions and he suffered greatly: bereavement, blindness, and captivity.

My challenge: Proverbs 28:1 (KJV) says, "The wicked flee when no man pursueth: but the righteous are bold as a lion." Choose wisely and prayerfully the issues for which you take a stand. Then, be bold as a lion for what is right.

Phony Commitment

Today's reading: Jeremiah 41:16-45:5

My selection: Jeremiah 42:5-6

[5] Then they said to Jeremiah, "May the Lord be a true and faithful witness against us if we do not act according to all the word with which the Lord your God sends you to us. [6] Whether it is good or bad, we will obey the voice of the Lord our God to whom we are sending you, that it may be well with us when we obey the voice of the Lord our God."

My reflections: Johanan and his allies had taken action and driven out Ishmael, the evil assassin of Gedaliah who was the appointed governor of Judah under Nebuchadnezzar.

So far so good.

Now Johanan and associates come to Jeremiah and want God's direction for the next step. They emphatically commit themselves to obey God's word to them through Jeremiah. When Jeremiah delivers the word to them, they reject it out of hand.

It turns out, they already had their minds made up to go to Egypt in an attempt to avoid the dangers of further war and famine. They had made a phony commitment to obey God, and it became obvious, once the Lord gave them different instructions than they were seeking. They did what they wanted to and went to Egypt, but Jeremiah persisted in warning them of the judgment that would fall on them even there, where they thought they would be safe.

Jesus confronted some of his phony followers with this question: "Why call ye me, Lord, Lord, and do not the things which I say? (Luke 6:46 KJV).

My challenge: Are you seeking direction from God with a truly willing heart? Do not pretend to be obedient while actually seeking God's endorsement of your own plan. God's way is perfect (Psalm 18:30). Trust Him to lead you to the best.

A Warning to Slackers

Today's reading: Jeremiah 46:1-48:47

My selection: Jeremiah 48:10

Cursed is he who does the work of the Lord with slackness, and cursed is he who keeps back his sword from bloodshed.

My reflections: In his prophecy against Moab, Jeremiah delivers this dire declaration. God told Jeremiah that the Babylonians would do His will against the neighboring nations to which He sent them (Jeremiah 27:1-11). Now Jeremiah addresses Moab with this message of judgment to be administered by Nebuchadnezzar and the Babylonian army. The Babylonians would not be merciful but fully carry out God's will against the Moabites. The Moabites ought to recognize this as God's punishment and submit to it.

If a pagan emperor like Nebuchadnezzar can do God's work thoroughly, how much more should those who profess faith in Him!

My challenge: It is not enough merely not to commit evil. It is not enough to do the work of the Lord in a perfunctory manner. Slackness in doing the work of the Lord brings a curse. If we are called to do His work, we are called to do it with wholeheartedness. We may not simply go through the motions.

What has God called you to do? Do you do it with all your might? Grandpa used to say, "That's good enough for government labor" and we all laughed.

But it is not good enough for the Lord's work. Do His work with excellence. Never be a slacker.

Jesus Christ: the Judge and Savior of All Nations

Today's reading: Jeremiah 49:1-39

My selection: Jeremiah 49:2

Therefore, behold, the days are coming,
declares the Lord,
when I will cause the battle cry to be heard
against Rabbah of the Ammonites;
it shall become a desolate mound,
and its villages shall be burned with fire;
then Israel shall dispossess those who dispossessed him,
says the Lord.

My reflections: God's rule is not limited to Israel and Judah. Here Jeremiah proclaims God's judgment against the neighboring nations of Judah. No one escapes. At the same time, the Lord Jesus Christ, who will judge the world (John 4:19-29), called His people to make disciples of all nations (Matthew 28:19-20).

My challenge: Are you conscious of God's purpose in all the world? Make world missions a priority in your prayer, giving, sending, and even going, if God wills, that the entire world may hear that Christ is Lord and Savior of all who believe in Him.

The False Confidence of Pagan Nations

Today's reading: Jeremiah 50:1-51:64

My selection: Jeremiah 50:7

All who found them have devoured them, and their enemies have said, 'We are not guilty, for they have sinned against the Lord, their habitation of righteousness, the Lord, the hope of their fathers.'"

My reflections: God uses all the forces and powers of the earth for His purposes, even those nations who officially do not believe in Him, like Babylonia in Jeremiah's day. These unbelieving peoples had enough theological knowledge to understand that Israel had sinned against her God, but not enough to realize that they too stood guilty before the Lord. Their day of judgment would come as today's reading shows.

My challenge: It is possible to know just enough truth to be dangerous or, in some cases, blissfully ignorant. God is a God to be feared. He will not be manipulated. We may not assume, as the enemies of Israel did, that our sin will not catch up with us.

Walk before God in reverent fear and awe. Do not grow complacent or comfortable in your sin. Worship Him in humility and repentance. He rules all, including you and me.

August 27/Day 239

Learning from Fools

Today's reading: Jeremiah 52:1-Lamentations 2:22

My selection: Jeremiah 52:7

Then a breach was made in the city, and all the men of war fled and went out from the city by night by the way of a gate between the two walls, by the king's garden, while the Chaldeans were around the city. And they went in the direction of the Araba.

My reflections: Humor and pathos. I am not sure whether to laugh or cry. I find the phrase "The men of war fled ... by night" as funny. An oxymoron. Were they men of war or did they flee? Don't real men of war fight to the death? So, I chuckle.

But the next paragraph wipes the smile off my face as I read of the sad specter of Zedekiah. The last thing he saw, before having his eyes put out, was the slaughter of his sons. So, I weep. Well, OK, maybe I don't literally weep, but I feel sad.

All of this was, of course, unnecessary. Jeremiah had spent his life crying out to the kingdom that God had sent Nebuchadnezzar against them to defeat them. There was a way out: surrender. But they would not submit to God's discipline through Nebuchadnezzar any more than they submitted to God's law which would have brought them blessing and security in the land.

My challenge: It's easier to see the grave failures of historic fools than to detect and avoid our own failures. Learn the lessons of those who refused to listen and obey. [See 1 Corinthians 10:6-13.]

August 28/Day 240

God's Absolute Control

Today's reading: Lamentations 3:1-5:22

My selection: Lamentations 3:37

Who has spoken and it came to pass,
unless the Lord has commanded it?

My reflections: God is sovereign, that is, He rules absolutely over all things and all events of human history and the cosmos. Nothing is out of His control, not one "rogue molecule," as R.C. Sproul often said. People can say what they will, but their promises and decisions are still in God's hand.

Knowing and believing in His sovereignty should free us from the fear that anything bad can come to us apart from God's direction. It should relieve the Christian from anxiety that he could ask for something bad and get it or fail to ask for something good and not get it. We do not control God like some genie in a bottle. God is completely free and acts according to His purposes and infinite wisdom.

My challenge: Believe God. Trust Him to send what is right into your life: punishment and correction, blessing and prosperity, trials and discipline. All are from His hand. All He sends is for good.

August 29/Day 241

God of Great and Small Things

Today's reading: Ezekiel 1:1-5:17

My selection: Ezekiel 1:3

The word of the Lord came to Ezekiel the priest, the son of Buzi, in the land of the Chaldeans by the Chebar canal, and the hand of the Lord was upon him there.

My reflections: Ezekiel was exiled as part of the people of Israel, by God's will. Ezekiel was sent visions in a foreign land, by God's will. Ezekiel was commanded to proclaim those visions to God's people, by God's will. God, according to His will, works in the great events of history like the conquest of Jerusalem by King Nebuchadnezzar of Babylonia and in the small events of one individual man's life, like Ezekiel.

God reveals Himself as powerful and glorious, a God to be feared and worshiped, not a dead idol.

My challenge: Never lose sight of the power of God in world history and in personal history. Never lose sight of His glory and power over all things and all people. Has He called you to His service? Serve Him with awe.

Lessons from Dead Worshipers

Today's Reading: Ezekiel 6:1-10:22

My selection: Ezekiel 6:13

And you shall know that I am the Lord, when their slain lie among their idols around their altars, on every high hill, on all the mountaintops, under every green tree, and under every leafy oak, wherever they offered pleasing aroma to all their idols

My reflections: Israel had trusted in idols, rejecting the exclusive worship of the true God. In the end, they would lie dead among their idols in the places where they made offerings to the false gods. Idols had no power to protect their worshipers from the living God. Ezekiel would gain new and deeper knowledge of the Lord upon seeing the grotesque spectacle of dead idol worshipers scattered among their gods.

Today in western society our idols tend not to be the little wooden or stone images of yesteryear but other more subtle idols, all the things that take the place of the one true God. Our idols may be financial security, prestige, materialism, power, pleasure, etc. These will fail us.

My challenge: Learn from the foolish practices of those who worship false gods. Flee from idolatry. Worship the Triune God of Scripture revealed in Jesus Christ and give thanks to Him.

August 31/Day 243

A New Heart

Today's reading: Ezekiel 11:1-14:11

My selection: Ezekiel 11:19-20

[19] And I will give them one heart, and a new spirit I will put within them. I will remove the heart of stone from their flesh and give them a heart of flesh,
[20] that they may walk in my statutes and keep my rules and obey them. And they shall be my people, and I will be their God.

My reflections: The problem with Israel was their hearts. They could go through the motions of sincere religion, but their hearts were like stone. Their elders had taken their idols into their hearts, yet presumed to get guidance from the Lord through the prophet (Ezekiel 14:3). Their hearts were divided and hardened. Only God could give them a tender, undivided heart and a new spirit. That is precisely what He promised to do. The result would be they would obey His statutes. They would be His people, and He would be their God. God makes this same change through His Holy Spirit when He regenerates unbelievers today. [Ephesians 2:1-10; John 3:1-8]

Pastor Fred Greco quotes J.C. Ryle on his email signature:

"The heart is the main thing in true religion...It is the hinge and turning-point in the condition of man's soul. If the heart is alive to God and quickened by the Spirit, the man is a living Christian. If the heart is dead and has not the Spirit, the man is dead before God."

My challenge: Beware of the condition of your heart. Pray that God may put within you and keep within you a heart that is tender and eager to obey Him.

September 1/Day 244

Depth of Mercy

Today's reading: Ezekiel 14:12-16:63

My selection: Ezekiel 16:62-63

[62] I will establish my covenant with you, and you shall know that I am the Lord, [63] that you may remember and be confounded, and never open your mouth again because of your shame, when I atone for you for all that you have done, declares the Lord God.

My reflections: In vivid and grotesque images, unparalleled in the entire Bible, God describes to Israel their sin. This sin is not merely neglect of God's law, but a rejection of His mercy and love which was poured out on them. They took God's gifts and used them to sin against Him. Facing obliteration, they benefited from His kindness, but gave Him no thanks or worship. Indeed, they glorified other gods. This is the depiction of spiritual adultery. It is a painful thing to contemplate. Yet this is what God's people had done. It is what you and I have done.

The only solution for them is for God Himself to atone for their sin. God alone is able to make a sacrifice sufficient to cover such horrendous evil. This is precisely what He did in sending the Messiah, the Lord Jesus Christ, the Lamb of God who took upon Himself the sin of God's covenant people.

My challenge: Have you seen the pervasiveness of your own sin? Have you grieved over your spiritual adultery before your Creator? Do not think your sin is less abhorrent than that of the ancient Israelites. Remember how you have been drawn away from the Lord by the lust of the flesh, the lust of the eyes, and the pride of life.

You might ask, as Charles Wesley did:

Depth of mercy! Can there be
Mercy still reserved for me?
Can my God His wrath forbear,
Me, the chief of sinners, spare?

The answers to those penetrating questions are a resounding no and yes! No, because there is no limit to God's mercy. Yes, because God, who is rich in mercy, has Himself made an offering for sin which completely satisfies His wrath against us. Repent and believe. Trust in the only offering for sin that can atone for you. Do not let guilt for forgiven sin rob you of your joy in Jesus Christ. Rejoice in the Savior you trust, the One who bought you with His blood.

Personal Responsibility before God

Today's reading: Ezekiel 17:1-19:14

My selection: Ezekiel 18:20

The soul who sins shall die. The son shall not suffer for the iniquity of the father, nor the father suffer for the iniquity of the son. The righteousness of the righteous shall be upon himself, and the wickedness of the wicked shall be upon himself.

My reflections: The people of Israel and Judah erred in their view of the justice of God. They either took false hope in their standing before God as a right of inheritance, or they considered God an unjust judge who would hold the sins of their ancestors against them no matter what they did. Here the Lord, through Ezekiel, spells out clearly the basis on which all will be judged. They would not be exonerated on the basis of their fathers' righteousness nor would they be condemned for their fathers' sins. Each one would stand on his own before the God of judgment. In other words, each one would be personally responsible for his or her own sin.

One implication of this truth is that there are limits to what a parent can do to influence his child toward or away from faith in God. At times, we see adult children veer from the truth of God even though they have been taught God's word from birth. At other times, we see adult children, raised without the gospel, turn to Christ in their youth or adulthood.

My challenge: The first sign of a changed heart is recognition of one's own corruption before God. Have you owned your own sin? Do not trust in the good name of your family for acceptance before God. Throughout the Bible, we are taught that there is no one who does good and never sins. Romans 3:9-20 quotes extensively from Psalms. Our only hope of acceptance and forgiveness before God is faith in the Lord Jesus Christ, who came to save His people from their sin (Romans 3:21-31).

Are you owning other people's sin for which you have no responsibility? If you teach and live God's truth in your home, do not condemn yourself if your family members do not all believe.

Own your own sin. Do not own that of others. Trust Jesus Christ for your forgiveness. Pray that all those you love may do the same.

September 3/Day 246

The Futility of Using God

Today's reading: Ezekiel 20:1-21:32

My selection: Ezekiel 20:31

When you present your gifts and offer up your children in fire, you defile yourselves with all your idols to this day. And shall I be inquired of by you, O house of Israel? As I live, declares the Lord God, I will not be inquired of by you.

My reflections: The elders of Israel came to the prophet Ezekiel to seek guidance from the Lord (20:1). God flatly refused to be used by the hypocritical leaders whose hearts were still bent on idolatry. They wanted to be like the pagan nations while still having all the advantages of getting things from the true and living God of Israel.

My challenge: We cannot have the "best of both worlds," that is, to be seen as hip and popular in the culture of the day as well as faithful to the Lord God of the Bible. God calls us to be His own people or, as the King James Version puts it, "a peculiar people" (1 Peter 2:9 KJV). Be faithful to God's word and His commands, even if you end up looking "peculiar."

September 4/Day 247

The Ugliness of Sin

Today's reading: Ezekiel 22:1-23:49

My selection: Ezekiel 23:28-29

28 For thus says the Lord God: "Behold, I will deliver you into the hands of those whom you hate, into the hands of those from whom you turned in disgust, 29 and they shall deal with you in hatred and take away all the fruit of your labor and leave you naked and bare, and the nakedness of your whoring shall be uncovered.

My reflections: I once heard Paul Tripp speak to a small group of pastors; he challenged us to be faithful in our marriages. Our sexual relationship, he said, should be characterized by "tenderness and beauty." I relayed this thought to a men's group later and one of the members said, "I understand tenderness, but what does he mean by beauty?" Whatever it means, certainly, Ezekiel 23 does not describe beauty in sex. It describes ugliness in every possible way. Here God again tells His people that they have sinned against Him by being unfaithful to Him. They have committed spiritual adultery by having many other gods over the course of their lifetime. They have not been satisfied by these gods. They have used them and been used by them. They have had uncontrolled lust, and it has brought them nothing but bitterness and disgust.

The Bible does not hesitate to discuss sin, but, unlike most of our media, it never makes sin look attractive. Sin brings judgment. Sin never satisfies. Sin continues to create more longing for what has proven empty over and over again.

My challenge: Do you hate sin and love righteousness? Samaria didn't. Jerusalem didn't. Learn from them.

Illustrating Your Message

Today's reading: Ezekiel 24:1-27:36

My selection: Ezekiel 24:27

On that day your mouth will be opened to the fugitive, and you shall speak and be no longer mute. So you will be a sign to them, and they will know that I am the Lord.

My reflections: When God called Ezekiel to be His prophet, He gave him a message, and, in some instances, God made Ezekiel's own life an illustration of that message. The Lord took his wife, whom he apparently loved deeply, and made this incident an object lesson for Judah. God told the prophet that as a result he himself would be a sign to them and they would come to know the Lord in truth.

What would they learn about the Lord through this?

that He is God and that He would not tolerate their idolatry forever

that He is God and that their ritualistic use of the temple to give superficial worship to God was unacceptable

that He is God and is not confined in the building they think of as His temple

Meanwhile, Ezekiel is going through a real crisis of his own as he has to endure the loss of his wife while serving as a message to the nation.

My challenge: If God is God, He has the right to use us as He will. He has the right to use our pain for His purposes. Do you desire that He be made known, even though it cost you the dearest person on earth? Everyone suffers pain, but not everyone makes the most of it. As Author and Pastor John Piper has said, "don't waste your pain." Pray that He will use your suffering and trials to make His name known to you and to the watching world.

September 6/Day 249

A Warning against Pride

Today's reading: Ezekiel 28:1-31:18

My selection: Ezekiel 28:2

Son of man, say to the prince of Tyre, Thus says the Lord God:
"Because your heart is proud,
and you have said, 'I am a god,
I sit in the seat of the gods,
in the heart of the seas,'
yet you are but a man, and no god,
though you make your heart like the heart of a god."'

My reflections: Ezekiel brings God's indictments against foreign nations. There is a common thread among these indictments. Tyre and other nations have been proud and lifted themselves up as gods. They have not recognized the true God, Maker of heaven and earth. For this they will be brought down.

My challenge: Isn't pride at the heart of all sin? Pride manifests the violation of the first commandment: "Thou shalt have no other gods before me" (Exodus 20:3 KJV). It was the essence of the serpent's temptation to Eve: "ye shall be as gods, knowing good and evil" (Genesis 3:5 KJV). Pride is a desire to ignore God and to replace ourselves as God.

Pride is an ugly thing. Do not let it take root in your heart as it did in the condemned nations of Ezekiel's day. Flee from pride. Replace it with the fear of the Lord.

September 7/Day 250

Hope for the Wicked; Warning to the "Righteous"

Today's reading: Ezekiel 32:1-34:31

My selection: Ezekiel 33:12

Son of man, say to your people, "The righteousness of the righteous shall not deliver him when he transgresses, and as for the wickedness of the wicked, he shall not fall by it when he turns from his wickedness, and the righteous shall not be able to live by his righteousness when he sins."

My reflections: Only perfect righteousness can save a person. One may be generally righteous but one slip into injustice is enough to wipe out all the good deeds he has done. Yet a wicked man may live by repentance and by acting consistently with that repentance.

Here we see the foundations of acceptance before God and of the salvation of repentant sinners. Only the Incarnate Son of God, Jesus Christ, could perfectly fulfill the demands of God's holy law. He did that and His offering of Himself on the cross is the basis for our salvation.

My challenge: If you are weighed down by your sin, do not despair but turn from it to Jesus Christ. Are you confident in your own good works? Be warned; they are not sufficient to save you. Only Christ could be saved by His righteousness, for you and I and everyone else has failed. Trust in Christ's righteousness for forgiveness and life before God.

Miracle in the Valley of Dry Bones

Today's reading: Ezekiel 35:1-37:28

My selection: Ezekiel 37:6

I will lay sinews upon you, and will cause flesh to come upon you, and cover you with skin, and put breath in you, and you shall live, and you shall know that I am the Lord.

My reflections: There is no more vivid picture of the spiritual deadness of Israel than the one before us here. There is no more vivid picture of the power of God to bring new life to the spiritually dead than the one before us here. Side by side we see hopeless death overcome by God's life-giving power.

It is necessary for Israel to understand how helpless and destitute she is. She is not merely weak or sick; she is dead. It is necessary to see that God alone can bring her life. And He will.

Paul in Ephesians 2:1-9 (KJV) pointed out that the Christians to whom he wrote had been "dead in trespasses and sins" before being saved by grace through faith. But God made them alive together with Christ. God brings life to the dead by the preaching of His Word to dry bones and by His Spirit breathing life into those skeletons.

My challenge: Preachers must faithfully proclaim the gospel even when the hearers are dead. They must rely on the Spirit to breathe life into those dead hearers. God delights in showing His power in bringing the dead to life so that those who see this miracle know that He is the Lord.

Do not neglect the preaching of the word of God. Do not neglect to pray for the Spirit to breathe life into the dead. He delights to show His power in the most hopeless situations. Miracles still happen in the valley of dry bones.

Why God Judges His People

Today's reading: Ezekiel 38:1-40:37

My selection: Ezekiel 39:23

The nations shall know that the house of Israel went into captivity for their iniquity, because they dealt so treacherously with me that I hid my face from them and gave them into the hand of their adversaries, and they all fell by the sword.

My reflections: God, through Ezekiel, foretold His wrath and judgment upon Israel through Gog, the king of Magog. But He also foretells the final outcome of this punishment: the nations would understand the reason for it, Israel would be re-established in the land, and God's glory would be set among the nations.

Again, we see that God is faithful to His covenant people, Israel, both in bringing judgment on them and also in fulfilling His purposes to ultimately bless them. God uses the wicked powers of this world to discipline and correct His own people. In the end, God is glorified, and His people are restored.

My challenge: Whatever the current circumstances of our world, God rules and is faithful to His covenant promises to His people. Do not fear the powers of this world, but fear the Lord. There is wisdom in fearing Him alone. Trust in His power, faithfulness, and love. There is peace in trusting Him alone. He is glorified when you fear and trust Him, walking in wisdom and peace.

September 10/Day 253

The Glory and Grace of God

Today's reading: Ezekiel 40:38-43:27

My selection: Ezekiel 43:5

The Spirit lifted me up and brought me into the inner court; and behold, the glory of the Lord filled the temple.

My reflections: Ezekiel hears and sees the glory of the Lord coming back into the temple. It is like the sound of many waters. Great light reflects off the earth as He comes. Ezekiel must have been dazzled by the sight and deafened by the sound that impacted his eyes and ears. He seems to have fallen on his face before the Lord, but the Spirit lifted him up and brought him into the inner court.

Here we see both the glory of God and the grace of God. God's glory is overwhelming to the senses. Even the faithful prophet sees his need to bow before this glorious Being. The Lord shows His mercy to Ezekiel. He brings His prophet into His presence. God draws Ezekiel to Himself.

My challenge: If thinking accurately, the believer in the God of the Bible holds in tension the Lord's glory and grace. The glory of God makes us fear and worship Him as we should. The grace of God makes us trust and rest in Him as we should.

Your understanding of His grace should never eclipse His glory. His glory should never eclipse His grace. Call Him "Father" for He accepts you, although He is far above you. Because He is glorious and gracious, He is both able and willing to provide for you, guide you, and keep you all the days of your life until He calls you into His presence.

September 11/Day 254

Orderly Worship

Today's reading: Ezekiel 44:1-46:24

My selection: Ezekiel 46:20

This is the place where the priests shall boil the guilt offering and the sin offering, and where they shall bake the grain offering, in order not to bring them out into the outer court and so communicate holiness to the people.

My reflections: The temple would be rebuilt, and God gave Ezekiel a clear vision of how it would be built and how it would be used. There was a time and place for everything. There were designated priests and Levites to handle the work to be done. Care was to be taken, because the people of Israel and Judah had failed to keep God's law carefully prior to the captivities of Assyria and Babylon.

My challenge: I have heard people disclaim the importance of an orderly approach to the worship and service of God, indeed, to all of life. For some it seems too regimented. It lacks spontaneity and freedom. Yet worship in Israel was not to be conducted willy-nilly according to each person's own whims. Order, according to God's instructions, shows reverence and submission, not coldness and heartlessness. God was clearly not pleased with superficial, perfunctory worship, nor with worship that disregarded His law.

We ought not be "frozen chosen" but neither ought we be disorderly in worship. Seek to serve God in private and public worship in spirit, truth, and order (John 4:23; 1 Corinthians 14:40).

September 12/Day 255

Prepared for Life

Today's reading: Ezekiel 47:1-Daniel 1:21

My selection: Daniel 1:19

The king spoke with them, and among all of them none was found like Daniel, Hananiah, Mishael, and Azariah. Therefore they stood before the king.

My reflections: The king of Babylon wisely chose, from his captives from Judah, an elite group to educate for his service. These included Daniel and his three friends. Imagine the pressure that was on them as they entered into the life in the court of Babylonia! Nevertheless, these four men proved to be wiser than those Nebuchadnezzar had always relied on.

For starters, Daniel negotiated an experiment with the king's steward to try a healthier diet for ten days, and, then, evaluate the results. The evaluation proved Daniel right. What made the difference in these young captives who had to adjust to a foreign land and strange pagan culture?

Is there any doubt, they knew and believed what David wrote: "O how love I thy law! it is my meditation all the day. Thou through thy commandments hast made me wiser than mine enemies: for they are ever with me. I have more understanding than all my teachers: for thy testimonies are my meditation" (Psalm 119:97-99 KJV).

My challenge: Do you know the Word of God well enough that it makes you wiser than your enemies and your teachers? Show your trust in His Word by making it a priority in your mind and heart. It has been given to equip you fully for the work He has for you (2 Timothy 3:16-17). You can be prepared for life.

Prepared for Death

Today's reading: Daniel 2:1-3:30

My selection: Daniel 2:19

The mystery was revealed to Daniel in a vision of the night. Then Daniel blessed the God of heaven.

My reflections: As we saw yesterday, the key to Daniel's success and wisdom before the court of Nebuchadnezzar was his knowledge of God's Word. In today's reading, He is not merely faced with a difficult diplomatic challenge but is faced with the threat of imminent execution. He does not become confused or irrational, but stays steady, no doubt, because he continues to trust the Lord. His prayer of thanks to God reveals a mind and heart deeply filled with truth from the Word of God which was available in ancient Israel: The Law, the Psalms and the historical books along with, perhaps, some of the prophets.

My challenge: There is no substitute for knowledge of Scripture which holds us steady even when there is an impending crisis. In the Bible we find the accurate source of God's truth. Read it. Study it. Pray it. Apply it. You may be faced with a life and death situation in which you will need it.

September 14/Day 257

Be a Daniel

Today's reading: Daniel 4:1-6:28

My selection: Daniel 4:34-35

34 At the end of the days I, Nebuchadnezzar, lifted my eyes to heaven, and my reason returned to me, and I blessed the Most High, and praised and honored him who lives forever,

for his dominion is an everlasting dominion,
and his kingdom endures from generation to generation;
35 all the inhabitants of the earth are accounted as nothing,
and he does according to his will among the host of heaven
and among the inhabitants of the earth;
and none can stay his hand
or say to him, "What have you done?"

My reflections: God showed grace and mercy to Nebuchadnezzar in giving him an explanation through Daniel, so he could grasp what was going on in his life as he descended into madness. Nebuchadnezzar deserved more severe judgment but was allowed discipline and instruction. He proved a teachable disciple to Daniel.

As a result, Nebuchadnezzar correctly understood his punishment and responded wisely. He makes one of the most succinct statements about the sovereignty of God to be found anywhere. As we saw yesterday, Daniel knew the word of God and he conveyed it to this pupil, King Nebuchadnezzar.

My challenge: Daniel was fearless in telling Nebuchadnezzar the truth. Do you fear God more than men, even men of high rank and power who could condemn you to death if they chose? Know God well. Fear not man. Proclaim God's truth. Be a Daniel.

September 15/Day 258

Confession of Sin

Today's reading: Daniel 7:1-9:27

My selection: Daniel 9:20-23

He made me understand, speaking with me and saying, "O Daniel, I have now come out to give you insight and understanding."

My reflections: Daniel's vision from the Lord was not completely clear to him. What was clear to him was his sin, the sin of his people Israel, and the need for confession. God sent him Gabriel to convey reassurance of God's love and to clarify what the vision meant.

My challenge: When God's people meet the Lord, they are always overwhelmed by His holiness and their own sinfulness. A measure of your growth in the knowledge of God is the level of your confession of sin (1 John 1). Do your prayers include a serious time of confession of sin? Here again Daniel models the kind of prayer that is offered by those who know God best. In the New Testament, we have even more assurance of forgiveness than Daniel. Take time to confess your sin.

September 16/Day 259

Brutal Reality

Today's reading: Daniel 10:1-12:13

My selection: Daniel 11:32-35

Some of the wise shall stumble, so that they may be refined, purified, and made white, until the time of the end, for it still awaits the appointed time.

My reflections: God never gives believers a false, rosy picture of life on this earth. God does promise to be with His own children, but He tells the truth about what awaits them. He does not seduce them with flattery and empty hopes. He tells them they will be tested, but He also shows them, as in this passage, that their trials will serve to purify their faith and character.

My challenge: Reality may be brutal, not what we want to hear; but thank God He has promised to be with us to the end of the age (Matthew 28:20). Resist the false teachers who say God only wants you to be comfortable and wealthy. God has purposed to make His people holy and that will only come through trials of faith (James 1:2-4). Be faithful and joyful in the midst of brutal reality.

Love So Amazing, So Divine

Today's reading: Hosea 1:1-5:15

My selection: Hosea 3:1

The Lord said to me, "Go again, love a woman who is loved by another man and is an adulteress, even as the Lord loves the children of Israel, though they turn to other gods and love cakes of raisins."

My reflections: What a poignant illustration the Lord uses to show the enormous sin of His people and the even greater vastness of His love and mercy. Israel is like an adulteress who has shamelessly betrayed her marriage vows! God is like a merciful and loving husband who seeks his unfaithful wife and actually pays her prostitution fees to get her back for a time.

Who would ever do such a thing, to show such blatant rebellion to a loving spouse? It describes the sin of Israel and Judah, but does it not also depict my sin as well? It does. Who would ever show such mercy in the face of such unfaithfulness? Hardly a human alive would do so, but God does it.

I think of Paul's words in Romans 5:6-8 (KJV): [6] For when we were yet without strength, in due time Christ died for the ungodly. [7] For scarcely for a righteous man will one die: yet peradventure for a good man some would even dare to die. [8] But God [demonstrates] his love toward us, in that, while we were yet sinners, Christ died for us.

My challenge: Even Hosea's depiction of God's mercy fails to reach the level of the salvation the believer has in Christ. Gomer sinned against her human, also sinful, husband, Hosea, but we sinned against a Holy God serving our idols whether literally or figuratively. Do you not see, more clearly, how despicable is your sin? Confess and turn from the sin in your heart today. Hosea paid money to buy back his adulteress wife, but Jesus Christ paid for the sin of His people with His life. Do you see how great God's love is for you? If you are a believer, give Him your heartfelt praise and selfless service for His forgiveness shown to you in His Son. As Isaac Watts expressed it in his great hymn, "When I Survey the Wondrous Cross":

Were the whole realm of nature mine,
That were a present far too small;
Love so amazing, so divine,
Demands my soul, my life, my all.

How We Look to God

Today's reading: Hosea 6:1-11:12

My selection: Hosea 9:10

They came to Baal-peor and consecrated themselves to the thing of shame, and became detestable like the thing they loved.

My reflections: When you love something, you become like the thing you love. God indicted Israel for their idolatry laying out in vivid form, through the marriage of Hosea to the prostitute, Gomer, how repugnant they had become. Here He tells them that they had become like what they loved and worshiped. They had become detestable.

In Romans 1:18-31 Paul fills this out even more. Men see themselves as wise but have become fools. They lose the ability to enjoy the blessings of normal sexuality. They become so degenerate that all relationships are broken down into evil and selfishness.

My challenge: It is a good thing to see ourselves as God sees us: sinful, rebellious, despicable, but also, if you are a believer, chosen, loved, and forgiven by Him. Never let one of those contrasting realities about your identity overshadow the other. Do not become presumptuous of your acceptance before Him, as if He were obligated by any merit in yourself to extend forgiveness. Do not become so overwhelmed by your propensity to lapse into sin that you doubt the sufficiency of His power, mercy, and grace through Christ to redeem and preserve you for Himself for ever.

Not Too Late

Today's reading: Hosea 12:1-Joel 2:27

My selection: Joel 2:25

I will restore to you the years
that the swarming locust has eaten,
the hopper, the destroyer, and the cutter,
my great army, which I sent among you.

My reflections: The same God who sent the locust plague on His people also promised to reverse the impact of that plague if His people would repent and turn back to Him. God is not time-bound as is man. He can restore what was lost.

My challenge: Never say, "I have sinned beyond restoration. There is no hope for me." God is able to restore the years that the locusts ate. It is always best to repent, believe in Him, and to return to His ways. He is able to restore the most wasted life. While you live, it is never too late for God to redeem you and give you back the lost years.

September 20/Day 263

Prepare to Meet Your God

Today's reading: Joel 2:28-Amos 4:13

My selection: Amos 4:12

Therefore thus I will do to you, O Israel;
because I will do this to you,
prepare to meet your God, O Israel!

My reflections: Israel did not respond to the series of plagues and trials that God sent their way. They did not return to the Lord even when they saw Him overthrowing some of their people. Those God spared were like brands plucked out of the fire but, in their presumption, they did not come to Him. Now God tells them they will meet Him but, on His terms, not their own.

My challenge: A final meeting with God is inevitable for every human being throughout history. You cannot avoid it. Nor can I.

[27] And as it is appointed unto men once to die, but after this the judgment: [28] So Christ was once offered to bear the sins of many; and unto them that look for him shall he appear the second time without sin unto salvation (Hebrews 9:27, 28 KJV).

How will you meet God? Will you come to Him in faith and repentance now and receive forgiveness and salvation or will you resist to the end and defiantly face Him as your judge? Prepare to meet your God, my friend. The day will come sooner than you imagine.

September 21/Day 264

The Undaunted Prophet

Today's reading: Amos 5:1-9:15

My selection: Amos 7:14-15

[14] Amos answered and said to Amaziah, "I was no prophet, nor a prophet's son, but I was a herdsman and a dresser of sycamore figs. [15] But the Lord took me from following the flock, and the Lord said to me, 'Go, prophesy to my people Israel.'"

My reflections: Amaziah, the priest in Bethel in Israel, felt secure in his own land--secure enough to order Amos, God's prophet, out of the land. He foolishly believed that the land of Israel was his forever. He called it his king's sanctuary. So, he attempted to deport Amos to Judah.

Amos, though admittedly a farmer and herdsman and not a member of the professional prophets' guild, did not back down. He had been commissioned by God, and he did not flinch in the face of official opposition.

My challenge: All things come from God and are entrusted to us as stewards—whether positions or possessions. Amaziah failed to recognize this. We use God's gifts subject to His pleasure and purposes. Although the land I live on has been in our family for over seventy years, one day I will leave it behind. God is eternal. Only He controls all there is. Walk before Him in humility. Know His commands and calling, as Amos did, and be undaunted to do God's will with what He has given you.

September 22/Day 265

The Deceitfulness of Pride

Today's reading: Obadiah 1-Jonah 4:11

My selection: Obadiah 3-4

3 "The pride of your heart has deceived you,
you who live in the clefts of the rock,
in your lofty dwelling,
who say in your heart,
'Who will bring me down to the ground?'
4 Though you soar aloft like the eagle,
though your nest is set among the stars,
from there I will bring you down," declares the Lord.

My reflections: The people of Edom took advantage of Babylon's invasion of Judah mercilessly capturing those fleeing from Nebuchadnezzar. They turned those captives over to him. How could they be so heartless? Easy. They were deceived by their own pride. Like Amaziah in yesterday's reading, they felt secure in their kingdom and willing to use their position to win favor with the Babylonians.

My challenge: Nothing is more deceptive than pride. Beware of false security which leads to pride and can make you hard-hearted toward the suffering of others. Keep humble before a holy, sovereign God. You are not invincible.

September 23/Day 266

Thy Kingdom Come

Today's reading: Micah 1:1-7:7

My selection: Micah 4:2

Many nations shall come, and say:
"Come, let us go up to the mountain of the Lord,
to the house of the God of Jacob,
that he may teach us his ways
and that we may walk in his paths."
For out of Zion shall go forth the law,
and the word of the Lord from Jerusalem.

My reflections: Once again we see the worldwide scope of God's covenant with Israel. Although the times of Micah were bleak, a better day was coming, a day in which many nations would be drawn to worship the true God in sincerity. They would come to Jerusalem seeking to know the Lord's ways so that they might walk in them.

My challenge: Some of us who love the Lord and believe the Bible will disagree as to when this will take place, whether in a literal millennial kingdom or in a figurative sense in the present age, but we will not disagree that this is a glorious description of the victory of the Lamb of God who takes away the sin of the world.

Whatever is going on in the world today, God rules and will ultimately be vindicated in His truth. God will have a people of His own from every tribe, tongue, and nation, a people zealous for good works. Do not despair as you await that moment of revelation. That glory to come far outweighs this present momentary affliction. Meanwhile, keep praying "Thy kingdom come."

Who Else?

Today's reading: Micah 7:8-Habakkuk 2:1

My selection: Micah 7:18

Who is a God like you, pardoning iniquity
and passing over transgression
for the remnant of his inheritance?
He does not retain his anger forever,
because he delights in steadfast love.

My reflections: I echo Micah's cry, "Who is a God like You?" This God is holy, so He would be completely just to bring to judgment all mankind for its sin, but He has a remnant to which He shows forgiveness. He does not remain angry because He delights to show steadfast love. He is the one who will take our sins from us and cast them into the depths of the sea.

When men conceive of God, they tend to think either of a god who has failures and sin much like their own and so cannot rightly judge man, or one who is morally perfect but wrathful and unrelenting in judgment. The God of Abraham, Isaac, and Jacob, the Father of our Lord Jesus Christ, is neither of these. He is holy but also compassionate. He judges justly but shows forgiveness to those who turn to Him in faith and repentance. This is not a god conceived by man but rather One who reveals Himself to man through His Son, born in the obscure town of Bethlehem (Micah 5:2).

My challenge: Praise God for His infinite wisdom in saving the believing remnant of His people. Praise God for His compassion, for casting your sins into the depths of the sea because of His steadfast love. Who else? No one else. There is no god like Him!

The Safe Place

Today's reading: Habakkuk 2:2-Zephaniah 3:20

My selection: Zephaniah 2:3

Seek the Lord, all you humble of the land,
who do his just commands;
seek righteousness; seek humility;
perhaps you may be hidden
on the day of the anger of the Lord.

My reflections: How should God's people respond to the announcement of the coming day of the anger of the Lord? Here they are commanded to seek righteousness and to seek humility. One would think that righteousness would include humility, but experience shows that people can be outwardly righteous while lacking inward humility. We can be proud of our humility, so to speak. This ruins everything.

Zephaniah tells them that by seeking righteousness and humility, they may be hidden on the day of the Lord's anger. In spite of seeking righteousness and humility, they will still need to be hidden when the wrath of God is unleashed. All their seeking will not suffice to protect them from His justice.

Nor will ours.

My challenge: It is good to hunger and thirst after righteousness. It is good to be humble but, from the New Testament, we learn that this is not enough to save us from the just wrath of God: "Set your affection on things above, not on things on the earth. For ye are dead, and your life is hid with Christ in God. When Christ, who is our life, shall appear, then shall ye also appear with him in glory" (Colossians 3:2-4 KJV).

Ultimately our only safe place from the wrath of God is the hiding place with Christ in God. He is our life. Lay aside any trust in your own righteousness. It is all of Him. Seek righteousness and humility, but trust in Christ's righteousness and humility. That is the safe place.

September 26/Day 269

A Taste of Heaven

Today's reading: Haggai 1:1-Zechariah 3:10

My selection: Zechariah 3:9

"Behold, on the stone that I have set before Joshua, on a single stone with seven eyes, I will engrave its inscription," declares the Lord of hosts, "and I will remove the iniquity of this land in a single day."

My reflections: After picturing the state of God's people as represented by a high priest in filthy garments who must receive new, clean clothes, the Lord promises a day of cleansing and restoration. The removal of iniquity occurs in a single day. This is the work of God, not man.

How does that renewal look? "In that day, saith the Lord of hosts, shall ye call every man his neighbour under the vine and under the fig tree" (Zechariah 3:10 KJV). There will be prosperity and unity among the people.

My challenge: When God's kingdom comes in its fullness, none will suffer want and all will extend hospitality. What a picture of joyful and peaceful life together! Today, in the church, we should see the beginnings of this expected life. Does your fellowship with other believers show that you have been cleansed of sin? Do you freely share what you have with others in anticipation of a day when peace will reign in the new heavens and earth? Think about how you can give a taste of heaven to others.

September 27/Day 270

The Day of Small Things

Today's reading: Zechariah 4:1-9:8

My selection: Zechariah 4:10

For whoever has despised the day of small things shall rejoice, and shall see the plumb line in the hand of Zerubbabel."

My reflections: When the rebuilding of the temple began, there were many who thought that nothing would come of it, that it would be insignificant, a pale shadow of the original temple. They thought it would be a "small thing" and they despised that "day of small things." But God delights to work in unpromising situations and through weak human instruments effecting His will by His Spirit (4:6). God shows His power in small things and small people so that the glory goes to Him alone. Zerubbabel would be the general contractor to rebuild the temple, but the glory would go to God, not Zerubbabel.

My challenge: What kinds of apparently small things are you despising today? Be faithful in the small things in your life that seem unimportant, mundane, tedious, and unpromising. They may be like a mustard seed that will grow and overwhelm the more impressive "big things" you see.

As Jesus said, "He that is faithful in that which is least is faithful also in much: and he that is unjust in the least is unjust also in much" (Luke 16:10 KJV).

September 28/Day 271

The Cleansing Fountain

Today's reading: Zechariah 9:9-14:21

My selection: Zechariah 13:1

On that day there shall be a fountain opened for the house of David and the inhabitants of Jerusalem, to cleanse them from sin and uncleanness.

My reflections: What a picture of the mercy and grace of God toward His sinful, filthy people! The fountain, gushing continuously, would be a reminder of the ongoing need for cleansing. Our problem is not only sin, those individual acts of rebellion against a holy God, but also the residual stains it leaves on our souls, the uncleanness it leaves behind. We need a fountain that cleanses and that never runs dry. That fountain is Jesus Christ, in Whom alone we find forgiveness and cleansing. He washes His people by regeneration, a new spiritual birth, and He renews them by His Holy Spirit resulting in an inheritance of hope of eternal life.

Here's how Titus 3:4-7 (KJV) describes that process: [4] But after that the kindness and love of God our Saviour toward man appeared, [5] Not by works of righteousness which we have done, but according to his mercy he saved us, by the washing of regeneration, and renewing of the Holy Ghost;[6] Which he shed on us abundantly through Jesus Christ our Saviour; [7] That being justified by his grace, we should be made heirs according to the hope of eternal life.

My challenge: If your sin weighs heavily upon you, if you are painfully aware of the corruption of sin on your soul, come to the fountain flowing abundantly to rid you of every stain. Rejoice in the truth that this fountain will never run dry. God poured out His Spirit richly so that, being declared righteous, you would become an heir to the hope of eternal life.

The Best News Ever

Today's reading: Malachi 1:1- Matthew 1:25

My selection: Matthew 1:20-21

[20] But as he considered these things, behold, an angel of the Lord appeared to him in a dream, saying, "Joseph, son of David, do not fear to take Mary as your wife, for that which is conceived in her is from the Holy Spirit. [21] She will bear a son, and you shall call his name Jesus, for he will save his people from their sins."

My reflections: There is no passage in the Bible that thrills me more than this one. The message was authoritative: from an angel of the Lord. The message was supernatural: a virgin was pregnant by the Holy Spirit. The message was anticipated: the fulfillment of the prophecy of Isaiah 7:14. The message was gracious: He would save His people from their sins.

Joseph needed this reassurance. He would not have put Mary to the shame normally reserved for those who break their marriage vow, but neither would he forgive, accept, and support her. He would divorce her, quietly. Joseph was reassured by the command to take Mary as his wife. He obeyed, and he obeyed immediately.

My challenge: This was arguably the best news ever spoken to anyone. Jesus would be born, and He would save His people from their sins. If you are a believer in Him, you trust Him for forgiveness of your sins. Rejoice in Him. Praise God for His mercy to His people, including you. If you are not trusting in Him for the forgiveness of sins, He calls you to repent and trust in Him.

September 30/Day 273

Blessing: Ends and Means

Today's reading: Matthew 2:1-5:20

My selection: Matthew 5:2-5 (KJV)

2 *And he opened his mouth, and taught them, saying,*
3 *Blessed are the poor in spirit: for theirs is the kingdom of heaven.*
4 *Blessed are they that mourn: for they shall be comforted.*
5 *Blessed are the meek: for they shall inherit the earth.*

My reflections: In the Beatitudes, Jesus teaches that blessing comes to those who have the kingdom of heaven, are comforted, inherit the earth, are satisfied, receive mercy, see God, are called His sons, and are persecuted for the sake of righteousness. These things, except for persecution, are the things that many, if not all, humans desire. What Jesus says that is new and different is *how* these things are obtained.

The kingdom of heaven is not for those who are proud, arrogant, and have enormous self-esteem. It is for those who are "poor in spirit," who recognize their sin, need, and unworthiness. Comfort is not for those who have hardened themselves against pain but for those who "mourn." The earth will be inherited not by the powerful ones who use every means to cheat and steal, but by those "meek" souls who faithfully do what is right. Satisfaction will not come to those who seek every imaginable pleasure, but by those who seek righteousness. And so on, the Lord goes.

My challenge: Our problem is not so much that we desire the wrong things, but that we pursue them in the wrong ways. Why all the restlessness in us? Begin by examining the things you long for. Are these what Jesus holds up as the most important? How are you seeking them? Seek them by the means He has indicated. You may even find yourself longing for more persecution.

October 1/Day 274

Why Being Good Is Not Good Enough

Today's reading: Matthew 5:21-7:23

My selection: Matthew 7:23

Then will I declare to them, "I never knew you; depart from me, you workers of lawlessness."

My reflections: Jesus explodes the myth that acceptance by God is based on mere outward conformity to the law or by the performing of good works. He told them that the righteousness of the scribes and Pharisees was not sufficient to enter the kingdom of heaven (5:20). He gave examples of how outward conformity to the law did not eradicate the guilt of inner sin. He tells them that many mighty works done in God's name would not open heaven to them.

Before we can be received into God's presence, we must come to grips with the enormity of our sin, including our outward actions and inward thoughts. We are hopelessly lost in our sin with no way to earn passage to glory. There is no way except through the One who perfectly kept the law and then died for the sins of all His people (Matthew 1:21). The problem with the people in today's selection was that they had no relationship with God. Why? Because they trusted in their works not in Jesus Christ.

My challenge: Being good is not good enough to insure eternal life. By faith you can know the One whose works were good enough to save both Himself and you. Be sure you are trusting in Jesus Christ today and always. To know Him is to have eternal life (John 17:3). Is it useless to seek to do good? No, but the one who knows God does good works out of gratitude to God and in His strength, never as an attempt to earn forgiveness.

The Authority of Jesus

Today's reading: Matthew 7:24-9:38

My selection: Matthew 7:29

He was teaching them as one who had authority, and not as their scribes.

My reflections: It was not just the content of Jesus' teaching that astounded the crowds, but also the authority with which He taught. In Matthew 7:24-27, Jesus concluded His sermon with the challenge not merely to hear but to *do* His words. Hearing alone is not sufficient. One must act on what he hears. It was an individual responsibility that applies to everyone who hears His words (vss. 24, 26). It has personal benefits or consequences for each person: survival or destruction (vss. 25, 27).

My challenge: The question of "who was Jesus Christ?" continues to resurface regularly in our time. That question needs to be considered in light of two other questions: who did He claim to be? and who do I believe Him to be? It is not enough to say He was a great teacher and miracle worker. He claimed to have authority that goes far beyond that. If He claimed that kind of authority and that obedience to His words was a matter of life and death, then He was either a lunatic, a charlatan, or God Incarnate.

I believe He was and is God Incarnate. Do you? How will this belief change your actions today? Hearing is necessary but not sufficient. If you trust Him, obey Him. Your house will be unshakeable in the floods and winds.

October 3/Day 276

The Call to Repentance, Rest, and Service

Today's reading: Matthew 10:1-12:14

My selection: Matthew 11:24-26

[24] But I tell you that it will be more tolerable on the day of judgment for the land of Sodom than for you. [25] At that time Jesus declared, "I thank you, Father, Lord of heaven and earth, that you have hidden these things from the wise and understanding and revealed them to little children; [26] yes, Father, for such was your gracious will."

My reflections: Some claim that Jesus presented a message strictly of forgiveness, love, and peace to all with no expectations of personal responsibility. But Jesus' teaching included warnings of impending judgment on the unrepentant and calls to the salvation found in Him alone.

Others say they can grasp truth through their superior intellect. But Jesus called His listeners to childlike simplicity and humble repentance as the key to understanding.

It's not unusual to hear from those who are not well-informed biblically that belief in Jesus rids one of any need to do good works. Here Jesus issues the invitation to come to Him for rest to take on His yoke which, though not heavy nor disagreeable, is still a yoke of submission to Him and of service for Him.

Who will come to the truth? Little children. Those who labor and are heavy laden. Not the proud. Not those who see themselves as wise and intellectual.

My challenge: Are you laden by sin? Are you weary of the burden of guilt which never goes away because you cannot find relief through your efforts to please God? If so, you are the kind of person Jesus calls to find rest in Him (Matthew 11:28-30). You are the kind of person to whom He gives a new and light yoke to bear, a yoke that links you to Him always. Jesus calls you to repentance, rest, and service. Come to Him. Be joined to Him. Walk with Him.

Bringing Justice to Victory

Today's reading: Matthew 12:15-13:46

My selection: Matthew 12:17-21 (KJV)

*[17] That it might be fulfilled which was spoken by Esaias the prophet,
saying, [18] Behold my servant, whom I have chosen; my beloved, in whom my
soul is well pleased: I will put my spirit upon him, and he shall shew judgment
to the Gentiles. [19] He shall not strive, nor cry; neither shall any man hear his
voice in the streets. [20] A bruised reed shall he not break, and smoking flax shall
he not quench, till he send forth judgment unto victory. [21] And in his name
shall the Gentiles trust.*

My reflections: Matthew emphasizes the continuity between the Old Testament prophecies and the person and work of Jesus Christ. Here we get a glimpse into the eternal decrees of God who from the fall of man promised that the seed of the woman would crush the serpent's head (Genesis 3:15) and that in calling Abraham all the families of the earth would be blessed (Genesis 12:3). This promise of a victorious deliverer for all mankind, including the Gentiles, continued through the prophets, like Isaiah, cited here.

Jesus, God's Chosen One, filled with the Spirit, is the name in whom the Gentiles trust (vs. 21). He has brought justice to victory through His death and resurrection. In Him, all who believe have a firm hope of eternal life.

My challenge: Do you marvel at the greatness of God's mercy to the world? Justice has been brought in Christ because sin has been paid for and the elect of God have been forgiven and set free. Never forget. Praise Him that He is just and the justifier of all who trust in Him, including, I hope, you. [Romans 3:26.]

October 5/Day 278

Discovering Who Jesus Really Is

Today's reading: Matthew 13:47-15:39

My selection: Matthew 14:33

Those in the boat worshiped him, saying, "Truly you are the Son of God."

My reflections: The disciples got it! Jesus is the Son of God. Their response? They worshiped Him right there in the boat.

Jesus multiplied food for 5000, healed people, cast out demons, walked on the water, allowed Peter to walk on the water, and calmed the storm. After all this, they got it.

Matthew started his gospel by reporting the conversation of the angel of the Lord with Joseph. The baby was conceived by the Holy Spirit. He would save His people from their sins. He could only do that because He Himself was the Son of God, sinless, perfect, without guilt of His own.

My challenge: Do you believe that Jesus is the Son of God? He deserves our complete worship, including the daily tasks we do before Him, and the directed worship and prayer to Him. Worship Him. Serve Him. Trust Him.

October 6/Day 279

Hearing Before Doing

Today's reading: Matthew 16:1-18:35

My selection: Matthew 17:5,6

5 He was still speaking when, behold, a bright cloud overshadowed them, and a voice from the cloud said, "This is my beloved Son, with whom I am well pleased; listen to him." 6 When the disciples heard this, they fell on their faces and were terrified.

My reflections: Once again, Peter, James, and John receive powerful evidence of the deity of their Master. Peter's nervous reaction turns to terror when he hears a voice from the cloud. Suddenly, he and his fellow disciples realize that, besides Jesus, Moses, and Elijah, God is present with them testifying to Jesus as His beloved Son, with whom He is well pleased. "Listen to Him," they hear.

Peter was eager to do something for Jesus, but before doing something for Him, Peter needs to listen to Him. Jesus is not one among equals with Moses and Elijah. He is God's Son. Peter still hadn't quite gotten that.

My challenge: Are you a lot like Peter? Your motto is "Don't just stand there, do something." Our first task is to hear Jesus. Know who He is. Know what He has said. Then act in obedience to Him.

The Unlikely Path to Greatness

Today's reading: Matthew 19:1-21:22

My selection: Matthew 20:26-27

[26] It shall not be so among you. But whoever would be great among you must be your servant, [27] and whoever would be first among you must be your slave.

My reflections: The disciples show again and again how out of sync they are with the Lord. Peter tried to pin Jesus down on a maximum requirement for extending forgiveness to others (18:21). Jesus showed him that those, who are forgiven, forgive freely. The twelve rebuked those who brought the little children to Jesus (19:13-15). Jesus welcomed and blessed them. The disciples jockeyed for positions of power among themselves (20:20; Mark 10:35-45). Jesus taught them that they should not be like the Gentiles, seeking to lord it over others, but that they should seek to serve and be slaves to others.

The disciples, minus Judas, would go on to learn these lessons and be faithful in the days following the death, resurrection, and ascension of the Lord. But the character changes were not instant.

My challenge: How are you out of sync with Jesus Christ? Is it your goal to forgive freely, to welcome others even though inconvenient, and to give your life as a servant and slave? Ponder what that means for you today. You may not attain greatness in this world, but you will before the Lord. That is the greatness that really matters.

October 8/Day 281

Heart Transplant

Today's reading: Matthew 21:23-22:46

My selection: Matthew 22:36-40 (KJV)

36 Master, which is the great commandment in the law? 37 Jesus said unto him, Thou shalt love the Lord thy God with all thy heart, and with all thy soul, and with all thy mind. 38 This is the first and great commandment. 39 And the second is like unto it, Thou shalt love thy neighbour as thyself. 40 On these two commandments hang all the law and the prophets.

My reflections: The various parties among the Jews (Pharisees, Sadducees, scribes, lawyers, etc.) hammered Jesus with questions seeking to entangle Him (22:15). In every case, He turned their questions into teaching opportunities and stumped them with questions.

Here Jesus exposes the Pharisees' error about law-keeping. Outward actions are insufficient. God sees inward attitudes. The supreme requirement by the law is love for God, first, and for others, second. Outward actions are a necessary expression of inward love as long as they reflect it. As 1 John 3:18 (KJV) says: "Little children, let us not love in word or talk but in deed and in truth."

My challenge: To love this way, we need changed hearts. Our natural, sinful, human disposition is to love ourselves first, leaving only the leftovers for God and others. The gospel of Jesus Christ focuses on the problem of our hearts and the need for a new spiritual birth by the Holy Spirit (John 3:3-8; Titus 3:4-7). How is your heart today? Do you love God with all your being? Do you love your neighbor as yourself? Do a heart check. Ask the Holy Spirit to produce in you His fruit toward God and others (Galatians 5:22-23).

Warnings to Church Leaders

Today's reading: Matthew 23:1-24:51

My selection: Matthew 23:2-3

[2] The scribes and the Pharisees sit on Moses' seat, [3] so practice and observe whatever they tell you— but not what they do. For they preach, but do not practice.

My reflections: In these two chapters, Jesus prepares His disciples for the difficulties ahead of them: corrupt religious authorities and political opposition. It is not a bright picture, but it is a true one. It is important that those who will be the apostles of His Church are forewarned and prepared.

Interestingly, Jesus tells them that the teaching of the scribes and Pharisees should be obeyed. The problem of the scribes and Pharisees is not their teaching but their practice. They teach one thing, but do another. They do what they do for show, to impress others.

Leaders, to be faithful to Christ, must serve. Christian leaders must do what they tell others to do. Christian leaders must assume a humble attitude, not with the goal of impressing others or of receiving titles and honors.

My challenge: Jesus was the ultimate example of godly leadership. He served others unto death. In your leading, serve others humbly for Christ's sake without thought of reward or honors.

God's Timing

Today's reading: Matthew 25:1-26:35

My selection: Matthew 26:4-5

[4] *[They] plotted together in order to arrest Jesus by stealth and kill him.* [5] *But they said, "Not during the feast, lest there be an uproar among the people."*

My reflections: God is sovereign over every action of man, including the timing of that action. The plot to kill Jesus seemed foolproof. It was concocted by the chief priests and the elders in the palace of the high priest, Caiaphas. There was no higher human authority among the Jews who could veto the plan. They agreed to do it *after* the Passover, but God had decreed that it would be *during* the Passover, to make the point that Jesus was the Passover Lamb whose blood would cover the people and save them from death (1 Corinthians 5:7).

The crucifixion was carried out by human means but with God's providence and sovereignty. The leaders couldn't put Jesus to death when they wanted to and when they wanted to delay the death they were overruled by God and carried it out.

My challenge: All things are in God's timing. He is wise and sovereign. He rules over all people and all actions, including yours. Trust Him. You are in His hand. Trust the Passover Lamb, Jesus Christ, who saves His people from death.

Inner Turmoil at Jesus' Trial

Today's reading: Matthew 26:36-27:44

My selection: Matthew 27:17

When they had gathered, Pilate said to them, "Whom do you want me to release for you: Barabbas, or Jesus who is called Christ?"

My reflections: The whole episode of Jesus' arrest and trial brought unspeakable anguish to several people. Judas was so distraught he returned the betrayal payment and hung himself. Peter, who had denied Jesus as predicted, was overcome with grief. Pilate's wife was sleepless and tried to keep her husband from getting involved in the scheme. Pilate repeatedly tried to find a way to free Jesus.

Meanwhile the crowds, incited by the chief priests and elders, grew adamant and callous in their attitude, even saying to Pilate, "His blood be on us and on our children!"

My challenge: One's response to Jesus Christ was then and is now the most pivotal issue in all of life. To reject Him is disaster. As Jesus told them: "Therefore say I unto you, The kingdom of God shall be taken from you, and given to a nation bringing forth the fruits thereof. And whosoever shall fall on this stone shall be broken: but on whomsoever it shall fall, it will grind him to powder" (Matthew 21:43-44 KJV).

What is your response to Jesus? His blood saves those who trust in Him but condemns those who consider Him worthy of death. Believe in Him. May His blood cover your sins.

Implications of Jesus' Resurrection

Today's reading: Matthew 27:45-Mark 1:45

My selection: Matthew 28:8-9

[8] They departed quickly from the tomb with fear and great joy, and ran to tell his disciples. [9] And behold, Jesus met them and said, "Greetings!" And they came up and took hold of his feet and worshiped him.

My reflections: The resurrection of Jesus Christ from the dead is the greatest proof of His deity and of His authority to save His people from their sin. Death is a universal experience. That is undeniable. It is the great problem of mankind. Individually and collectively, we cannot permanently postpone our date with death. Here is the one hope for humanity. Someone who claims to be the Son of God, God Incarnate, has come into the world, lived, died, and risen from death and tells us that there is an answer, a solution to our mortality in Him.

The religious and political authorities of the day colluded in an attempt to paint the resurrection as a hoax. Why did they want to take away the one solid hope that death could be overcome? Was it not to avoid the implications of having to admit that Jesus was who He said He was? Why is so much ink spilled to this day to attempt to show that Jesus was a mere man and did not rise from the dead? If it can be shown that Jesus is not God, that He did not rise from the grave, then His teachings, claims, and commands may be dismissed with no further thought.

My challenge: Trust in the One who conquered death. Sing with sincerity the old hymn.

My hope is built on nothing less
Than Jesus' blood and righteousness
I dare not trust the sweetest frame
But wholly lean on Jesus' name.
On Christ the Solid Rock, I stand
All other ground is sinking sand,
All other ground is sinking sand.

Why Jesus Came

Today's reading: Mark 2:1-4:20

My selection: Mark 2:17

When Jesus heard it, he said to them, "Those who are well have no need of a physician, but those who are sick. I came not to call the righteous, but sinners."

My reflections: There are three kinds of people with relationship to Jesus Christ. First, there are tormented souls who think that they are too evil to be saved. They are wrong. Second, there are proud fools who believe they are good enough and don't need saving. They feel no need for help. They too are wrong.

Then there are those who know they are sick and sinful and, in themselves, hopeless. It is the sweetest music they have ever heard when Jesus says He came for sinners. While on earth, Jesus ate with this kind of people. He befriended them. They flocked to Him and held onto His teachings. These were the kind of people Jesus came for. They came to Him and found salvation. They still do.

My challenge: In which of these three groups are you? Do you see yourself as too far gone even for Jesus to save? If so, you underestimate His power and love. Do you see yourself as good enough not to need a Savior? If so, you overestimate your holiness before a Perfect God who will judge the secrets of men's hearts. I hope you see yourself as a sick and sinful person and Jesus as a mighty Savior who forgives the repentant, believing sinner. He came for people like that. Trust Him for forgiveness, healing, hope, and eternal life.

October 14/Day 287

The Mysterious Growth of the Kingdom

Today's reading: Mark 4:21-6:29

My selection: Mark 4:26

And [Jesus] said, "The kingdom of God is as if a man should scatter seed on the ground.

My reflections: The growth of the kingdom of God is mysterious. Like the example of the planter, there is a human component: seed is scattered and harvesting is done. There is a time factor: it's a process, no instant results. There is a hidden aspect: the seed grows unseen. There is a termination component: the results are obvious.

For over 2000 years, the kingdom of God has been growing in the world. Its mark is unmistakable. Persecution only makes it stronger. In fact, it thrives in adversity and languishes in acceptability.

My challenge: Do not lose hope when you see apparent delay to the kingdom. It is the threshold of a new growth season. Keep sowing, watering, praying, waiting, and trusting.

Making the Connection

Today's reading: Mark 6:30-8:2Mark 6:30-8:211

My selection: Mark 8:17

Jesus... said to them, "Why are you discussing the fact that you have no bread? Do you not yet perceive or understand? Are your hearts hardened?"

My reflections: Reading this, you have to smile. However, the disciples were not very different from us. They had seen Jesus multiply five loaves and two fish to feed five thousand. They had seen Him do the same for another crowd of 4000. They had a loaf with them, so they were not completely out, just in low supply. When Jesus made a comment about the "leaven" of the Pharisees and of Herod, a reference to the sin of those in power, they immediately got nervous and worried about the lack of literal bread.

What do we do? We see the Lord answer prayer, provide in amazing ways, and show His faithfulness to sparrows and to us. We see, but what do we do when our financial security is threatened? What do we do when our job is in jeopardy? What do we do when our freedoms seem threatened? What do we do when our culture moves further away from the moral foundations of the Bible?

Answer: I am afraid, we generally talk among ourselves and worry.

My challenge: If we made the connection between the power of God and our daily lives, better than the disciples did in the boat that day, we would pray and trust more and talk and worry less. Are you praying or talking? Are you trusting or worrying? Make the connection.

Erratic Disciples

Today's reading: Mark 8:22-10:16

My selection: Mark 8:33

Turning and seeing his disciples, [Jesus] rebuked Peter and said, "Get behind me, Satan! For you are not setting your mind on the things of God, but on the things of man."

My reflections: Jesus' patience with the disciples is legendary. That doesn't mean He wasn't firm and forthright as well. Yesterday, we saw how they failed to grow in trust of Him from one situation to another (Mark 8:16-18). Now, Peter no sooner makes his bold and clear statement that Jesus is the Christ, then he turns around and rebukes Jesus for the idea that He will suffer, be killed, and rise again after three days.

This is the height of absurdity: rebuking the Son of God, the One he just called "the Christ." Again, we see how prone Peter and the rest were to trust themselves in a tough situation.

My challenge: One of the fundamental commands of the Christian life, designed to keep us out of trouble, is Proverbs 3:5 (KJV): "Trust in the Lord with all thine heart; and lean not unto thine own understanding."

Have you learned this basic truth? When you find your own understanding completely reasonable and sensible, yet in conflict with trusting God, beware. Flee to the wisdom of God. Keep trusting Him. Don't be an erratic disciple.

October 17/Day 290

Jesus Christ: Faithful to the Truth

Today's reading: Mark 10:17-12:17

My selection: Mark 12:14

[The Pharisees and the Herodians] came and said to him, "Teacher, we know that you are true and do not care about anyone's opinion. For you are not swayed by appearances, but truly teach the way of God. Is it lawful to pay taxes to Caesar, or not? Should we pay them, or should we not?"

My reflections: The Pharisees and Herodians were not natural allies, but here they had a common cause: to defeat and destroy Jesus. All the normal means of controlling upstart rabbis had failed. The subtle pressure had not affected Jesus at all. Now they try flattery. They tell Him they know He is not concerned about what anyone thinks. He gives the truth straight. They tell Him they realize that appearances don't sway Him. He sticks to the "way of God."

So, they try to sway Him, while telling Him that nothing sways Him. He will not change His message to gain acceptance from people. Of course, they turn right around and ask Him a knotty question about taxation that would potentially get him in trouble with one faction or the other.

My challenge: Are you struck by the firmness of Christ's character? Because He was true and told the truth, He perfectly glorified God the Father and kept the law without compromise. He did what we do not do. His perfection meant He was sinless and free from any condemnation and free to take upon Himself the sins of His people. Praise God that Jesus' perfection was evident even to those who tried to destroy Him.

October 18/Day 291

Common Errors about Heaven, Angels, and Truth

Today's reading: Mark 12:18-14:26

My selection: Mark 12:24

Jesus said to them, "Is this not the reason you are wrong, because you know neither the Scriptures nor the power of God?

My reflections: In this brief paragraph, Jesus corrects the error of the Sadducees, but also the errors of Islam, Mormonism, and many Biblically ignorant or unbelieving people today. Note:

1. There is a resurrection. The common belief that there is nothing after this life is false. The Sadducees were wrong on this and so are people today who prefer not to face God and so deny the final judgment.

2. Earthly, human marriage does not continue in heaven. As much as I enjoy my marriage, that relationship will not extend into the eternal state. God must have something better. Here Mormons and Muslims err. This does not imply that marriage is somehow an inferior relationship unworthy of heaven. The relationship between Christ and the Church is compared to a marriage. There will be a marriage supper of the Lamb in heaven, but no marriage between humans.

3. The dead do not become angels. The believing dead are like angels (with regard to marriage), but Jesus did not say they become angels. Angels have been confirmed in righteousness (i.e. they are unable ever to sin) but they have never been humans. In heaven, believers will be confirmed in righteousness and enjoy perfected bodies and souls, but will not be angels.

4. God is all-powerful, His word is infallible, and people wander into foolishness and error, who lose sight of these truths.

My challenge: Do your beliefs conform to a right knowledge of God's Word and God's power? The Sadducees were wrong in so many ways. Don't be like them. Check your theology about heaven with the Scriptures.

October 19/Day 292

Ceaseless Amazement

Today's reading: Mark 14:27-15:41

My selection: Mark 15:37-39

[37] Jesus uttered a loud cry and breathed his last. [38] And the curtain of the temple was torn in two, from top to bottom. [39] And when the centurion, who stood facing him, saw that in this way he breathed his last, he said, "Truly this man was the Son of God!"

My reflections: Mark records succinctly these events around Jesus' death: a cry, a final breath, the curtain tearing in the temple, and the centurion exclaiming that He was truly the Son of God. Although Mark doesn't expound on the meaning of the curtain being torn in two, Jewish readers would have understood immediately that this referred to the curtain which separated the Holy Place from the Holy of Holies in the temple. The curtain hid the place where the High Priest entered with fear and trembling annually, on the day of atonement, to offer a blood sacrifice for the sins of the people. Jesus' death opened the entrance into the place where God's presence was accessed.

Here is the most significant event of human history, the event upon which the salvation of a vast host from every tribe, tongue, and nation depends.

It is hard to say anything more about this, but rather to sit, silently, and stare in wonder at the words on the page.

My challenge: Are you not overwhelmed to think God took on flesh and lived among us, but even more overwhelmed that He died opening the way for us to the Holy of Holies in the temple? Let us never lose that sense of amazement and wonder!

October 20/Day 293

The Ministry of John the Baptist

Today's reading: Mark 15:42-Luke 1:56

My selection: Luke 1:15

He will be great before the Lord. And he must not drink wine or strong drink, and he will be filled with the Holy Spirit, even from his mother's womb.

My reflections: John's life purpose and work was spelled out to his father, Zacharias the priest, by the angel of the Lord. As the last of the prophets, John would be charged with preparing people for the coming of the Lord, that is, Jesus Christ. His ministry was extremely important, and it would be successful, unlike so many of the previous prophets of the Old Testament era whose messages were largely ignored or rejected. John would do all this because he would be filled with the Holy Spirit, so much so that even in his mother's womb he would rejoice when Jesus, also in His mother's womb, would come near to him.

What kind of preparation was needed by the nation that was about to receive the Messiah? We get a clue in the phrase "to turn the hearts of the fathers to the children, and the disobedient to the wisdom of the just" (Luke 1:17). There needed to be a change in the hearts of negligent fathers and rebellious fools.

My challenge: The generation gap did not begin in America in the 20th Century. It existed since the first family. Pray that God will prepare people today for the Lord, who will return in judgment, that they may see their negligence as fathers and mothers and the folly of their ways. Without a clear sense of sin, there will be a foolish presumption of innocence even in the face of impending judgment.

Understanding the Identity of Jesus

Today's reading: Luke 1:57-2:52

My selection: Luke 2:49

He said to them, "Why were you looking for me? Did you not know that I must be in my Father's house?"

My reflections: Here we learn some important things about Jesus.

1. His self-awareness. He knew at an early age that the God of Israel, who was worshiped in the temple, was His Father.

2. His mission. Even at age 12, He understood that His Father had an agenda for Him that took priority over other matters and relationships.

3. His knowledge. He amazed the teachers and others in the temple with His understanding and His answers.

My challenge: Jesus is God the Son. He existed eternally with the Father and the Spirit, but He became flesh and dwelt among us in space and time. He has given us a certain revelation of the Father. Be sure you know Who He is. Worship Him and trust Him for He alone could reveal God to us and bring us to the Father. [See John 1:1-18; 14:6; 1 Peter 3:18.]

October 22/Day 295

Jesus: Tested and Victorious

Today's reading: Luke 3:1-4:44

My selection: Luke 4:13

When the devil had ended every temptation, he departed from him until an opportune time.

My reflections: Jesus' ministry did not begin smoothly and without opposition. After His baptism, He was led by the Spirit in the wilderness for forty days. There He was tempted by the devil. The temptations were all related to Jesus' preservation and position. The devil was extremely shrewd and strategic in his approach and timing. Jesus was physically weak from fasting. His ministry was about to begin so this was Satan's time to defeat Him before He got started. Would Jesus protect Himself from physical need or danger? No. Would He take a short cut to gain the kingdoms of this world? No.

Jesus triumphed over the direct attacks of the devil, precisely where our first parents, Adam and Eve, failed. They listened to the lies of the devil and believed them. Jesus overcame a triple attack and, for a time, was left alone by the devil.

My challenge: Jesus is our Savior because of who He is, the Son of God, but also because He was victorious over the devil. He deserves all our worship. Our salvation, if we believe Him, is secure because He did what we did not do and leads us, who were captives, to freedom and glory. Lift your heart in unceasing praise to Him.

October 23/Day 296

Jesus' Authority to Forgive Sin

Today's reading: Luke 5:1-6:45

My selection: Luke 5:20

When he saw their faith, he said, "Man, your sins are forgiven you."

My reflections: Jesus assumed authority to forgive sins. The scribes and the Pharisees rightly perceived that this was a claim to divinity. Jesus was either God or He had blasphemed shamelessly. Other prophets had healed the sick, raised the dead, and suspended natural laws, but none had ever even claimed authority to forgive sins. The religious leaders of the Jews did not miss the significance of this claim.

Since forgiveness of sin is not visibly demonstrable, Jesus proved His authority by healing the man. The results were the onlookers "were all amazed, and they glorified God, and were filled with fear, saying, 'We have seen strange things to day'" (Luke 5:26 KJV).

My challenge: If you trust in Jesus for the forgiveness of sin, should you not be continually filled with praise to Him for that blessing? Should you not be amazed and filled with awe that God has come to us and brought hope and salvation from the wrath we justly deserve? May we never lose that sense of amazement and awe!

October 24/Day 297

Beware of Self-Delusion

Today's reading: Luke 6:46-8:25

My selection: Luke 8:18

Take care then how you hear, for to the one who has, more will be given, and from the one who has not, even what he thinks that he has will be taken away.

My reflections: When the final judgment comes, "God shall judge the secrets of men by Jesus Christ" (Romans 2:16 KJV). A warning is sounded here, because what is secret will come to light, and because what a person thinks he has may be a delusion. For one who has heard much preaching, or is very familiar with the Bible, there is a danger that he has not heard carefully. Some typical delusions are:

1. Head knowledge--possessing the facts about the Bible and theology without personally trusting God. Merely being a Bible trivia champ will be of no advantage when the secrets of our hearts are made manifest. A lot of seed falls on bad soil.

2. Outward conformity--thinking that compliance with church requirements brings salvation. Raising one's hand, going forward at an "altar call," baptism, or joining a church is not the basis for salvation. Faith is. Those outward actions may indicate faith, but they may also be done without holding true faith.

3. Complacency--presuming that God's love covers everyone and that ultimately all will be saved. The Bible teaches that only those who repent and believe in Jesus Christ will be saved and that those who do will show their faith by a changed life.

My challenge: Be careful how you hear. Do not be deluded by mere head knowledge of the truth. Seek to know the truth truly so that there is a changed life that confirms it. Always beware of the deceitfulness of your own heart.

Following Christ; Bearing a Cross

Today's reading: Luke 8:26-9:56

My selection: Luke 9:23

He said to all, "If anyone would come after me, let him deny himself and take up his cross daily and follow me."

My reflections: The disciples had seen Jesus' mighty acts. Three of them even saw His transfiguration. Now Peter confesses clearly what they must all have been thinking that Jesus is "the Christ of God" (9:20).

But Jesus' response is not what they might have expected.

1. They are not to tell who He is. This was a temporary command which would be suspended after His resurrection when He commissioned His disciples to go and make disciples of all nations (Matthew 28:19-20).

2. He is going to suffer, be rejected by the elders, chief priests, and scribes, be killed, and on the third day be raised.

3. If they want to come after Him, they must deny themselves, take up their cross daily, and follow Him.

The disciples probably thought that the full establishment of the kingdom would come at any moment, but instead there would be suffering ahead. They knew who Jesus was, but they must wait to announce it and suffer with Him in the meantime.

My challenge: The King has come and revealed Himself. We are in the last days, but these last days are not few. The final culmination of His kingdom will come, but meanwhile we are to be faithful, waiting for the end. This reality is further shown in Revelation. Be patient. Be faithful. Bear your cross. Repeat daily until further instructions.

Why Unbelievers Resist Truth

Today's reading: Luke 9:57-11:36

My selection: Luke 11:20

But if it is by the finger of God that I cast out demons, then the kingdom of God has come upon you.

My reflections: For the unbeliever, any excuse, no matter how flawed, will suffice to continue in unbelief. If Jesus hadn't cast out demons, they would have doubted His power. When He did cast out demons, they said He used Satan's power to do it. Jesus showed them that their reasoning would not hold up. A divided house cannot stand. Beelzebul cannot be at war with his own forces.

The real reason the doubters did not believe is that if Jesus truly had power over the demons, they would have to admit that the kingdom of God had come upon them. This was precisely what Jesus was asserting.

My challenge: Does it seem that the reasoning of those who find fault with the gospel and with the authority of Jesus Christ is unassailable? Stand for the truth. Doubters do not believe because, in themselves, they cannot believe. Pray that God may change their hearts, make them as little children (Luke 10:21), and grant them faith and repentance before the judgment falls.

October 27/Day 300

Fear: Proper and Improper

Today's reading: Luke 11:37-13:9

My selection: Luke 12:5

I will warn you whom to fear: fear him who, after he has killed, has authority to cast into hell. Yes, I tell you, fear him!

My reflections: For most people, the greatest fear is fear of death, and, by extension, fear of those who could kill them. Jesus taught that there is something worse than physical death in this world, which is condemnation into hell, and, by extension, fear of the One who has authority to cast us into hell.

Fear of God is not an outmoded, primitive concept superseded somehow by the gospel of Christ. Fear of God is very much a correct mindset for the Christian. Yet we are comforted in knowing that the One who has authority to cast into hell is the same One who died for all who believe in Him to deliver us from hell. We ought to fear the wrath of God, but not lose sight that He knows and cares for His own.

My challenge: Never become presumptuous and arrogant before God as if you were good enough in yourself to escape His judgment. Rest in His mercy and grace, but rest humbly and gratefully. Never despair that He has forgotten or overlooked you. You are of more value than all the sparrows of which He keeps track. Fear God, but trust God. Do not fear man. Do not trust in yourself.

October 28/Day 301

The Safety-in-Numbers Myth

Today's reading: Luke 13:10-15:32

My selection: Luke 13:24

Strive to enter through the narrow door. For many, I tell you, will seek to enter and will not be able.

My reflections: Apparently a burning question for at least one person who heard Jesus teach was "will few people be saved?" (Luke 13:23). We might ask it this way, "How many will be saved?" or "Who will be saved?" Jesus confirmed that many would seek to enter and not be able. He was warning not to go with popular trends and opinions or you will be left out in the cold. His subsequent teachings as recorded by Luke elaborate on the subject.

The narrow door would exclude those who trusted in their own good deeds or connections with Israel. Significantly, it did not exclude repentant sinners who return to the Father for mercy (15:11ff).

In the gospel, things are generally turned upside down from popular opinion. Some are last who will be first, and some are first who will be last.

My challenge: In our society, we are increasingly enamored with public opinion polls. When the majority agrees with us, we assume our view is correct, especially when the majority is overwhelming, but even if the majority is only barely 51%. There is a false sense of confidence in being in the majority on a given issue. Jesus warned against it. Do not be duped just because "everyone" agrees on an issue. Many will not enter in to salvation in the last day.

There is no safety in numbers. We will stand before God alone. I want to be like the prodigal son, in the sense of recognizing my sin and unworthiness before the Father, not the older brother who knew nothing of the grace and mercy of God. Enter through the narrow door. Don't miss it by trusting in popular opinion.

October 29/Day 302

Stubborn Unbelief

Today's reading: Luke 16:1-18:17

My selection: Luke 16:31

If they do not hear Moses and the Prophets, neither will they be convinced if someone should rise from the dead.

My reflections: In Jesus' parable (or was it a true story?) He describes a man who had lived selfishly and without belief. After death he was in torment in Hades, but he thought of his five brothers and had enough concern for them to ask Abraham to send Lazarus, his poor former neighbor now in heaven, to warn them to repent so as not to come to torment as well. Abraham tells him that if they do not hear Moses and the Prophets they will not believe even if someone should rise from the dead before them.

Unbelief is not reversed with mere signs and wonders, like someone rising from the dead. Indeed, Jesus Himself would soon rise from the dead and not everyone would believe. Without the regenerating work of the Holy Spirit in the heart, an unbeliever will not accept any kind of warning of the judgment to come.

My challenge: Are you resisting the obvious evidence that God has come to us in time and space as a human, lived a perfect life, died, been buried, and rose again from the grave to demonstrate His divinity? Do you ask for more signs than these to authenticate His identity and the truth of His teaching? If you do not believe, it is because you cannot believe without God's work in your heart. You could end up like the rich man and his six brothers. Call to God for mercy and grace that His Spirit may transform your heart and grant you faith.

Meeting God in His Word

Today's reading: Luke 18:18-20:8

My selection: Luke 18:29-30

[29] Truly, I say to you, there is no one who has left house or wife or brothers or parents or children, for the sake of the kingdom of God, [30] who will not receive many times more in this time, and in the age to come eternal life.

My reflections: As a young Christian, I was surprised (well, "stunned" would be a better word) by this passage one summer morning while reading my Bible on a rock in a lake in upstate New York. My surroundings that day added to the drama. I had paddled my canoe to that rock, climbed onto it with my Bible, and begun my daily reading. But my heart was weighed down with grief. Over the previous 8 months, I had come to faith in Jesus Christ, but, through obedience to Him, had also walked away from almost all my previous goals and plans. It felt to me like I was very alone with only a rock under me in this world.

I dutifully opened my Bible to read. I came to Luke 18 not by random reading. It was scheduled for that day as I made my way through the Bible, much as we are doing now. God in His goodness knew I needed reassurance, and reassurance He gave me. I totally identified with Peter at that moment who said precisely what I was feeling (Luke 18:28). "Lord, I have left everything to follow You."

But then came Jesus' comforting words, "there is not one who has left [all this] who will not receive many times more in this time, and in the age to come eternal life." Those words jumped off the page at me and my heart soared high above the rock in the lake. I read them again. And again. And again. I memorized them. They became like an anchor to me over the months and years ahead.

They have continued to sustain me for the past 49 years. So far they have proven abundantly true. I am sure they will prove true even beyond this life into eternity.

My challenge: Have you seen how God meets you in His Word, bringing comfort and reassurance to your heart and mind? Keep reading. Bring your life, your pain, your confusion, your grief to Him as you read and let Him speak to it through His word. This is what sustains our faith in Him and walk with Him. In times of discouragement, confusion, and despair never neglect daily Bible reading and prayer. Those are precisely the means He uses to encourage, direct, and renew you.

October 31/Day 304

Staying Alert

Today's reading: Luke 20:9-22:6

My selection: Luke 21:36

Stay awake at all times, praying that you may have strength to escape all these things that are going to take place, and to stand before the Son of Man.

My reflections: Jesus was teaching that the day of the coming of the kingdom of God was near, that it would happen before that generation would pass away. Was He referring to His death, resurrection, and ascension? Was He referring to the coming of the Holy Spirit on the Day of Pentecost? Was He referring to the fall of Jerusalem in 70 AD? Was He referring to His still yet-to-come second coming and the final judgment? Was He referring to all of the above?

There will be disagreement about this among Bible scholars and students, but there will be much agreement that the final consummation of the kingdom is still before us and that we need to "watch" ourselves that our minds not be consumed with the things of this life from distractions, escapes, and worries.

How near are we to the end of this age? It has been 500 years since Europe colonized the New World. The physical earth is largely populated and, since the 20th Century, is linked together by communication, transportation, economics, politics, and culture. Evil has not been reduced, indeed, it is more widespread and entrenched than ever with rampant abortion, sexual trafficking, and the normalization of various kinds of behaviors the Bible has declared sinful for thousands of years.

As the country song goes, "It's Five o'clock Somewhere." Let's kick back and party. Let's give ourselves to dissipation and drunkenness. This is what we hear.

My challenge: Now is the time to seek the Lord, to pray, and to proclaim the truth of the gospel and the need to flee the wrath to come by repentance and faith in the Savior, the Lord Jesus Christ. Check your priorities today. Prepare to stand before the Son of Man.

November 1/Day 305

What We Learn from Jesus' Prayer

Today's reading: Luke 22:7-23:25

My selection: Luke 22:42

Father, if you are willing, remove this cup from me. Nevertheless, not my will, but yours, be done.

My reflections: Here Luke gives further insight into prayer and Jesus' prayer life in particular:

1. Not my will, but yours be done. Jesus showed His trust in the Father even if the cup of suffering should not be taken from Him. He bowed to the Father's wise will.

2. Strength in suffering. The immediate answer to Jesus' prayer came by the appearance of an angel who strengthened Him to endure but did not take away the agony and the pain.

3. Prayer answered in the negative. God did not give what His Son requested. It is not a sin nor a shame to get a prayer request answered in the negative. Jesus did.

My challenge: Prayer is a vital part of the life of a disciple of Jesus Christ. Does it not seem that God is quick to strengthen His children as they call upon Him, even if He does not answer their requests in the positive?

Persevere in prayer even when the answer is "no" or "wait". Scripture promises "Draw nigh to God, and he will draw nigh to you" (James 4:8 KJV). Jesus did not attempt to face the cross without prayer; can we face our trials without it?

November 2/Day 306

What Jesus Gave His Disciples

Today's reading: Luke 23:26-24:53

My selection: Luke 24:45

He opened their minds to understand the Scriptures.

My reflections: The disciples always showed themselves to be a very needy and, often, unstable group of men. Here we can see both their needs and the way Jesus equipped them to carry out the super-human task that they were given.

1. The disciples needed Jesus to open their minds to understand the Scriptures. It was not that they were unbelieving or unwilling to believe, they simply could not see what was being said in the Law of Moses, the Prophets, and the Psalms about Christ and how this had been fulfilled in His death, burial, and resurrection.

2. The disciples needed direction for their future. Jesus gave them that direction through what we commonly call "the Great Commission" (v. 47; Matthew 28:18-20; Acts 1:8). It included a what (the content of the message) and a where (all nations beginning from Jerusalem).

3. The disciples needed power to carry out this commission. Jesus promised that they would receive power from on high, the fulfillment of the promise of His Father, the Holy Spirit (Acts 2).

My challenge: Just as Jesus' disciples were weak, confused, and dependent, so are we. Pray that the truth of God's word, that is permeated with the person and work of Jesus Christ, may be clear to you. Start in your Jerusalem, where God has you now, and continue the work of proclaiming repentance and forgiveness of sins in the name of Christ who suffered, died, and rose for the redemption of sinners who believe in Him.

What John Thought about Jesus

Today's reading: John 1:1-2:25

My selection: John 1:34

I have seen and have borne witness that this is the Son of God."

My reflections: There is hardly a more powerful statement in the entire Bible about the identity of Jesus Christ than this one. John (aka John the Baptist whose words are recorded here by John the disciple of Jesus who authored this gospel) gives these claims as to who Jesus is and what He does:

1. He is eternal. This is, at least, implied by John's words that Jesus was before him although we know that John was born before Jesus (John 1:30).

2. He has the Holy Spirit and baptizes others with the Holy Spirit.

3. He takes away the sin of the world in His role as the Lamb of God.

Bottom line: this is the Son of God.

These are either the most wildly bizarre claims ever made by one man of another or Jesus is to be taken as the one and only Son of God as John concluded.

My challenge: How do you see Jesus? Is He merely a good teacher, very advanced for His time? If He is not who He and His followers claimed Him to be, He cannot be considered good at all but delusional or deceptive. But if He is the Son of God, the Lamb of God, the One who baptizes with the Holy Spirit, we are left with no alternative but to worship Him, trust Him, follow Him, and obey Him. You cannot be neutral about Him. The question of "Who is Jesus Christ?" is still the burning question of all history and of your life.

Jesus: Reliable Truth about Heaven

Today's reading: John 3:1-4:54

My selection: John 3:11

Truly, truly, I say to you, we speak of what we know, and bear witness to what we have seen, but you do not receive our testimony.

My reflections: A theme running throughout the Gospel of John (as well as the other gospels) is the authority of Jesus. How does He know what He is teaching? Who is He to speak this way? Can we trust Him and His words?

Nicodemus seems honestly to want to know the answers. Jesus tells Nicodemus that He (Jesus) is the only one who has come down from heaven and is in the unique position to speak knowledgeably of heavenly things.

What is at stake? It is not merely a matter of satisfying our curiosity about the world to come or the invisible, spiritual world. It is about seeing our need to believe in Him and have eternal life.

My challenge: Jesus Christ is the way to the Father and to life eternal. He has descended from heaven into this world. He speaks truth. Hear Him. Believe Him. Worship Him. Through Him, by faith, aristocrats, like Nicodemus, and Samaritans, like the woman at the well, gain true life, a spring of water that wells up within to eternal life. They enter the Kingdom of God. Have you?

November 5/Day 309

Father and Son

Today's reading: John 5:1-6:24

My selection: John 5:22,23

[22] The Father judges no one, but has given all judgment to the Son, [23] that all may honor the Son, just as they honor the Father. Whoever does not honor the Son does not honor the Father who sent him.

My reflections: The Gospel of John is rich in information about the Trinity. In this section, we get important insight into the relationship between God the Father and God the Son, Jesus Himself. In verses 19-21, Jesus describes His dependence on the Father, His unity of action with the Father, and the bond of love between Him and the Father.

In **My selection:** , Jesus states further aspects of the Father-Son relationship related to the eternal destiny of mankind:

1. All judgment has been delegated to the Son in order that the Son be given the same honor as the Father. Here Unitarians, Mormons, Jehovah's Witnesses, Oneness Pentecostals and others err.

2. Deliverance from judgment and the receiving of eternal life depends on hearing the word of Jesus and believing the "One who sent" Him, that is, the Father.

My challenge: The message of the gospel is clear and simple. Believe who Jesus is and what He says and you will be saved. Reject Him and His words, and you can expect judgment ahead. There is a sure way of salvation, not by works but by faith. The Word became flesh and dwelt among us (John 1:14). Do you believe Him? Hold to Him and to His promises today and all the way to the end of this life until you enter His presence. Nothing else matters, really. Flee the wrath of God and the judgment of the Son by fleeing to the Son who will save all who come to Him and judge those who will not.

November 6/Day 310

Rivers of Living Water

Today's reading: John 6:25-7:44

My selection: John 7:38

Whoever believes in me, as the Scripture has said, "Out of his heart will flow rivers of living water."

My reflections: Jesus boldly proclaims His power to impart the Spirit of God to those who come to Him. The process is open to all who meet the conditions:

1. Must thirst. It is by God's grace that one senses a need, an insatiable craving, for what only Jesus Christ can supply.

2. Must come to Christ and drink. Many, if not most, feel empty and needy, but that alone will not bring a lasting solution. We come to Him as we read His Word, hear His Word preached, and call upon Him in faith.

3. Must believe in Him. Faith in Christ is more than merely intellectual assent to His existence or trusting Him for immediate needs. It is to rest upon Him alone, to trust Him completely for forgiveness of sin and adoption as God's child. That faith will express itself in an obedient, albeit still imperfect, life.

The result of this is to receive the Spirit that Christ gave to His people, the Spirit that is like rivers of living water flowing out of the believer's heart.

My challenge: Jesus' call and claim are unparalleled by any sane person in human history. Have you thirsted, come to Him, believed in Him and received His Spirit? If so, seek to abide in Him and bear the fruit of the Spirit today. Seek to be satisfied by the living water of His Spirit alone.

November 7/Day 311

Salvation Depicted

Today's reading: John 7:45-9:12

My selection: John 8:36

If the Son sets you free, you will be free indeed.

My reflections: Salvation in Jesus Christ is described in John's gospel with several poignant analogies: water, light, bread, sight, and, here, freedom. Spiritual slavery, unlike political or physical slavery, is imperceptible to the natural man (that is, man with only his human faculties unaided by the grace of God). The Jews, who heard Jesus refer to it, were not aware of their enslaved condition (8:33).

Without the regenerating work of the Holy Spirit in a person, he will not be aware that he is enslaved by sin nor will he be aware that there is any hope of spiritual freedom. After all, one of Satan's deceptions is to keep people blind, but thinking they can see. Blindness is the new 20-20 vision (2 Corinthians 4:3-4).

Jesus came to make the Father known. He came so that those who believe in Him and abide in His Word would be free (8:31-32).

My challenge: Have you known what it is to thirst? To grope in the darkness of this world? To hunger? To be blind? To be enslaved? Have you found in Christ water, light, bread, sight, and freedom? John wrote his gospel "that ye might believe that Jesus is the Christ, the Son of God; and that believing ye might have life through his name" (John 20:31 KJV).

If you have not found this in Jesus Christ, call upon Him for mercy and grace and faith to see your real condition and to believe in Him. If you have found life in Christ, walk today as a true disciple, abiding in His Word.

November 8/Day 312

Safe Sheep

Today's reading: John 9:13-11:16

My selection: John 10:28, 29

[28] I give them eternal life, and they will never perish, and no one will snatch them out of my hand. [29] My Father, who has given them to me, is greater than all, and no one is able to snatch them out of the Father's hand.

My reflections: For the Christian, Christ's sheep, there is hardly a more comforting or reassuring passage in all the Bible. What do the sheep have?

Eternal life, the assurance they will never perish.

Security in being held in Christ's hand and in the Father's hand.

Personal intimacy with the Lord, the Good Shepherd, who says He knows His sheep.

In other words, there is certainty of salvation and relationship with God, a certainty which cannot be lost.

How can you tell if you are one of His sheep? His sheep hear His voice. His sheep follow Him.

What is the basis for this promise? God the Father has given Jesus His sheep. The Father and the Son are one. They are agreed about this and this purpose cannot be defeated.

My challenge: Obedience to Christ is a trait of His sheep. Other Scriptures (Romans 7; 1 John 1) indicate that there is a battle with sin which continues in believers until they enter into the Lord's presence (1 John 3:1-2). Yet Christ's sheep cannot go long and far from their Shepherd. They are drawn back to Him in repentance and renewed obedience over and over again. He seeks His own who wander away (Luke 15:1-7).

Praise God for His promises of eternal life. If you are one of His sheep, rejoice in His knowledge and care of you.

November 9/Day 313

A Death to End Death

Today's reading: John 11:17-12:50

My selection: John 11:50

Nor do you understand that it is better for you that one man should die for the people, not that the whole nation should perish.

My reflections: The true motivations of the chief priests and Pharisees are laid bare here. They were concerned about maintaining their power and their esteem before the public (12:42-43). This is the danger which power and position brings: to be so blinded by the allurement of the kingdom of this world as to be unable to see the obvious truth. What would Jesus have to do to be more convincing as to His identity? He raised a man from the dead. The miracle was completely credible so that it could not be denied.

The authorities desperately consult about how to stop Him. The high priest unwittingly makes a true statement. Jesus will die for the people. More than that, John adds, He died "to gather into one the children of God who are scattered abroad." Jesus' death, rather than defeat His purposes and ministry, would catapult Him onto the stage of human history as the true Savior of the world. His cause goes on as He calls to Himself His people from every tribe, nation, and tongue.

My challenge: Be confident in the Lord's victory. No earthly power can stand against Him. He has triumphed, and His conquest will ultimately be revealed. Every knee will bow and every tongue confess that He is Lord, to the glory of God the Father! John Owens' classic title says it well, "The Death of Death [has come] in the Death of Christ." Tell the news!

November 10/Day 314

The Fruitful Christian

Today's reading: John 13:1-15:17

My selection: John 15:5

I am the vine; you are the branches. Whoever abides in me and I in him, he it is that bears much fruit, for apart from me you can do nothing.

My reflections: The life of the Christian is intended to be fruitful. This fruit comes from a relationship with Jesus Christ which is described as one of abiding, as a branch bears fruit by its connection to a vine. How does that abiding, connected relationship look?

1. Dependence. A Christian does not produce fruit merely by his own power or ability. There is a dependence on the Lord evidenced, in part, by prayer (15:7, 16).

2. Love-motivated obedience (14:21). Neither is the Christian passive in producing fruit. He is called to demonstrate his love for Christ by knowing and obeying the commands of his Lord, for example, to love others as Christ loved (13:34, 35; 15:12).

3. God-glorifying works. The ultimate purpose of fruit is to bring glory to God. Jesus even said His disciples would do "greater works" than He did through His going to the Father and sending the Spirit (14:12).

My challenge: Jesus showed unequaled love toward His disciples. If you think the people in your life are hard to love, check out the twelve disciples. Impetuous Peter. Doubting Thomas. The traitor Judas. And these were His closest friends. Jesus loved by speaking the truth in love. Love is not telling others what they want to hear but telling them what they need to hear. Abide in Christ and love as He loved. You will be fruitful.

Peace and Glory after Tribulation

Today's reading: John 15:18-18:18

My selection: John 16:33

I have said these things to you, that in me you may have peace. In the world you will have tribulation. But take heart; I have overcome the world.

My reflections: Jesus shows His tender and forgiving love toward His disciples, unreliable as they are, and His confidence in the presence of the Father as He faces the cross. He has no illusions about the twelve. They will abandon Him, but He continues to reassure them by His promises of peace in the world where they will experience tribulation.

The Lord also reveals the depth of His unity with and dependence on the Father. The world is against Him. His disciples will desert Him. He remains steadfast, trusting His Father to be with Him. He is not alone.

My challenge: None of us will ever face the suffering which Jesus faced, but believers face tribulation in the world. Do not think you can completely escape it. Do you believe that the Father is with you? He is! Not only that, but Jesus has promised that He will be with His own and that the Spirit will be with His people (Matthew 28:19-20; John 16:4ff). Believer, know that though your trials and suffering are great, the Triune God is with you, that Christ has overcome the world, and that He has plans to bring you into His glory (17:24). Though you are weak and unreliable, His plans cannot be defeated.

November 12/Day 316

Paid in Full

Today's reading: John 18:19-20:23

My selection: John 19:30

When Jesus had received the sour wine, he said, "It is finished," and he bowed his head and gave up his spirit.

My reflections: Jesus finished His work, the redemption of His people, by His atonement. His death satisfied the wrath of God as He bore the sins of His elect. The condemnation that His people deserve was paid in full. There was and is nothing that can be added to it. Nothing need be added to it.

To think we need to add our works to Jesus' death in order to secure our salvation is to diminish the value of His agony and pain. His perfect life and His offering of His body and blood cannot be supplemented by anything we do.

It is finished.

My challenge: Stand in awe of what Jesus did. Speechless but grateful. Amazed and humbled. That is the hope of the world for salvation. Never doubt that what He did fully and completely accomplished the purpose of salvation for His own. As the old hymn goes,

Jesus paid it all,
All to Him I owe,
Sin had left a crimson stain,
He washed it white as snow.

The Great Commission

Today's reading: John 20:24-Acts 2:13

My selection: Acts 1:8

But you will receive power when the Holy Spirit has come upon you, and you will be my witnesses in Jerusalem and in all Judea and Samaria, and to the end of the earth.

My reflections: Jesus' disciples were focused on the restoration of the kingdom to Israel (Acts 1:7). The Lord quickly redirected their attention away from the kingdom of Israel to the Kingdom of God which has global scope and supernatural power.

The disciples were to be about witnessing for and to Christ, the One who lived, died, and rose again for the salvation of the world. They were to do it in the power of the Holy Spirit. They were to carry this out on a worldwide basis. So are we.

There is a what, where, and how to this Great Commission: witness to Christ in the power of the Holy Spirit to all the world.

My challenge: What is your focus as a believer in Christ? Is it mere local issues and passing concerns? Christ has sent us to the ends of the earth with a message of eternal importance. Let your focus be as broad and deep as His, but don't let your contribution be diluted by the failure to lift up the cross where you are. Recognize your need for the power of His Holy Spirit. Depend on Him. Be ready to move out to wherever He may call you: Jerusalem, Judea, Samaria, or the ends of the earth.

November 14/Day 318

Why Bad Things Happened to a Good Person

Today's reading: Acts 2:14-4:22

My selection: Acts 2:23, 24

[23] This Jesus, delivered up according to the definite plan and foreknowledge of God, you crucified and killed by the hands of lawless men. [24] God raised him up, loosing the pangs of death, because it was not possible for him to be held by it.

My reflections: God is never surprised, never out of control, never defeated, never frustrated. The crucifixion of God the Son, the Lord Jesus Christ, was carried out by men but planned by God. It was the most evil act ever perpetrated, because it was done against the only perfectly good person, the Creator Himself.

The reason why this happened is that it was the means by which God satisfied His wrath against sinful humanity which He had purposed to save. With apologies to Rabbi Kushner, bad things happened to <u>the</u> Good Person so that good things could happen to bad people, sinners who repent and believe in Christ.

My challenge: All of us experience some unjust suffering, but believers in Jesus Christ also experience undeserved blessing. Forgive those who inflict unjust suffering on you, if you have a God who has poured out undeserved mercy and blessing on you.

Severe Opposition; Unshakeable Commitment

Today's reading: Acts 4:23-6:15

My selection: Acts 4:29

Lord, look upon their threats and grant to your servants to continue to speak your word with all boldness.

My reflections: This period of history of the early church was characterized by powerful apostolic preaching, radical commitment on the part of believers, miraculous signs and wonders performed by God, and relentless opposition by the authorities.

Following the healing of a paralytic man at the temple, the chief priests and elders arrested Peter and John and ordered them to desist from preaching in Jesus' name. Notice their reaction to this.

1. They refused to stop preaching. They invoked their obligation to obey God over any human authority.
2. They prayed for boldness to keep preaching.
3. They continued preaching in the power of the Holy Spirit.

The result of this was not an easing of persecution, but the high priest and Sadducees ramped up opposition and imprisoned the Apostles.

My challenge: What would you do if faced with such severe opposition? What would you pray for? The Apostles did not pray for the opposition to diminish, but for their ability to continue to speak the word with boldness. The church of Jesus Christ in the Western World may be on the brink of severe opposition, such as we have never seen. Be ready to proclaim Christ in the face of official resistance. Ask for relief from persecution, but, even more, for boldness to bear whatever consequences come your way, and keep on preaching.

Martyrdom and Forgiveness

Today's reading: Acts 7:1-8:25

My selection: Acts 7:58-60

58 Then they cast him out of the city and stoned him. And the witnesses laid down their garments at the feet of a young man named Saul. 59 And as they were stoning Stephen, he called out, "Lord Jesus, receive my spirit." 60 And falling to his knees he cried out with a loud voice, "Lord, do not hold this sin against them." And when he had said this, he fell asleep.

My reflections: There are not a lot of details about the martyrdom of Stephen, the first one to die for the gospel in the post-ascension era. Luke does include two interesting facts.

1. Stephen's attitude. Nearly parroting Jesus' words, Stephen prayed for God's forgiveness for his executioners. A disciple is never more Christlike than when he prays for the forgiveness of those who persecute him. [See Matthew 5:43-48.]

2. Saul's presence. Here we are first introduced to Saul, later to be converted and called Paul. In modern literature, this comment would be seen as a tease, as bait to keep the reader turning pages to find out who this person is. We don't know much of what was going through Saul's mind as he witnessed and supported the stoning of Stephen, but it is safe to say that Stephen's attitude was not lost on Saul.

My challenge: Tertullian (160-220 AD) is credited with the saying, "The blood of the martyrs is the seed of the church." This truth is demonstrated here as well. This persecution would result in the expansion of the Church. Stand firm. Be encouraged and expectant. If persecution comes with the same results as it has historically, you may see a great growth in the size and vibrancy of the Church.

Unintended Benefits

Today's reading: Acts 8:26-10:22

My selection: Acts 9:22, 23

[22] But Saul increased all the more in strength, and confounded the Jews who lived in Damascus by proving that Jesus was the Christ. [23] When many days had passed, the Jews plotted to kill him.

My reflections: Two developments grab my attention here.

1. Saul's very rapid emergence as a powerful voice for Jesus Christ. He was strengthened, and he confounded the Jews in Damascus as he proved that Jesus was the Messiah, the Christ. His conversion was a complete about-face and his early growth as a Christian and a preacher was stunning. The energy and boldness he had once used against the Church, he now used for his Lord and the gospel.

2. The Jews chronic knee-jerk reaction to seek to kill whoever opposed them in the name of Christ. When they crucified Jesus, the Church was born and testified to the resurrection. When they stoned Stephen, the Church was dispersed and grew. Now they set their sights on the latest target, Saul. They inadvertently contributed to the growth of the gospel whenever they attempted to defeat it.

My challenge: Few, if any, match Saul (aka Paul) for worldwide impact for the gospel, and we should praise God for His powerful work in and through that great missionary and church planter. Ask God to use you, as well, for His purposes to continue to proclaim that Jesus is the Christ to your generation. Do not be disheartened by opposition, as it is a sign that your message is effective. Know that God will bless you when you suffer persecution and opposition. May you also experience the law of unintended benefits.

November 18/Day 322

Unlikely Converts

Today's reading: Acts 10:23-13:3

My selection: Acts 10:42-43

[42] He commanded us to preach to the people and to testify that he is the one appointed by God to be judge of the living and the dead. [43] To him all the prophets bear witness that everyone who believes in him receives forgiveness of sins through his name.

My reflections: Here is a succinct statement by Peter to Cornelius and his friends, all Gentiles, about Jesus' life and ministry: who He was, what He did, and what the significance was of these things. The historic facts about His life were clear: His anointing by the Holy Spirit, His good works and healing, His death by crucifixion, His resurrection, and His appearance to witnesses. Jesus sent the apostles to preach and testify to two things:

1. That Jesus was the One appointed by God to judge the living and the dead.

2. That everyone who believes in Him receives forgiveness of sins through His name.

Jesus is Judge and Savior. His judgment extends to all mankind. His salvation extends to all who believe, to all mankind without distinction whether Jew or Gentile.

Peter here was the preacher, but he was also the learner, because God was showing him the truth that *all* who believe would be saved.

My challenge: Are there groups or individuals whom you have difficulty envisioning among the saved? Perhaps they are people who are very different from you or who seem to be very unresponsive to the gospel. If so, you can understand how Peter viewed Gentiles before the vision from God and the experience with Cornelius and his friends.

Give out the gospel to all who will hear. Never underestimate the power of God to bring to Himself those who you think most unlikely to respond.

November 19/Day 323

The Right Question

Today's reading: Acts 13:4-14:28

My selection: Acts 14:21-23

[21] When they had preached the gospel to that city and had made many disciples, they returned to Lystra and to Iconium and to Antioch, [22] strengthening the souls of the disciples, encouraging them to continue in the faith, and saying that through many tribulations we must enter the kingdom of God. [23] And when they had appointed elders for them in every church, with prayer and fasting they committed them to the Lord in whom they had believed.

My reflections: It was another roller-coaster time for Paul. He was driven out of Iconium, almost worshiped in Lystra after a man was healed, then stoned in Lystra when his enemies arrived.

What did he do? He went to Derbe briefly before returning to the site of the trouble, Lystra, Iconium, and Antioch. Why? To strengthen the souls of the disciples, and to encourage them to continue in the faith. Paul told them that "we must through much tribulation enter into the kingdom of God" (Acts 14:22 KJV). Paul was relentless in his ministry to the believers. He modeled the boldness and willingness to suffer that he preached to others.

My challenge: Are you growing in willingness to suffer for the gospel or are you seeking to avoid dangerous and threatening situations? The work of the kingdom of God is advanced by faithful men and women who lose their lives for the gospel of Jesus Christ. Pray for willingness to risk suffering. Ask not "Will I suffer if I do this?" but "Will God be glorified if I do this?" That is the right question.

November 20/Day 324

The Main Thing

Today's reading: Acts 15:1-17:9

My selection: Acts 17:2, 3

[2] Paul went in, as was his custom, and on three Sabbath days he reasoned with them from the Scriptures, [3] explaining and proving that it was necessary for the Christ to suffer and to rise from the dead, and saying, "This Jesus, whom I proclaim to you, is the Christ."

My reflections: Paul's ministry strategy and message did not vary based on circumstances. It was his custom to go to the synagogue and reason with the Jews. Paul's message focused on the essential issues of connecting the person and work of Jesus Christ with the Old Testament scriptures. Jesus suffered. Jesus died. Jesus rose from the dead. Jesus is the Christ, the Anointed One of God.

My challenge: Paul understood how to keep the main thing the main thing. Do you? The gospel of Jesus Christ is about whom He is and what He did. Do not allow this to fade out in the midst of all the distracting themes that bombard us in the media and the marketplace today. Sure, there are important political and economic issues. There are moral issues to be addressed, but never let these replace the gospel. God is holy. Man is sinful. Jesus is the Savior. Repent and believe the gospel that you may be saved from the wrath of God. Everything else is secondary.

November 21/Day 325

Idolatry Unmasked

Today's reading: Acts 17:10-19:41

My selection: Acts 17:30, 31

[30] The times of ignorance God overlooked, but now he commands all people everywhere to repent, [31] because he has fixed a day on which he will judge the world in righteousness by a man whom he has appointed; and of this he has given assurance to all by raising him from the dead.

My reflections: In these closing words of Paul's famous sermon on Mars Hill, he argues that idolatry ought to be obviously rejected merely on the basis that God cannot be adequately represented by a mineral or gem crafted by a man's imagination and skill. Man, as God's creation or offspring, reflects God's greatness and what man devises dimly reflects man's ingenuity, but it cannot reflect, even dimly, God's grandeur.

Now a time for repentance has been granted. Judgment is coming. Jesus, who rose from the dead, is the judge. His judgment will be righteous.

My challenge: Are you ready for the judgment to come? The gospel has been proclaimed for 2000 years and millions have turned to Christ for forgiveness of sin. The only day we have is today. Believe in the One who rose from death and will one day judge all the earth. Repent of your idolatry, subtle as it may be. Turn from the trust in material things. Worship the true God who revealed Himself in Christ. In Him is salvation.

Discipleship: Purpose and Commitment

Today's reading: Acts 20:1-21:36

My selection: Acts 20:24

But I do not account my life of any value nor as precious to myself, if only I may finish my course and the ministry that I received from the Lord Jesus, to testify to the gospel of the grace of God.

My reflections: This is the classic statement by Paul of his view of life. He has done what Jesus commanded, not to save his life in this world. He thinks of his life as a resource only for the purpose of fulfilling the ministry given to him by God. He is clear about what that ministry is: to testify to the gospel of God's grace.

Notice what Jesus said:

Then said Jesus unto his disciples, If any man will come after me, let him deny himself, and take up his cross, and follow me. For whosoever will save his life shall lose it: and whosoever will lose his life for my sake shall find it. For what is a man profited, if he shall gain the whole world, and lose his own soul? or what shall a man give in exchange for his soul? For the Son of man shall come in the glory of his Father with his angels; and then he shall reward every man according to his works. Matthew 16:24-27 (KJV)

My challenge: How can any believer not be completely challenged by this statement? How do you view your life? Do you jealously guard it against any unpleasant demands or do you offer yourself as a living sacrifice to Christ each day (Romans 12:1-2)? How do you view your purpose for life? Are you vague about what God wants you to do or do you have a clear vision of His calling and the gifts He has given you to use for His glory?

Take time to pray and think about what God has called you to do. Take steps to bring your actions and attitudes in line with the purposes you know He has for you.

The Cost of Integrity

Today's reading: Acts 21:37-24:27

My selection: Acts 23:4-5

[4] Those who stood by said, "Would you revile God's high priest?"[5] And Paul said, "I did not know, brothers, that he was the high priest, for it is written, 'You shall not speak evil of a ruler of your people.'"

My reflections: Paul, in spite of the unfair and untrue charges being made against him, held himself to the highest standard of the law. He put himself in a weakened position by reviling the high priest, albeit, inadvertently. However, he did not try to diminish his sin, but confessed, quoting the law he had violated. Paul modeled the reality of the claim he had just made. "Paul, earnestly beholding the council, said, 'Men and brethren, I have lived in all good conscience before God until this day'" (Acts 23:1 KJV).

My challenge: Do you keep a good conscience before God even when it weakens your case or makes you look foolish? When you are confronted with a failure or a weakness, do you immediately recognize it? Seek today to walk before God with a good conscience, no matter what the cost.

November 24/Day 328

Simplicity and Steadfastness

Today's reading: Acts 25:1-27:26

My selection: Acts 26:18

To open their eyes, so that they may turn from darkness to light and from the power of Satan to God, that they may receive forgiveness of sins and a place among those who are sanctified by faith in me.

My reflections: Jesus had given a clear commission to Paul. Paul knew exactly what it was and he kept it in front of him over the years. He was not intimidated by opposition and persecution. He was not distracted by other attractive goals or activities. He focused on one thing, the thing God gave him to do.

My challenge: Do you know what God has called you to do? Are you seeking daily to fulfill His purpose for you? Do not lose heart. Do not become distracted. Seek first His kingdom and His righteousness. Glorify God and enjoy Him today. Keep it simple. Be steadfast.

November 25/Day 329

Morality by Majority Vote

Today's reading: Acts 27:27-Romans 1:32

My selection: Romans 1:32

Though they know God's decree that those who practice such things deserve to die, they not only do them but give approval to those who practice them.

My reflections: In an editorial in the Roanoke Times (April 8, 2013), the writer cited C.S. Lewis and argued that Christians ought not to impose their moral standards on the rest of the society. Everyone, this writer said, should be free to decide right and wrong for himself.

In a democracy like ours, moral, ethical, and legal standards are more or less determined by popular opinion or by majority vote. We do not have a theocracy or a Christian nation. Therefore, Christians in this nation have no more influence at the ballot box than atheists, Muslims, or any other group. But neither do they have less.

Paul says that God has given a decree that those who practice the evils mentioned here deserve death. Paul also condemns not only the practice of these evils, but the approval of them. Christians, if asked for their opinion or their vote on a moral issue, may not abdicate their responsibility to affirm that the sins which violate God's law are worthy of condemnation. Christians may not be able to stop the instituting of immoral behavior, but they certainly ought to voice opposition by the legitimate means they have.

My challenge: Do you stand for morality based on the law of God, the Ten Commandments? If you do, be bold and loving in proclaiming your opposition to the fast-paced breakdown in moral standards that will sooner or later lead to the judgment of God. If you are defeated in this purpose, prepare to suffer along with the rest of our culture. Ultimately, the Christian's hope is not in this world but the one to come.

November 26/Day 330

Dangerous Presumption

Today's reading: Romans 2:1-4:25

My selection: Romans 2:3

Do you suppose, O man—you who judge those who do such things and yet do them yourself—that you will escape the judgment of God?

My reflections: What is the mindset of the judgmental person? Paul says here that one who judges others while doing the same things may hold two very dangerous thoughts:

1. I am an exception to the rule. Judgment is for others, not me. God will not judge me. I will escape the judgment of God (Romans 2:2).

2. God is love, and His present blessing on me proves I will always be blessed, never judged.

These thoughts are dangerous because, first, the one who has them ignores the fact that God's present kindness is intended to lead to repentance, not to false security. Secondly, while the present life of the judgmental person may seem blessed and pleasant, his hard and impenitent heart is resulting in a mounting up of wrath for himself "against the day of wrath and revelation of the righteous judgment of God (Romans 2:5 KJV). This judgment will be complete and just, because it will be based on the "secrets of men" (Romans 2:16 KJV).

My challenge: Check your heart. Do you hold one or both of these dangerous presumptuous thoughts? Do you judge others who seem more evil than you? Could you be guilty of a hard and impenitent heart? Repent of your sin, daily. Make confession of sin a part of your daily prayer. Recognize that you deserve His wrath. Ask God's forgiveness. He justifies, that is, declares righteous by grace. That grace is His undeserved favor, His gift to believers. This gift was secured for us through the redemption, or purchase of freedom, made by Christ. He gave Himself as a propitiation, or an offering to satisfy the wrath of God. All this is received by faith alone (Romans 3:21-26). Do you believe?

Deliverance of the Wretched

Today's reading: Romans 5:1-8:17

My selection: Romans 7:24-8:1

[24] Wretched man that I am! Who will deliver me from this body of death?
[25] Thanks be to God through Jesus Christ our Lord! So then, I myself serve the law of God with my mind, but with my flesh I serve the law of sin. [1] There is therefore now no condemnation for those who are in Christ Jesus.

My reflections: One reality of life for the Christian is that sin is still very much a part of his daily life. His flesh is dead, unable to obey consistently God's law despite his desire to do so. The other reality is that he is delivered from his body of death by God through Jesus Christ resulting in a state of non-condemnation.

My challenge: No condemnation! What wonderful, comforting, precious words! Perfection is not possible but, by faith in Christ, salvation is certain. We err if we expect to attain sinless perfection in this life, but we also err if we fail to embrace by faith the justification and adoption that God grants to those who repent and believe the gospel.

Fellow Christian, confess your sin. Confess it fully and receive God's forgiveness in Christ. Do not join Satan's chorus of accusing the brethren, including you. Seek to grow in obedience, knowing you are not condemned.

November 28/Day 332

The Freedom of Glory

Today's reading: Romans 8:18-11:10

My selection: Romans 8:21

The creation itself will be set free from its bondage to decay and obtain the freedom of the glory of the children of God.

My reflections: The children of God have freedom. That freedom is related to glory.

The glory of no condemnation (8:1). Free from guilt.

The glory of being led by the indwelling Spirit of God (8:14). Free from abandonment.

The glory of being God's children (8:16). Free from worthlessness.

The glory of being heirs of God (8:17). Free from poverty.

The glory of being redeemed from dying bodies (8:11). Free from death.

We still suffer, but there is the hope of glory to come. In that day, we will experience fully the glory God has given us now as a foretaste, and we will be free from the desire or need to escape the present suffering which we are leaving behind. We will truly lack nothing because we will be completely filled with the glory of God.

My challenge: If you know God through Jesus Christ, praise Him for the glory and freedom that is yours and that is still to come. Reject any lesser distracting glories of the kingdoms of this world. Let your heart be filled with Him and His glory. You will be free, free from discontentment, free from emptiness, free from the longing for other things that can never satisfy.

Overwhelmed by God

Today's reading: Romans 11:11-15:13

My selection: Romans 11:33-36 (KJV)

[33] O the depth of the riches both of the wisdom and knowledge of God! how unsearchable are his judgments, and his ways past finding out![34] For who hath known the mind of the Lord? or who hath been his counsellor?[35] Or who hath first given to him, and it shall be recompensed unto him again?[36] For of him, and through him, and to him, are all things: to whom be glory for ever. Amen.

My reflections: Paul is overwhelmed by who God is. Words fail. God's resources are deep. He has all things in the universe at His disposal. God's wisdom is without limit. He knows how to make all things work together for good. God's knowledge is infinite. He not only knows what has happened, is happening, and will happen in time and space, He has decreed all that happens. He controls all things.

No one knows what God knows. No one can inform Him of anything. No one can give Him anything that He needs or lacks. God is not indebted to anyone. He is not dependent on anyone or anything.

He is the ultimate end of all things. He deserves all glory. Always.

My challenge: Although we do not know all that God knows, He has chosen to reveal truth to us, not exhaustively, but as fully as we need to know. Make it your goal to know well the truth about God that He has revealed to us both in general revelation (Psalm 19:1-6; Romans 1:18) and special revelation (Psalm 19:7-14; 2 Peter 1:19-21; 2 Timothy 3:14-17).

November 30/Day 334

Preaching Christ Crucified

Today's reading: Romans 15:14-1 Corinthians 2:5

My selection: 1 Corinthians 1:23

We preach Christ crucified, a stumbling block to Jews and folly to Gentiles.

My reflections: Why do some respond to the preaching of the gospel of Christ while others do not? Paul indicates that, on a human level, Jews don't "get" the gospel because they demand signs and Greeks don't "get" the gospel because they seek wisdom. Apparently, the sign of a Man rising from the dead in human history does not suffice for the Jews and other sign seekers. On the other hand, for Greeks and other wisdom seekers, the simplicity and complexity of the Holy, Creator God taking on human flesh, living a perfect life, dying as an atoning sacrifice to satisfy His own just wrath, and rising from the dead for the salvation of all who believe is not profound enough to meet their expectations.

But the ultimate answer, as to why some people do respond in faith while others do not, is that the former are called, and the latter are not. When God calls Jews, they get the gospel, that Christ is the power of God. When God calls Greeks (i.e. non-Jews of all kinds), they get the gospel, that Christ is the wisdom of God. God changes the natural skepticism of human hearts when He calls a man or woman to Himself.

My challenge: Are you tempted to try to downplay the centrality of Christ in winning those who want impressive signs or who want high-sounding wisdom? Do not be embarrassed by the gospel. Paul could argue philosophy with the best (Acts 17:16-34). He had performed signs and wonders (Romans 15:19), but that same Paul concluded that he was called to "preach Christ crucified." The response of the hearers to his message would reveal whether or not they were called. Those who heard would either stumble or they would find Christ to be the power of God and the wisdom of God.

Preach Christ crucified. God will use the truth to draw His called, elect ones to Himself.

Rock Stars and Spiritual Leaders

Today's reading: 1 Corinthians 2:6-6:20

My selection: 1 Corinthians 3:3

You are still of the flesh. For while there is jealousy and strife among you, are you not of the flesh and behaving only in a human way?

My reflections: One clear sign of spiritual immaturity is exclusive allegiance to a teacher or preacher. There is nothing wrong, in itself, with allegiance to godly leaders, but what Paul is indicting is an exclusive allegiance that leads to divisions in the church. Groups form around a Paul or an Apollos and there is jealousy and strife between them.

One clear sign of spiritual maturity in a leader is the unwillingness to encourage that kind of exclusive allegiance in those to whom he ministers. Paul saw that even those who said "I follow Paul" were not spiritual people but infants in Christ, unable to receive solid food. Paul demonstrated his own spiritual maturity by pointing his followers to Christ, and away from adulation of a mere servant of God.

My challenge: Do you identify yourself exclusively with one teacher or leader so that you create divisions in the body of Christ? Beware. If you are a leader in the church, do you seek to encourage that kind of identity with you? Beware. The glory belongs to God. A faithful minister is a servant of God, not a rock star building a fan club.

Contentment in God's Service

Today's reading: 1 Corinthians 7:1-9:27

My selection: 1 Corinthians 7:17

Only let each person lead the life that the Lord has assigned to him, and to which God has called him. This is my rule in all the churches.

My reflections: In this chapter, Paul admonishes the believers in Corinth not to be restless, but to be focused on the work of the kingdom of God. Marriage, with all the joys it can bring, is not heaven. For some it has brought little joy, and it always distracts, even as it helps, the disciple who is seeking to serve the Lord.

Here is a call to contentment and discipline to serve the Lord in the state in which He has called you. One should not think that by changing one's marital status or social status he can suddenly be delivered from all the trials of this life. It's okay to marry. It's okay to gain freedom from slavery. But life will still have problems.

My challenge: Are you content? Accept the things you cannot change about your life and press on in the service of the Lord.

Why We Need the Old Testament

Today's reading: 1 Corinthians 10:1-12:11

My selection: 1 Corinthians 10:11

These things happened to them as an example, but they were written down for our instruction, on whom the end of the ages has come.

My reflections: This passage tells us that one of the purposes of the Old Testament is to instruct Christians by example. Some of these examples are negative, as in the case of the people of Israel who engaged in drunkenness, idolatry, sexual immorality, and grumbling. Even though the Corinthian believers lived, as we do, at the end of the ages, they could not assume that they were exempt from the same kinds of temptations as the Israelites.

There is a warning here to Christians, of all times, not to presume to be above falling into temptation and sin. There is also a promise to believers today to remember the sovereignty and providence of God who always holds in check the intensity of the temptations which come their way, and to provide a way of escape from those temptations so that no believer need succumb to them.

My challenge: Do not neglect the study of the Old Testament which contains examples, both positive and negative, for our growth in faith. Avoid the extremes of cheap grace, which downplays the importance of a daily pursuit of holiness in life, and perfectionism, which expects the attainment of a sinless life in this world. Seek to be holy. Expect progress but also ongoing struggles and failures. Confess sin and receive forgiveness and cleansing. Your standing before God is, and always will be, based on Christ's atoning work, not your own achievements and merits.

What to Do While Waiting for World Unity

Today's reading: 1 Corinthians 12:12-15:11

My selection: 1 Corinthians 12:12-14

[12] For just as the body is one and has many members, and all the members of the body, though many, are one body, so it is with Christ. [13] For in one Spirit we were all baptized into one body—Jews or Greeks, slaves or free—and all were made to drink of one Spirit. [14] For the body does not consist of one member but of many.

My reflections: In this first letter of Paul to the Corinthians, he addresses the problems of divisions in the church. Here he shows that there is diversity and unity in the body. The diversity allows for each member to make a unique contribution, and for there to be a colorful variety within the body. The unity promotes acceptance of one another, even though we differ in race, culture, and socioeconomic status. That unity is based on the spiritual connection which all people in Christ have. God's Spirit makes all believers one.

In the world, there is a push to obliterate distinctions, to bring all cultures together in some kind of unity, political (United Nations, communism, benevolent dictatorships) or cultural and religious (Islamic fundamentalism, ecological causes). All of these efforts are done without the gospel and the Triune God of the Bible, so they will not succeed. But the idea of universal harmony and peace is not contrary to God's ultimate purpose for His people. The problem is partly the goal (unity for Man's benefit not God's glory) and also the means (human methods without dependence on God).

My challenge: Are you discouraged with the on-going strife between nations and within our nation between political and cultural ideologies? Have you placed more hope in secular forces than in the gospel to bring about true unity and peace? Remember Paul's words to the Philippians: "Wherefore God also hath highly exalted him, and given him a name which is above every name: That at the name of Jesus every knee should bow, of things in heaven, and things in earth, and things under the earth; And that every tongue should confess that Jesus Christ is Lord, to the glory of God the Father" (Philippians 2:9-11 KJV).

When that day comes, there will be unity around the worship of Jesus Christ. Meanwhile, keep shining as lights in the world (Philippians 2:14-16).

Does Prayer Matter?

Today's reading: 1 Corinthians 15:12-2 Corinthians 1:11

My selection: 2 Corinthians 1:11

You also must help us by prayer, so that many will give thanks on our behalf for the blessing granted us through the prayers of many.

My reflections: Paul has been through great trials. In one case, he and those with him were so burdened beyond their strength that they "despaired of life itself." But God delivered them then and Paul knew He would do it again (2 Corinthians 1:8-10). He did not assume that no more trials would come his way, but he did assume that as God had been with them in the past, He would be with them in the future.

Perhaps surprisingly, we see that Paul counted on the prayers of his friends in Corinth to help him. This does not indicate a lack of trust in God or a view that God can do nothing unless we pray. It did indicate that Paul knew that God uses means to accomplish His purposes, and He is glorified when His people draw together in prayer to Him and, thus, become part of the means God uses to fulfill His will.

My challenge: Are you convinced that your prayer for others is a vital and essential means through which God blesses and helps them? When it comes to prayer, keep at it (Romans 12:12). Remember your prayer does matter because God works through it to accomplish His purposes.

What to Do While Longing for Heaven

Today's reading: 2 Corinthians 1:12-6:2

My selection: 2 Corinthians 5:2

In this tent we groan, longing to put on our heavenly dwelling.

My reflections: There are several important contrasts between our present life and the life that comes after death:

1. Temporary vs. permanent. Here we have an earthly home (a tent). There we will have a heavenly house (a building).

2. The destructibility of this body vs. the eternality of that body.

3. Groaning and nakedness here and now vs. clothing and not groaning (implied) then and there.

Often when a loved one dies we hear the comments, "Well, he's in a better place" or "She's free from suffering now." This is a firm hope that believers have. Christians are promised that they will enter into the Lord's presence at death. Meanwhile, Paul's example was to be engaged in the task of persuading others to be reconciled to God (2 Corinthians 5:11). Those who are not reconciled to God through Christ have no hope of approval before the judgment seat of Christ (2 Corinthians 5:10).

My challenge: Be urgent in calling unbelievers to faith and repentance before it is too late. Beware of giving false hope to unbelievers. Admittedly, we do not know the condition of anyone's soul in life or in death. Only God knows this, but those who finally and definitively reject Christ as Savior and Lord are not in a better place when they die. Be about the ministry of reconciliation.

Never stop longing to be fully clothed and in the Lord's presence.

December 7/Day 341

The Test of Ministerial Integrity

Today's reading: 2 Corinthians 6:3-10:18

My selection: 2 Corinthians 6:3-5

3 We put no obstacle in anyone's way, so that no fault may be found with our ministry, 4 but as servants of God we commend ourselves in every way: by great endurance, in afflictions, hardships, calamities, 5 beatings, imprisonments, riots, labors, sleepless nights, hunger.

My reflections: Paul was completely committed to the ministry of the gospel. He saw himself as a servant of God. His desire was to be sure there were no obstacles in anyone's way.

What kind of obstacles?

We get a clue by what he says next (6:6-10). If the attitudes, characteristics, and experiences he mentions were not descriptive of his ministry, there would be a basis for discounting the validity and authenticity of his life and work. If Paul's life did not match his message, that would create an obstacle, for those who heard him, to believe what he preached. For example, he says that he and his fellow-workers have demonstrated great endurance. They did not give up when faced with opposition, even severe opposition, like: afflictions, hardships, calamities, beatings, and imprisonments. Furthermore, their lives were characterized by the godly virtues of purity, knowledge, patience, kindness, the Holy Spirit, genuine love, and truthful speech. He does not credit himself for this but, rather, the power of God and the weapons of righteousness on which he elaborates in Ephesians 6.

In western evangelical Christianity today, there is a tendency to point to material success as a badge of authenticity of a ministry. Huge mega-churches with impressive buildings, edgy music, exciting programs, and entertaining sermons are often considered to enjoy God's presence and blessing. Yet Paul's ministry was carried out under the worst conditions of opposition. Paul did not point to his success as the badge of authenticity of his ministry. Enduring imprisonment and hunger, not successful TV ratings and the applause of man, were Paul's proof of God's blessing.

My challenge: How do you evaluate God's hand upon a preacher or a church? Does that preacher endure opposition and buck the tide of popular opinion, or does he flow along with the culture, telling people what they want to hear? Beware of being seduced by the superficial and temporary success of ministers and ministries that lack both the willingness to endure opposition and the godly qualities that combine truth and love. Beware of churches that succeed by human means but lack the power of God.

Prone to Wander, Lord, I Feel It

Today's reading: 2 Corinthians 11:1-Galatians 1:24

My selection: Galatians 1:8

Even if we or an angel from heaven should preach to you a gospel contrary to the one we preached to you, let him be accursed.

My reflections: The temptation to stray from the true gospel was powerful to the Galatians. They began to doubt that salvation was by grace alone through faith alone in Christ alone. They were drawn back to trust in the ceremonial law of the Old Testament, such as circumcision, for acceptance before God.

This dependence on self for salvation appeals to human nature, but, for the Galatians, it also offered the advantage of not coming into conflict with the Jews who still trusted in their keeping of the law for their standing before God.

My challenge: What temptations lure you away from the truth of the gospel? Be vigilant in resisting the attraction of human reasoning or the allurement of popularity and social acceptability that can make you prone to wander and desert the true gospel.

December 9/Day 343

The Dangers of Misusing the Law

Today's reading: Galatians 2:1-4:31

My selection: Galatians 4:21

Tell me, you who desire to be under the law, do you not listen to the law?

My reflections: The reader of this epistle to the Galatians, if he ignores the rest of the Bible, could easily reject the doctrine of the third use of the law, that is, that the moral law is given as a means of guidance for the believer. The moral law shows us our sin and leads us to Christ (first use). The moral law restrains evil in society (second use).

Context is important. Paul is dealing with the problem of the Galatians reverting to the ceremonial law, exemplified by circumcision, as a means to salvation. So, the errors to avoid are:

1. Reliance on the law as a means of being reconciled to God.
2. Confusing the ceremonial law (the law of sacrifices, circumcision, feasts, etc.) which was fulfilled in Christ perfectly and must no longer be observed, and the moral law which, though unable to justify us, guides the believer in God's ways and must be observed.

It is clear, as we see in the Galatians 5-6, that Paul was not advocating antinomianism (the belief that the moral law is suspended and need not be observed by Christians), nor was he advocating disregard for holiness in life. What he opposes in Galatians 1-4 is trust in circumcision, and by extension the Old Testament ceremonial law, as a basis for justification before God.

My challenge: Never trust in your works for acceptance before God. Trust in Christ's perfect keeping of the law for us. Never disregard God's moral law, embodied in the Ten Commandments, as the basis for knowing God's will. Study, know, and obey His law if you would walk wisely before Him.

December 10/Day 344

The Big Picture

Today's reading: Galatians 5:1-Ephesians 2:22

My selection: Ephesians 1:13,14

[13] In him you also, when you heard the word of truth, the gospel of your salvation, and believed in him, were sealed with the promised Holy Spirit, [14] who is the guarantee of our inheritance until we acquire possession of it, to the praise of his glory.

My reflections: Here we get a glimpse of God's great eternal purposes for mankind. God is uniting all things in Christ (Ephesians 1:10). His purpose is the praise of His glory (Ephesians 1:12,14). Those who hope in Christ have an inheritance in all this that God is doing. The guarantee of that inheritance, of which we have not yet acquired possession, is the Holy Spirit. Those who believe have been sealed with the Holy Spirit.

How should we respond to this? We should keep this great view of the purposes of God before us continually, lest we become discouraged with the depressing news of the day, man's inhumanity to man, endless political corruption, war, deceit, etc. We should seek to grow in the knowledge of our ultimate hope in Him, as Paul prayed for the Ephesian believers (Ephesians 1:15-23).

My challenge: Walk in the Spirit with which He has sealed you. Do not lose heart. Keep the big picture before you, today, and every day. God has put all things under the feet of Christ and has given Him as head over all things to the Church. He will fulfill all His purposes to the praise of His glory. Never forget it.

Walking as Children of Light

Today's reading: Ephesians 3:1-5:33

My selection: Ephesians 5:5-6

5 For you may be sure of this, that everyone who is sexually immoral or impure, or who is covetous (that is, an idolater), has no inheritance in the kingdom of Christ and God. 6 Let no one deceive you with empty words, for because of these things the wrath of God comes upon the sons of disobedience.

My reflections: Paul makes a powerful statement here of warning to the Christians in Ephesus and to us in the twenty first century. In this passage, we see:

1. Certainty. You may be sure of this.

2. Absolute terms. Everyone who...has no inheritance in the kingdom of Christ and God.

3. Specificity. Sexual immorality and impurity and covetousness (aka idolatry) are listed. Even talk that is foolish, and joking, that is crude, is condemned (5:4). Sin is defined by God's law, not by the latest public opinion polls.

4. Warning. Paul tells them to beware of deceiving words. Someone out there is attempting to contradict this teaching.

5. Consequences. Because of these things the wrath of God comes upon the sons of disobedience.

How clearly is this truth being preached in American evangelical churches today? As the issue of redefining marriage to include homosexual relationships rages, many Christian leaders err either by caving in to public pressure to approve this new definition or by arguing against it based on historic traditions rather than Scripture. Some seem to have ignored the general level of sexual immorality in the church, refusing to discipline open fornication, while rising to condemn the equally sinful approval of homosexual conduct in the general society.

My challenge: As you have opportunity, seek to influence our society to respect the moral law of God. A vote against homosexual marriage is not the imposition of your morality on unbelievers, but the protection of our society against evil so blatant that it will bring down the wrath of God on us all. Meanwhile, work to strengthen a fear of God and His law in your home and church. Walk as a child of the light.

Having the Mind of Christ

Today's reading: Ephesians 6:1-Philippians 2:30

My selection: Philippians 2:5-7

[5] Have this mind among yourselves, which is yours in Christ Jesus, [6] who, though he was in the form of God, did not count equality with God a thing to be grasped, [7] but made himself nothing, taking the form of a servant, being born in the likeness of men.

My reflections: Paul commanded the Philippian Christians to have the mind of Christ among them. What is that mind? It is the mind of One who gave up the greatest glory in the universe to assume the lowest form of humankind, a servant. It is the mind of One who, after becoming a man and a servant, humbled Himself submitting to the most horrific death possible: crucifixion. Indeed, He was honored by God for all this and will be recognized by every person in heaven and on earth and under the earth.

That is the mind, says Paul, which Christians are to have.

My challenge: It should be a small thing for us to relinquish our position, prestige, and pride to serve others. We have so much less to give up than Christ had. We are already human, so we are partly there toward being servants and dying to ourselves for the good of others. Why is this so hard?

Jesus modeled what He taught. He who loses his life will find it. Do you believe that? Have you learned that by experience?

Look for the areas of your life where you put yourself first. Look for the ways that you are liable to get angry or depressed when slighted or underestimated. Confess sin and pray that you may have the mind of Christ in your dealings with others. Actively seek to serve others as Christ did.

Jesus Christ: His Person and Work in a Nutshell

Today's reading: Philippians 3:1-Colossians 2:23

My selection: Colossians 1:19-20

19 For in him all the fullness of God was pleased to dwell, 20 and through him to reconcile to himself all things, whether on earth or in heaven, making peace by the blood of his cross.

My reflections: Here in a few words is a concise statement of the Biblical teaching on the person and work of Jesus Christ.

Who is He? He is the God-Man in whom all the fullness of God was pleased to dwell. There is nothing lacking in His person that is in God the Father. Jesus told Philip that to see Him was to see the Father (John 14:8-11). Through Christ, we know fully and accurately God the Father.

What was His work? In a word, it was reconciliation. He came to reconcile fallen, sinful Man to God, but, not only that, His reconciliation includes all things as well. The creation was delivered from its bondage to corruption through Him. This reconciliation brought peace between the fallen world, including humanity, and God.

How did He do this work? All this was accomplished by the blood of his cross. By Jesus' death God's wrath was satisfied against sinners. Believers in Him trust His work as the basis for their peace with God.

My challenge: Do you glory in Christ Jesus? Is all your confidence in Him? Do you resist the temptation to look for new or novel ways of knowing God apart from Christ? If you believe in Him, give Him praise for His faithful submission to death on your behalf. Trust Him alone, not in any worthiness in you or your works, for your reconciliation and peace with God.

A Quick Guide on How to Do Everything

Today's reading: Colossians 3:1-1 Thessalonians 3:13

My selection: Colossians 3:17

Whatever you do, in word or deed, do everything in the name of the Lord Jesus, giving thanks to God the Father through him.

My reflections: All of life is to be lived in the name of the Lord Jesus Christ giving thanks to God the Father through Him. This implies that all of life is service to the Lord. Nothing we do that is good and true falls outside of our Christian life. This obviously includes our worship, but no less it includes our health, our eating, our work, our play, our relationships, our finances, everything. All of life is lived before Him. All of life is important. Many tasks are routine and commonplace, but nothing is meaningless or useless. "In every thing give thanks: for this is the will of God in Christ Jesus concerning you," wrote Paul to the Thessalonians (1 Thessalonians 5:18 KJV).

My challenge: Joni Eareckson Tada, who is a quadriplegic, has expressed longing to be able to plant vegetables or wash her own hair. It is easy for me to complain about tasks that she might find exhilarating if she could do them even once.

How about you? Do you consciously live before the Lord, giving thanks to God for the everyday, repetitive activities of your life? Live life fully as an act of perpetual worship and thanksgiving to God. That is your privilege, if you are a Christian. This is a quick guide to how to do everything.

Escape from Delusion

Today's reading: 1 Thessalonians 4:1-2 Thessalonians 3:18

My selection: 2 Thessalonians 2:11-12

[11] Therefore God sends them a strong delusion, so that they may believe what is false, [12] in order that all may be condemned who did not believe the truth but had pleasure in unrighteousness.

My reflections: I once heard Pastor Joe Novensen ask, "If you were deceived, would you know it?" The answer is, of course, "No." The nature of deception is that the one deceived is unaware of his state.

In this passage we can see that there are several factors working to create a deceived person: Satan, God, and the person himself or herself.

What are the characteristics of persons who are deceived? They refuse to love the truth or believe what would bring them to salvation. Often this takes the form of complacency, that is, they see no need to be "saved." They are not buying this idea that they are sinners, justly deserving the wrath of God. They are not buying that there is a Savior, Jesus Christ, who took upon Himself the sins of His people. The deluded are characterized by taking pleasure in unrighteousness. They break God's law and find pleasure in it.

The function of Satan is to make this deluded position seem totally reasonable by offering power, false signs, and wonders. He appeals to the person who is easily impressed with success, prestige, wealth, and apparent miraculous signs. Once Satan establishes his position, he can tell any lie and it becomes believable.

God confirms the state of the deluded by strengthening the delusion. God can save the most deluded, if He chooses to do so. He is free. But when He chooses not to save, the deluded one is further confirmed in his state and senses no urgency or danger. He is quite content to remain deluded.

My challenge: How can you tell you are deluded? If you thought you were deluded, you would, presumably, turn away from your erroneous beliefs and seek the truth. But you would be in a "Catch 22." You don't believe because you can't believe. You can't believe because you don't believe.

Is there no way out? Yes, the first step is to recognize your delusion. But how?

The hint is found in the observable characteristics of the deluded: they refuse to love the truth and they have pleasure in unrighteousness. The only possible way out for the deluded is to begin to seek to know the truth and to know what God calls unrighteousness. Listen to the preaching of the gospel. Read the Word of God and ask for grace to repent and believe. As my friend, Steve Slater, prayed in his youth before he believed: "God, show me the truth, and give me the courage to follow it." God answered that prayer for Steve. May He answer it for you, too.

Instructions for a Good Servant of Christ Jesus

Today's reading: 1 Timothy 1:1-6:2

My selection: 1 Timothy 4:6

If you put these things before the brothers, you will be a good servant of Christ Jesus, being trained in the words of the faith and of the good doctrine that you have followed.

My reflections: In a succinct statement (1 Timothy 4:6-10), Paul gives Timothy crucial commands for anyone who desires to be a good servant of Christ Jesus.

1. Put truth before those you serve--your brothers and sisters. Do not stray from the teaching you have received by getting into faddish or trendy teachings.

2. Practice what you preach. You yourself must be trained in the words of faith. You yourself must follow the good doctrine, not irreverent, silly myths. This means you not only believe the truth, but you train yourself in godliness with the intensity of an athlete

3. Set your hope on the living God, the Savior. Do not hope in anyone or anything else. Set your hope on Him. Keep your hope on Him. There is a life to come so keep that before you.

My challenge: Consider your service to the Lord today. Are you a good servant by these standards? What do you teach? How do you live? In whom do you hope? Teach the truth. Be godly in your life. Hope in God alone. Never swerve from this. You will someday hear the words, "Well done, thou good and faithful servant" (Matthew 25:21 KJV).

A Warning to Preachers and Churches

Today's reading: 1 Timothy 6:3-2 Timothy 4:8

My selection: 2 Timothy 4:2

Preach the word; be ready in season and out of season; reprove, rebuke, and exhort, with complete patience and teaching

My reflections: Paul's letters advise and warn Timothy about how to fulfill his pastoral ministry in Ephesus, but it also holds much instruction and admonition for Christians in general. It is obvious from the warnings given to Timothy that he was not an infallible super-Christian. Nor were his congregants models of holiness and integrity.

Timothy might be negligent in preaching truths that would challenge his hearers. He needed to be faithful to the Word especially when it ran counter to the thoughts and actions of the people. On the other hand, Timothy, having told the church the uncomfortable truth, might be impatient to see them think and act accordingly, but he was to have complete patience. Further teaching might be needed. Change does not come easily even to those who are sealed with the Holy Spirit.

A congregation might be guilty of rejecting truth that would challenge them. Sound teaching runs contrary to human passions. When church attendees hear and reject difficult truth, they either leave or try to replace the preacher with someone who will tell them what they want to hear, "chicken soup for the soul."

My challenge: Pastors, beware of soft-pedaling God's truth or of impatience with those you shepherd. Church members, beware of resisting the truth that runs cross grain to your flesh. All of us will have to answer to God for our faithfulness, or lack thereof, in heeding His Word.

What and Whom to Avoid

Today's reading: 2 Timothy 4:9-Philemon 25

My selection: Titus 3:9, 10

[9] Avoid foolish controversies, genealogies, dissensions, and quarrels about the law, for they are unprofitable and worthless. [10] As for a person who stirs up division, after warning him once and then twice, have nothing more to do with him.

My reflections: Paul warned both Timothy and Titus about avoiding foolish controversies and here he warns Titus also to avoid divisive people. Jesus taught His disciples how to handle sin in the church (Matthew 18:15ff), which in extreme cases of resistance to correction should result in excommunication.

Pastors and elders must know not only what to do but what not to do. There are many distractions such as controversial issues, stirred up weekly on blogs and social media, which have no merit. There are people who are bent on dividing congregations, often by criticizing the pastor (2 Corinthians 10-13). Paul said, basically, "Do not suffer fools gladly." According to Jesus (in the Matthew passage cited), there were to be three warnings culminating in a warning by the church and then, if there is no response, you administer excommunication and the individual is to be treated as an unrepentant outsider of the church.

My challenge: If you are a pastor, are you avoiding the distractions of foolish controversies that are unprofitable and worthless? Beware of being distracted by the latest novel theological idea floating around in cyberspace. Do you and your elders deal decisively with people who attempt to divide or distract the congregation? If you are a church member, are you a source of unity or of division in the congregation? Beware of seeking to show your intelligence by stirring up debates on worthless topics.

Pray that your role in the body of Christ will always be one of promoting the truth of the gospel and the unity of the saints.

December 19/Day 353

Getting Free from the Fear of Death

Today's reading: Hebrews 1:1-6:12

My selection: Hebrews 2:15

[Jesus] deliver[s] all those who through fear of death were subject to lifelong slavery.

My reflections: The writer of Hebrews is carefully laying out a case for the superiority of Jesus over angels, Moses, and Aaron. The salvation which Jesus accomplished for His people is great (2:2-3).

What is so great about this salvation?

First, in this salvation, Jesus destroyed the devil, the one who has the power of death. If you trust in Jesus for salvation, do not fear the devil. Though he continues to exercise dying powers, his final destruction has been assured through Christ.

Second, in this salvation, Jesus delivered all those who through fear of death were enslaved their entire lives. If you trust in Jesus for salvation, do not fear death. The power of death has been destroyed along with the one who had that power, the devil.

My challenge: Death and the devil are real threats to all those who are strangers to the salvation of Christ. If you know Him as Savior, rejoice in the great salvation which Jesus Christ achieved for His people. Never stop being amazed by it. Death has no power to paralyze with fear you who believe in Him. That is a great salvation, the greatest salvation!

December 20/Day 354

Jesus, Our High Priest

Today's reading: Hebrews 6:13-10:18

My selection: Hebrews 9:24

For Christ has entered, not into holy places made with hands, which are copies of the true things, but into heaven itself, now to appear in the presence of God on our behalf.

My reflections: The writer of Hebrews wanted his readers to know that Jesus is the High Priest of His people. Jesus Christ, as the High Priest to end all other priesthoods, offered Himself. His offering was made, not on earth in a mere human temple but, in heaven itself, literally before God. His offering was sufficient forever. He continues before God on our behalf.

As our High Priest, Jesus made a perfect offering perfectly in the heavenly temple. This was because He had no sin of His own for which He needed forgiveness and cleansing. The place of His offering was the temple of heaven, not the earthly temple made with human hands. His high priestly service was such that it would never need to be repeated; it was an eternally, effective offering. Now His continuing priesthood includes His making intercession to the Father on behalf of His people which He does continually.

My challenge: How would your life and character be different if you thought more often about Jesus' ministry for you before the Father? Do you not need to take more joy and comfort in knowing He is before God on your behalf? Think about that.

December 21/Day 355

Steering a Straight Path

Today's reading: Hebrews 10:19-12:29

My selection: Hebrews 12:14

Strive for peace with everyone, and for the holiness without which no one will see the Lord.

My reflections: In the Christian life, there are two important dangers to avoid. One leads to unwarranted confidence and pride, the other to unremitting guilt and despair. The first danger is to think ourselves acceptable to God by means of our good works and religious observances. The second danger is to downplay our responsibility to seek peace and holiness and to presume on the grace of God. The writer of the Hebrews calls his readers to seek peace in their relationships with all others and to pursue holiness in their daily lives.

How do we avoid these two dangers and maintain a safe course down the middle of the road?

On one hand, I cannot be proud of my spiritual and moral standing. If I am saved, it is not by my works, but by the work of Jesus Christ, my High Priest. Yet if I am saved, I am saved to do good works, to live at peace with others, and to grow in holiness. I cannot have Christ and be unchanged in my life, unperturbed by my persistent sin. If I have Christ, there must be evidence; there must be a hunger and thirst for righteousness.

My challenge: Are you not somewhat haunted by the words in the Hebrews 12:14? Beware of presuming on the grace of God. Assurance of salvation is based on God's promises, but also evidenced by a changed and changing life. Repentance will be a regular part of the life of one who knows that his or her holiness falls far short of God's glory and that there will never be enough holiness in us to merit God's favor. Ultimately, we are saved by faith in the One who offered the perfect sacrifice for sin and whose righteousness is credited to us; but, meanwhile, seek the holiness without which no one will see God. Pursue holiness while trusting in Christ's holiness.

Fighting Self-deception

Today's reading: Hebrews 13:1-James 3:12

My selection: James 1:22

But be doers of the word, and not hearers only, deceiving yourselves.

My reflections: James is concerned about wisdom, that believers be wise in the midst of the rough and tumble of life. A key part of wisdom is not to be deceived. One can be deceived about the dynamics of temptation (James 1:12-16), not seeing that there is blessing in remaining steadfast under trial but attempting to shift the blame for temptation to God. A wise person takes responsibility for his sin.

One can be deceived when he is a mere hearer of the Word of God and not a doer of it. He knows a lot but practices nothing. He fails to apply what the Scriptures tell him to his own life and behavior. He looks into the Word but presumes that it is not addressing any needed change in his life.

My challenge: Beware of self-deception. As we saw in our December 15 reading, self-deception and delusion often come masquerading in the proud thought, "I am an exception. Others need to obey, submit to the truth, but not me. Poor fools. I am unique." Don't be deceived. Apply the word more strictly to yourself than to others. Oh, and be quick about it (James 1:19).

A Chosen Race; A Holy Nation

Today's reading: James 3:13-1 Peter 2:12

My selection: 1 Peter 2:9

9 But you are a chosen race, a royal priesthood, a holy nation, a people for his own possession, that you may proclaim the excellencies of him who called you out of darkness into his marvelous light.

My reflections: Here is a remarkable, even stunning, statement which connects God's purposes revealed to His people at Mt. Sinai to the Church of Jesus Christ (Exodus 19:5-6).

It was always God's plan and purpose to bless all the families of the earth through Abraham (Genesis 12:3). Certainly, the Israelites were given the Law, the Prophets, and the other Old Testament writings. Their mandate was to be obedient and, thus, fulfill their calling to be a nation of priests and a holy nation. Only Jesus Christ, the Messiah, perfectly obeyed God's voice and kept His covenant. In so doing, Jesus established His Church as the fulfillment of God's eternal, unchangeable purpose to bless all the families of the earth and to bring together a people for God's own possession.

This is not "replacement theology," as some disparagingly call it. This is "fulfillment theology." God's eternal purposes are perfectly fulfilled in Christ.

My challenge: God has only one people, saved by grace alone through faith alone in Jesus Christ alone for the glory of God alone as taught in His Word from beginning to end. Praise Him for His great wisdom in decreeing this efficiently. Praise Him for His sovereignty in executing this effectively. Praise Him, if you are in Christ, for calling you out of darkness into His holy nation by mercy. Proclaim His excellencies to all who will hear.

Saved by Grace; Assured by Fruit

Today's reading: 1 Peter 2:13-2 Peter 1:21

My selection: 2 Peter 1:10

Therefore, brothers, be all the more diligent to make your calling and election sure, for if you practice these qualities you will never fall.

My reflections: As a young Christian, I was taught to trust in the promises of the Bible that salvation is by grace through faith, for my assurance of salvation. Yet as I read this passage, it seems clear that while salvation is by grace through faith and not at all based on the character or works of the believer, assurance of salvation comes, at least in part, by a fruitful, changed life that is the result of that salvation. An unchanged, unfruitful, stagnant believer in Jesus Christ is a contradiction of terms.

In this one paragraph, there is reference to calling and election, God's choosing those whom He would save and calling them effectually to Himself, and a reference to the need to practice the qualities listed, character traits of one who has been forgiven and given the promises of God to partake of the divine nature.

My challenge: Perhaps you trust in God's grace alone for your salvation, but do you see the necessity of bearing fruit as an evidence of your salvation? Do not be passive in seeking the Lord, in abiding in Christ, and in bearing the fruit of a redeemed life. Seek to grow in the virtues of knowledge, self-control, steadfastness, godliness, brotherly affection, and love. Make your calling and election sure. A rich entrance into the eternal kingdom of our Lord and Savior Jesus Christ awaits you.

Christmas Light

Today's reading: 2 Peter 2:1-1 John 3:10

My selection: 1 John 1:7

If we walk in the light, as he is in the light, we have fellowship with one another, and the blood of Jesus his Son cleanses us from all sin

My reflections: As we celebrate the birth of the Light of the World, Jesus, notice some of the benefits of "walking in the light." [John 8:12]

1. Nearness to God. God is in the light (1:5) so walking in the light results, first of all, in living close to Him.

2. Cleansing from all sin. Light reveals sin and facilitates confession of it resulting in forgiveness and cleansing.

3. Fellowship with others. There is no fellowship to compare with the fellowship of those who are walking in the light. Nothing is hidden in the light, including our sin. Yet this makes for relationships which are open and honest, without hypocrisy or facades.

My challenge: As you celebrate the birth of Jesus today, remember He came to save His people from their sin (Matthew 1:21). If you believe in Him, you will want to live a life that reflects what He has done for you in taking your punishment on the cross and freeing you from the guilt of sin. Make a conscious effort to walk in the light, because, naturally, we love darkness rather than light (John 3:19-21). Walk in the light today, though your flesh resists it. Hear God's word. Trust Him. Obey Him. Confess sin. Be cleansed by Him. Enjoy Him and all those who walk with you in the light. May your Christmas be truly merry as you walk in the light and grow nearer to Christ.

Being Certain of Eternal Life

Today's reading: 1 John 3:11-3 John 15

My selection: 1 John 5:11-12

[11] And this is the testimony, that God gave us eternal life, and this life is in his Son. [12] Whoever has the Son has life; whoever does not have the Son of God does not have life.

My reflections: Death is the great universal problem of mankind. No one escapes death, although most people long for life that is unending, full of love, peace, and joy (Romans 5:12).

But there is one way out, through Jesus Christ, the Word of God Who became flesh, dwelt among us, and in Whom is life (John 1:1-4,14-18). The New Testament describes this salvation from death through Christ as being in Christ (Romans 8:1; 1 Corinthians 1:30; 15:22) or, as John terms it here, having Christ. He is essential to salvation.

We may say the saved, those who have eternal life, are in Christ or have Christ. These are not the only metaphors used to describe this relationship, but the conclusion is always that the relationship with Christ saves and without Him there is no salvation.

My challenge: Do you trust in Christ for your salvation? Do you rejoice in the certainty of eternal life that is promised to you in Him? Resist the temptation to rely on any other thing--such as your accomplishments, your church affiliation, or your theological knowledge--for the certainty of your eternal life.

As Augustus Toplady's great hymn, “Rock of Ages”, says it:

Nothing in my hand I bring,
Simply to Thy cross I cling;
Naked, come to Thee for dress;
Helpless, look to Thee for grace;
Foul, I to the fountain fly;
Wash me, Savior, or I die.

December 27/Day 361

The Sardis Syndrome

Today's reading: Jude 1-Revelation 3:13

My selection: Revelation 3:2

Wake up, and strengthen what remains and is about to die, for I have not found your works complete in the sight of my God.

My reflections: In these letters to the churches, there are several references to false teachings and teachers, sexual immorality, and lack of good works, problems that continue to plague the Church today.

Sardis shows a failure in the area of their works, but their problem is masked by the fact that they are known for being an alive, vibrant church. The perception is that they are zealous and active. The Lord tells them they are asleep, and they are about to lose what they have. Judgment is imminent, but they are resting on their laurels, on their press releases.

In our society, it is common to hold that perception is more important than substance, and that as long as your reputation is good there is no need to back that up with reality. This is not God's view. We suffer from the Sardis syndrome.

My challenge: In your personal life and character, are you concerned more with impressing others or with walking in integrity before God? God has called a people for Himself who are zealous for good deeds (Titus 2:14). Be fervent in doctrine and practice seeking to please God whether or not those around you are impressed. Beware of the praise of men. Beware of the lie that perception is above substance and reputation is above reality. God looks at the heart.

December 28/Day 362

The Church in Glory

Today's reading: Revelation 3:14-8:5

My selection: Revelation 7:14

These are the ones coming out of the great tribulation. They have washed their robes and made them white in the blood of the Lamb.

My reflections: John sees an innumerable multitude from every nation, tribe, people, and language worshiping God along with the angels (7:9-12). One of the elders asks John who they are, probably not to gain information, but as a teaching technique to impart knowledge to John and to ensure that John knows what he is seeing. John cannot answer so the elder informs him of the identity of these worshipers.

1. They have come out of the great tribulation. These are people who have suffered, it would seem, in every nation. The tribulation must be worldwide and the persecuted have been drawn from everywhere. Their faith did not exempt them from tribulation; it caused it.

2. They have washed their robes and made them white in the blood of the Lamb. They are not sinless beings; they are cleansed sinners, forgiven through the atonement of Christ on the cross. They stand before God and worship because of what the Lamb of God did for them.

3. They worship. The chief end of man is to glorify God and to enjoy Him forever (Westminster Shorter Catechism Question 1). They fulfill their purpose through worship. They have been made fit to worship by the cleansing blood of the Lamb.

My challenge: Do not think that faith in Christ will save you from suffering in this world. Be prepared for opposition, persecution, and even death for bearing the name of Christ. Be assured that He will sustain you and one day deliver you from every evil and sadness (7:15-17). Do not think that your own righteousness will ever be the basis for your standing and acceptance before God. If you are a believer, although you will be confirmed in righteousness and unable to sin in glory, you will still be dependent on the blood of the Lamb for your adoption as God's child. For that you will give praise to Him. Practice worship now, personally and corporately. It is a manifestation of your chief end and a foretaste of heaven.

The Smooth-talking Beast

Today's reading: Revelation 8:6-13:10

My selection: Revelation 13:8

Also it was allowed to make war on the saints and to conquer them. And authority was given it over every tribe and people and language and nation, and all who dwell on earth will worship it, everyone whose name has not been written before the foundation of the world in the book of life of the Lamb that was slain.

My reflections: The beast, contrary to what one might think, is articulate. "There was given unto him a mouth speaking great things and blasphemies," we read (13: 5 KJV). He is powerful, able to conquer the saints and holding power over every tribe and people and language and nation. He is glorious, eliciting worship from all but those whose names are written in the book of life of the Lamb.

Satan counterfeits every good thing of God: eloquent wisdom, sovereign power, and worship-worthy majesty. As the knowledge of the true God fades out in modern society, the vacuum left is filled by the counterfeit, a monolithic system which unites political-military power, academia, and religion. You can see why Bible-believing people are not willing to blindly follow existing political parties and charismatic leaders.

My challenge: Are you prepared to suffer for the truth of the gospel? Do you resist the seduction of political leaders who promise a perfect world? Can you see through the pseudo-intellectualism of those whose wisdom does not begin with the fear of the Lord but with the worship of Man? Beware of Satan's counterfeits. Do not be deceived, but, remember, you may suffer in this world. You will not in the next.

December 30/Day 364

The Longing Soul

Today's reading: Revelation 13:11-18:24

My selection: Revelation 18:14

The fruit for which your soul longed
has gone from you,
and all your delicacies and your splendors
are lost to you,
never to be found again!

My reflections: The final judgment of this world is symbolized in the fall of Babylon with its materialism and sensuality. The souls of deceived people longed for the pleasures and majesty which the earthly kingdom offered, but it will elude them and be lost forever. All they can do is stand in fear, weeping and mourning for their loss, never to be recovered (18:15). What a sad picture!

The writer to the Hebrews says that God's people, by faith, long for a better country, a heavenly one. They will not be disappointed. "But now they desire a better country, that is, an heavenly: wherefore God is not ashamed to be called their God: for he hath prepared for them a city" (Hebrews 12:6 KJV).

My challenge: Everyone longs for something. The question is what is the object of your longing? For what does your soul long? If it is not God and the heavenly country, it is this world with its pending destruction. Christian, you are called to long for that heavenly country, the city God has prepared for you. Do not long for anything less.

Remember the famous words of martyred missionary, Jim Elliot: "He is no fool who gives what he cannot keep to gain what he cannot lose" *(The Journals of Jim Elliot.* Revell, 2002).

December 31/Day 365

All Things Made New

Today's reading: Revelation 19:1-22:21

My selection: Revelation 21:5-7

[5] And he who was seated on the throne said, "Behold, I am making all things new." Also he said, "Write this down, for these words are trustworthy and true."[6] And he said to me, "It is done! I am the Alpha and the Omega, the beginning and the end. To the thirsty I will give from the spring of the water of life without payment.[7] The one who conquers will have this heritage, and I will be his God and he will be my son."

My reflections: Human history, as we know it with its fallenness, will have an end. The One who sits on the throne cannot fail. He will make everything new because it is corrupted. The heritage of the conqueror will be to belong as a son to God.

My challenge: The Bible ends on this high note of victory for God and His people, but the ominous warning of the second death for unredeemed sinners. Are you among those who will be found faithful, conquering? You will not do it in your own strength. Only by the blood of the Lamb will you conquer. Trust Him. The end draws nearer.

Until then may God bless you and may we meet at His throne!

Acknowledgements

The apostle James wrote: "Every good gift and every perfect gift is from above, and cometh down from the Father of lights, with whom is no variableness, neither shadow of turning" (James 1:17 KJV). Whatever is good in this book comes from God and to Him is due all the glory.

But He also uses means to give His good gifts—especially the people who have loved and encouraged me over the long and winding road of my life. Chief among these is my faithful wife, Mary, to whom I have dedicated this work. She prayed for me and unselfishly gave her constant encouragement and editorial skills.

I am grateful to my friend, the Rev. Dr. W. Duncan Rankin, for his gracious Foreword in this revised 2018 edition.

Several staff members of the Navigators played a crucial role in my conversion, subsequent growth in Christ, and training in service to Him. Over the first five years of my Christian life, Dwight and Ruth Hill challenged me to follow the Lord, to study His Word, and to proclaim the gospel from Blacksburg, Virginia to Quezon City, The Philippines. I treasure the lessons learned through my training with Dean and Dorothy Truog, Jim and Jeri White, Walt and Leete Henrichsen, Gene and Mary Denler, and Gene and Helen Tabor. On a visit to Cordoba, Argentina over thirty years ago, Dr. Jerry White, former president of the Navigators, encouraged me to write and planted a seed that kept growing.

Friends at Christ Church (PCA) in Katy, TX gave support—particularly Stella Davison who suggested I write a devotional. Dr. Don Clements formerly of Metokos Press launched my career as a writer. I am indebted to all who wrote reviews on Amazon. Brothers and sisters in Christ at Grace Church in Roanoke prayed for me as I have worked on this. One of them spent countless hours checking grammar and punctuation and giving me invaluable feedback. Thanks, Joel Gurley. (I take full responsibility for any and all errors).

You are reading this because Barbara Baranowski, president of the Roanoke Valley Christian Writers and Sandi Bird Aldridge supported me with their knowledge and expertise in writing, design, and publishing.

Above all, I am eternally grateful to Yaweh who revealed Himself in the Bible as the Triune God: Father, Son, and Holy Spirit. As Dr. Francis Schaeffer wrote, "He is there and He is not silent."

About the Author

John A. Carroll is a member (honorably retired) of the Blue Ridge Presbytery of the Presbyterian Church in America. He formerly pastored Christ Church in Katy, TX, and Central Presbyterian Church, Kingstree, SC. Dr. Carroll served for twenty-eight years as a staff member with the Navigators on university campuses in the Philippines, Argentina, and various locations in the United States. He blogs at http://ThistleDewFarm.us.

A graduate of Virginia Tech (BS), Columbia International University (M. Div), and the Reformed Theological Seminary (D. Min), John and, his wife, Mary, have three daughters and six grandchildren. They live on Thistle Dew Farm in the Blue Ridge Mountains of Virginia (with a pretty good dog named *Ocho*) where they enjoy hiking, gardening, time with family, friends and neighbors, touring historic sites and, of course, daily Bible reading.

Appendix: What is the Bible and why should we read it?

As a Christian in the reformed tradition, I believe that the Bible is the Word of God. It is one book containing sixty-six smaller books inspired by God and recorded by human writers over a period of many centuries. The thoughts are God's not those of the writers who recorded them. Thus, the Bible gives us information we could not have known (things that took place before human history began, things still in the future, or things that take place in invisible spiritual realms) apart from God revealing it. For example, we learn in Genesis how the earth began. We learn why it began and what mankind's role is in it. We also learn how evil and death came into the world and we begin to see what the solution is for it. In Revelation, we get a picture of what is going on in heaven and what will happen as human history ends, and the eternal state begins.

I read the Bible because it instructs me as to how I may be saved from the just consequences of my sin. I read the Bible to gain understanding as to how I should live my daily life in this world. I read the Bible because God has commanded it in the Bible.[2]

How should we read the Bible?

If I believe that the Bible is the Word of God, I will read it diligently. It is a very long book containing a variety of types of writing: history, law, poetry and prophecy. Some passages are easy to understand; others are not only difficult but controversial. I will not let this deter me but seek to read daily and attentively.

---

[2] For the classic statement on Scripture see the Westminster Confession of Faith Chapter 1.

When, as a college student, I began reading the Bible on a daily basis over fifty years ago, I was not certain I believed it and I gave little thought to obeying it. I read it merely to be educated but not necessarily to be changed. Despite my attitude through God's grace to me, I was changed by it.

There are a number of approaches to Bible reading, but the one used here is what I call "Cover to Cover." This is the simplest plan as it begins on page one and continues straight through to the end of the Bible with daily readings of approximately eighty-five verses. The reading schedule was set up using Logos Bible Software and uses paragraph (pericope) divisions not verse or chapter divisions (although the readings may end at a chapter break). The advantage of this is that the length of each daily reading is about the same.

There are many other Bible reading plans available online. Some have you read the books of the Bible in chronological order as they were written. Some have you read in several places each day working your way through different genres of the Biblical literature. I have used a number of approaches over the years and all are useful. If you read the Bible repeatedly you will probably want to use different approaches for variety.

Made in the USA
Coppell, TX
06 October 2021

63562535R00252